Praise for *Lead the Work*

"The new world of work has new ways of working. Boudreau, Jesuthasan, and Creelman brilliantly capture the increasingly granular and customized work world where more employees will be free agents. This forward-thinking book offers creative and relevant insights for managing employees as agents. It has implications for leaders, human resources, rewards, and employees."

—Dave Ulrich, Rensis Likert Professor of Business, University of Michigan, and Partner, The RBL Group

"Anyone leading an organization through the rapidly changing and challenging landscape of today's workplace will find *Lead the Work* tremendously valuable. Boudreau, Jesuthasan, and Creelman expertly chronicle how work has evolved into multiple methods of employment, focused less on managing employees and more on providing work-based leadership. They give concrete advice on how organizations can thrive in this environment. The concept of 'beyond employment' will soon be commonplace to business leaders."

—Henry G. Jackson, President and Chief Executive Officer, Society for Human Resource Management

"*Lead the Work* invites business leaders to free their minds from the shackles of traditional regular full-time employment. The book provides a framework that enables us to embrace examples like Elance-oDesk, Tongal, and Khazanah not as anomalies but as potential solutions to getting the work done and sourcing the best talent. *Lead the Work* pushes the boundaries of flexibility in work arrangements to a future where we not only just build or buy talent but also borrow and share talent."

—Johan Mahmood Merican, Chief Executive Officer, TalentCorp

"How leaders and organizations assemble the right teams of talent today is rapidly evolving to utilize teams of much more than just permanent employees, temporary help, and outsourcers. I have seen this to be true across the globe . . . a globe that has fewer and fewer borders when it comes to customers and talent. The focus on the 'workers,' the 'client,' and the 'work' in *Lead the Work* brings all the pieces together of how organizations need to deliver value to their customers, both today and tomorrow. Innovation of how to find and utilize talent is going to be a differentiator, both in professional services organizations and beyond. *Lead the Work* does an excellent job of describing what the trends are, brings them to life by showcasing real examples that expand your thinking, and helps to alleviate any fears about this new talent marketplace."

—Jill Smart, President,
National Academy of Human Resources, and
retired Chief Human Resources Officer, Accenture

"The world of work is changing fast—creating more complexity and breeding disengagement. Boudreau, Jesuthasan, and Creelman take a comprehensive look at the changes happening outside our companies that are affecting how we get work done together inside our companies. After exploring the diverse ways in which we now connect people with the work we need done, they offer us a convincing framework for designing our enterprises, organizing work, and constructing deals to offer workers. Fortunately, this framework clearly shows leaders the few critical levers to pull to create new work arrangements that deliver on the value agenda. Wisely, the authors also engage with tough questions about the impact this new framework will have on society and the roles of leaders, HR departments, and government. *Lead the Work* enlightens us all—as leaders, workers, and citizens—about how we can still accomplish great things together in the midst of this turbulence."

—Sandy Ogg, Operating Partner,
Private Equity Group, Blackstone

"*Lead the Work* explores a seismic shift in the very concept of work. For anyone looking for a fresh way to think about competing, innovating and leading, *Lead the Work* will stimulate your creativity and give you new ideas on how to tap into an emerging "free agent world." This new virtual workplace being built by a diverse, multi generation workforce hinges on individuals leveraging their skills to build portfolios of work that seamlessly integrate into the lives they want to lead.

The new book by Boudreau, Jesuthasan and Creelman makes an intriguing argument that traditional employment approaches are migrating to innovative and agile ways of tapping into new talent pools. The authors paint a compelling picture of workplace innovations that challenge convention to compete in an open, global and virtual talent marketplace. The challenge lies in how to lead in this new world.

The best managers in this new paradigm bring together flexible teams and distribute work to those best skilled to deliver, more quickly and cost effectively than traditional approaches. Convening and motivating a network of "followers" who you may never physically meet, requires new ways of leading, orchestrating and collaborating, along with new rules of engagement.

Lead the Work is a fresh, insightful way to think about work, how it is done and who does it. It challenges us to make potentially radical shifts in the way we need to lead and compete. The authors deliver a wake-up call with numerous real world business examples that make the case this is not a temporary trend, but rather a pivotal inflection point. The highest impact insight is that the basic concepts of work, employee and leader must be reinvented in a world where individuals seek to be the "CEO of me."

As a former Chief HR Officer and alum of five global fast paced consumer and technology companies, *Lead the Work* challenged my thinking about new ways to lead and innovate with the talent of today and tomorrow."

—Eva Sage-Gavin, Vice Chair, Aspen Institute's Skills for America's Future Advisory Board, formerly Executive Vice President, Human Resources and Corporate Affairs, Gap, Inc.

"Knowing how to manage the multitude of contractors, vendors, and temps who now work side by side with our regular employees is a crucial skill, and *Lead the Work* shows us how to do it right."

—Peter Cappelli, George W. Taylor Professor of Management and Director of the Center for Human Resources, Wharton School of Business, University of Pennsylvania

"The traditional employment relationship has evolved to a place of free agency where employees are the CEOs of 'self, incorporated' in a flat, interconnected, dynamic, and creative world. John, Ravin, and David take a new and refreshing look at how the relationship has evolved to better enable organizations and their leaders to achieve business objectives through employment relationships some may view as fickle, but which others appreciate as the new normal."

—Scott Sherman, Executive Vice President,
Human Resources, Ingram Micro

"The way in which work gets done, by whom, and how, is changing quickly and dramatically. Everything it seems is being "disrupted", including the process of workforce planning. The models of employment and organization that have evolved slowly and predictably, are soon to be extinct or irrelevant in whole or in part. *Lead the Work* is a must read for business leaders, particularly Human Resources executives, who must adapt or wither, even if they don't yet realize it. This book, greatly advances our understanding of what these changes are, what they will be, and most importantly, provides great insight into how to move your enterprise into this new world. This is an orientation to what is to become of HR and the management of human capital. A total "Aha" experience. I have seen no research which comes close to this."

—James J. Duffy, Chief Human Resources Officer,
Ally Financial Inc.

"Changing demographics, changing worker values and preferences, changing technologies...these all drive leaders to consider changing approaches to how work gets done in and through organizations. In *Lead the Work*, Boudreau, Jesuthasan, and Creelman detail how these trends have transformed work and caused many to question the traditional employment model. They provide examples of companies that have successfully leveraged innovative approaches to work arrangements to provide quicker, more efficient, and—more importantly—more effective means of competing. This book will give leaders strategies, tools, and ideas for how to do the same in their organization."

—Patrick M. Wright, Director,
Center for Executive Succession, and Thomas C. Vandiver
Bicentennial Chair in Business, Darla Moore School of Business,
University of South Carolina

"*Lead the Work* delivers revolutionary thinking about the emerging transformation in how work will be done in the future, as well as when, where, why, and by whom it will be done. This book contemplates a world beyond traditional employment models. It asks and answers the crucial yet frightening question—what would happen if the traditional employment model gave way to more bite-sized, freelanced, project-based, shorter-term gigs? It not only addresses this question, but also challenges us to rethink the implications of blowing up and refashioning long-held assumptions about leadership, organizational operating models, workforce engagement, culture and purpose, and the future of the human resources profession, to name a few.

"Imagine a world of work where most (or a significant percentage) of the people doing the work are not our employees, but rather freelancers who have complete control over what work they choose to do, when they choose to do it, where they choose to do it, with whom they choose to do it, and why they choose to do it. Imagine the implications of leading the work rather than the employees doing the work.

"Boudreau, Jesuthasan, and Creelman get our attention, question our assumptions, capture our imaginations, shake us up, and help us see all will be all right—but not before they teach us what we have to do to reshape the role of leaders and organizations. After reading *Lead the Work*, you will never think about leadership, work, or the workforce in quite the same way again."

—Ian Ziskin, President, EXec EXcel Group LLC, and former Chief Human Resources Officer of Northrop Grumman and Qwest Communications

"Finally a book that takes us into the rapidly evolving nature of work and how workers and organizations will respond! The authors have provided the first book to enable HR leaders and organizations to better understand where work is going and to create tools and methods to respond to these changes."

—Libby Sartain, former CHRO, Yahoo! and Southwest Airlines, and Director, Manpower Group and AARP

"As a board member of the Institute for the Future and a former CHRO in Silicon Valley, I have become very aware that we are moving from a world of hierarchical organizational structures toward a world where human resources can be digitally activated, deactivated, and reconfigured to come together as needed and where needed. In its best form, workers from all over the globe will be empowered to choose when, where, and how they work. Many will choose to be their own employers. Those who continue to align with a specific institution will expect equivalent opportunity and flexibility, and the challenge of building a productive work community in this kind of environment will call upon new forms of leadership. John, Ravin, and David's look at the evolution of work has arrived not a moment too soon. It is time that every person who occupies a position of leadership or aspires to be a leader fully appreciates this new world of work, and this well-grounded research is an important step in that direction."

—Debra Engel, board member, Institute for the Future, and former Senior Vice President of Corporate Services, 3Com

"The authors have very thoughtfully and clearly described the opportunity for companies to deconstruct work into 'tangible deliverables,' and then source the work from new and rapidly evolving labor pools. Those who are tracking the dynamics of these evolving labor pools understand that the 'free-agent workforce' is well represented by workers who are described as 'creatives.' Shopping in that labor pool is important if you believe creativity is critical to your future business performance. Executing these ideas will be nontrivial, and will require nontraditional thinking and methods. CHROs will have an important role in these transformations, but the success of changes of this scale requires the full alignment of the CEO and the executive team."

—John S. Bronson, Bronson Consulting LLC; formerly Vice President of HR, Williams Sonoma, and Executive Vice President, Pepsi-Cola Worldwide

"Boudreau, Jesuthasan, and Creelman invite us into the new world of work, where technology disrupts markets and businesses, where the democratization of work empowers the individual employee and drives enhanced employee choice, and where work models emerge from other domains, such as sports or moviemaking, where 'loaning talent,' free agency, or assembling project-based production teams is the norm. They introduce this world through a series of contemporary, diverse examples ranging from the established infrastructure of IBM to Topcoder, an online community that 'gathers the world's experts in design, development, and data science to work on interesting and challenging problems.' They urge today's leaders to step boldly into this complexity and ambiguity, and provide a framework to guide their journey. That framework is accessible and compelling, whether you are a chief executive officer, a business unit leader, an academic, or a human capital professional. As a former chief human resources officer, I suggest that HR leaders read this book with their CEOs, business unit leaders, and leadership teams. Use it as an organizational diagnosis and to develop a road map for this 'brave new world of work.'"

—Kaye Foster-Cheek, Senior Advisor, Boston Consulting Group, and former Chief HR Officer for Onyx Pharmaceuticals and Johnson & Johnson

"Future organizational challenges require rethinking fundamental assumptions, and some of the most important assumptions have to do with work and workers. Achieving success through talent is the job of corporate officers, boards, managers, workers, citizens, and governments. *Lead the Work* offers CEOs a thoughtful framework for navigating the rapidly evolving nature of how work gets done. It is a forward-looking guide to the future, with useful, important, and practical insights for operating in today's environment as well. CEOs should read this book together with their heads of HR, their extended leadership teams, and their boards. This book clearly describes a future that is approaching fast, with an important vision for leadership and human resource management."

—Laurie Siegel, Director, CenturyLink and Volt Information Sciences, and former CHRO, Tyco International

Lead the Work

Lead the Work

Navigating a World beyond Employment

John Boudreau
Ravin Jesuthasan
David Creelman

WILEY

Published by John Wiley & Sons, Inc., Hoboken, New Jersey.
Published simultaneously in Canada.

For general information on our other products and services or for technical support, please contact our Customer Care Department within the United States at (800) 762-2974, outside the United States at (317) 572-3993 or fax (317) 572-4002.

Wiley publishes in a variety of print and electronic formats and by print-on-demand. Some material included with standard print versions of this book may not be included in e-books or in print-on-demand. If this book refers to media such as a CD or DVD that is not included in the version you purchased, you may download this material at http://booksupport.wiley.com. For more information about Wiley products, visit www.wiley.com.

Library of Congress Cataloging-in-Publication Data
Boudreau, John W.
   Lead the work : navigating a world beyond employment / John Boudreau, Ravin Jesuthasan, David Creelman.
      pages cm
   Includes index.
   ISBN 978-1-119-04004-0 (hardback)
   ISBN 978-1-119-04006-4 (ePDF)
   ISBN 978-1-119-04007-1 (ePub)
   1. Contracting out. 2. Consultants. 3. Self-employed. I. Jesuthasan, Ravin, 1968- II. Creelman, David, 1957- III. Title.
   HD2365.B665 2015
   658.3'01–dc23

                                        2015018223

Cover Design: Wiley
Cover Image: ©iStock.com/george tsartsianidis

Printed in the United States of America

10 9 8 7 6 5 4 3 2 1

To the free agents and free-spirited employees and colleagues, including my daughter and wife, whose stories bring life to a new world of work
—John Boudreau

To my colleagues at Towers Watson and the members of St. Paul and the Redeemer Church in Chicago who continually inspire me with their random acts of kindness and love
—Ravin Jesuthasan

To the free agents of the world who are striving, not without difficulty, to invent a new way of work.
—David Creelman

Contents

Foreword

A few years ago I attended an HR conference where I found myself on a panel with a freelancer. He had no desire to work for a corporation, nor a manager for that matter. And he was clearly very good at his craft—someone my company would want to hire.

"I get that you love the independence," I said. "But what about your training and development? How do you stay on the leading edge of your craft?"

"Meet-ups," he said. Seeing my uninformed gaze, he went on. "We get together online and arrange festival-like gatherings, often on the campuses of Bay Area companies, inviting the best players to come and speak. Great for networking too."

I tried another tack. "What about a sense of community? Don't you get bored or stale working alone all day?"

"Co-working," came the reply. There are really cool workspaces that can be rented with other freelancers, and a Starbucks downstairs for meetings.

I was getting rather desperate at this point. "What about benefits?" I inquired. "What happens if you get sick?"

"The Freelancers Union," was the answer.

So there it was: a new and compelling paradigm for getting work done, no longer for those who are marginally employed, but for the very best talent in our industry, and pouring out of our universities every day. It forces all of us in corporations to rethink our value propositions, to provide the same kind of ad hoc opportunities to grow and expand skills inside our companies, and to incorporate alternative work arrangements into our talent strategies.

To be sure, the "organization" itself has been evolving. Once you could neatly distinguish insiders from outsiders, but today, the relationship between an organization and all its constituents is becoming more permeable and flexible. Its structure is evolving from a hierarchy to a network model of deep collaboration across the entire value chain, including suppliers, partners, and customers. Leadership is more collective and democratic, defined increasingly by expertise and the ability to energize others. Authority is increasingly bestowed by the community, not by a position.

Leadership still means achieving a mission through the efforts of talented people—but *how* you lead is changing.

This new form of organizational openness offers tremendous upside potential—empowered employees, free-flowing ideas, more creativity and innovation, happier customers, and better results. But with more openness also comes more risk. As rigid controls loosen, organizations need a strong sense of purpose and shared beliefs to guide decision making. Teams will need processes and tools that inspire collaboration on a massive scale. Skills need to be validated in some reliable way. Perhaps most important, organizations must help employees develop the capabilities to adapt and excel in this type of environment.

As you navigate these shifts, finding and developing the right talent and leadership is challenging. John Boudreau, Ravin Jesuthasan, and David Creelman pull together compelling evidence and tools to help you find your way. I'm pleased to say that you'll find a chapter in the book about our journey at IBM, and you'll read about other innovative organizations as well.

One of their key observations is about the changing nature of work. The talented people you lead will engage in new ways that look very different from regular full-time employment. They will work on tasks, projects, and assignments, not only in traditional jobs. They will contribute through a global network connected to your organization through remote platforms, alliances, contracts, and even online games. Sometimes, the best talent won't be your regular full-time employees, but freelancers, contractors, or even volunteers. One IBM study found that independent workers were actually more engaged with the organization they worked for than regular full-time employees. Your organization's transition toward work beyond employment will depend on your industry, region, size, and other variables. Yet, this evolution promises significant changes even for your regular full-time employees.

The book also explores the changing expectations of employees. Even regular employees want to work on projects they choose, much like freelancers. They expect careers that reach beyond your organization, just as contractors experience a wide array of industries and environments. They want discretion about where and when they work, and while they still value the security and stability of regular employment, they also know that nothing lasts forever, and the half-life of capabilities is constantly shrinking. Winning enterprises will help employees anticipate these shifts and adjust to them.

There are other interesting examples of innovative approaches to getting work done—a crowdsourced advertisement, a smartphone app built entirely by freelancers, an intriguing alliance of employees between two companies, a drug breakthrough discovered by volunteer online gamers.

Taken individually, these are interesting anecdotes, but string them together, and this book signals that something meaningful is happening. The convergence of the digital, social, and mobile spheres is connecting customers, employees, and partners in new ways to organizations and to each other. Leaders are recognizing that this connected era is fundamentally changing how people engage, and this puts pressure on leadership to adapt.

Let this book be your navigation guide to the new world of work.

If you are a corporate officer, investor, or manager, read this book to understand how to lead and engage the new workforce. Share the book with your HR leaders, and discuss how you can work with them to optimize the opportunities, and avoid the pitfalls, of the new global workplace.

If you are an HR leader, read this book to be inspired and guided on how you can contribute in new ways, as the evolving world of work will alter virtually every element of your profession. Please share this book with your colleagues outside of HR, and together craft your unique vision of a new kind of strategic partnership.

If you are a professional, read this book and be inspired by the expanding options for you to craft an even more fulfilling and rewarding work life.

If you are a policy maker, read this book and consider the role of governments, nations, and societies in ensuring that this evolution is fair, inclusive, and sustainable.

—Diane Gherson
Senior Vice President
Human Resources, IBM

Acknowledgments

This book is the result of tireless support from many friends and colleagues.

We thank our colleagues at Towers Watson, particularly Juliet Piekarski, who reviewed and read every chapter countless times, Jorn Janssens, who helped advance some of our original ideas, and Shatrunjay Krishna who helped us tell the intriguing story of Bharti Airtel.

We are also grateful for the sponsorship and support of Julie Gebauer, who embodies all the attributes of the engaging leader in her leadership of Towers Watson's Talent and Rewards segment.

We wish to thank the executives at each of our case study companies for sharing their stories with us.

We are also grateful for the comments and feedback from many trusted colleagues, particularly John Bronson, Jim Duffy, Doug Milroy, Sandy Ogg, Scott Sherman, Laurie Siegel, and Mara Swann.

In addition, we wish to acknowledge the editorial staff at Wiley publishing; Karen Murphy, Shannon Vargo, Judy Howarth, Tiffany Colon, and Abirami Srikandan, for their support.

Lead the Work

PART ONE

ONE

The Background

1

Leading Work—Not Managing Employees

We create boxes to make sense of the world. We talk about organizations and jobs as boxes. Employees sit inside jobs that sit inside organizations. This is how we think things get done. In practice, it's never really so cut and dried, but the simple mental model works—or at least it used to.

Now we are seeing those comfortably familiar boxes begin to disintegrate.

Have you heard phrases like "nonemployment work arrangements," "freelance talent platforms," and "labor market intermediaries?" They reflect an emerging trend in which work and workers exist "beyond employment." Many leaders have hardly noticed the rising frequency with which these terms crop up in discussions about the future of work. To leaders, "nonemployment work arrangement" may sound like something to be delegated to specialists in procurement or personnel. Or they might ask, "Are these new arrangements just simple extensions of cost-reduction techniques we've seen for years, such as outsourcing, temporary contract workers, and consultants?" Sometimes they sound familiar, but increasingly these new approaches to work are already fundamentally changing how you compete and achieve your organization's mission. Leaders who overlook them risk making the same mistake that taxi services made when they dismissed the emergence of the Uber ride-sharing service.

A world where work moves "beyond employment" will challenge fundamental strategic assumptions in virtually every industry and sector. The world is changing, and the role of a leader is not to stand back, or marvel at the change, or delegate the decisions to administrative rules. A leader's job is to achieve organizational goals through the work of others. Leaders must develop the tools to grapple with this new world. Work is escaping the confines of regular full-time employment, and it is leaving your organization. These changes create opportunities that should not be ignored.

This shift is reminiscent of the diversity movement that seeks out talent regardless of gender or ethnic origin. The beyond employment opportunity is to seek out talent among free agents, anywhere in the world, who prefer free agency to employment. In particular if you are looking for authentic innovators and creative agents, this is where they are likely to be found.

The problem for leaders is that they face a bewildering array of stories and examples of how work is changing, but no framework to guide their decisions. It's like seeing lots of bright shiny objects in the sky, with no framework of astronomy to guide you. The stories and examples tend to focus on two things, and have omitted a vital third element.

Many stories and examples focus on the *Workers*. You hear a lot about the plight of contingent workers, the exploitation of part-time workers, but also about the freelance coder who is earning $100,000 a year sitting on a beach in Bali, or the crowdsourced gamers that solved a thorny riddle in AIDS treatment. You wonder if you should be using such workers, or even whether you should become one yourself.

Other stories and examples focus on the *Client* for the work. You hear a lot about Netflix saying that "adequate performance gets a generous severance package,"[1] companies like Colgate-Palmolive producing ads for the Super Bowl through crowdsourcing,[2] and early-stage companies that consist of a few employees who lead the work by tapping a vast global network of workers connected through cloud technology and personal technology. You wonder if you should adopt some of these practices in your organization when you are the client for the work.

These examples and stories can appear like the lights on a Christmas tree in a dark room. If you can't see the shape of the tree that holds the lights, it's often difficult to understand their pattern. What you need is to see the tree underneath the lights. This book focuses on the decisions you make about the *Work*. It draws on the excellent ideas that others have proposed regarding the Worker and the Client, and then builds upon them by illuminating how understanding the Work helps to explain the stories and examples. More important, because a leader's job is to achieve a mission through the work of others, this book's focus on the work gives you a way to navigate this emerging world beyond regular full-time employment.

Work: Escaping Traditional Regular Full-Time Employment

Does being a leader mean leading your regular full-time employees? What does it mean to lead when workers are not employees? For example, should you and your leaders be the best at leading free agents or contractors?

Let's look at some examples of work being done by workers who are outside the confines of traditional regular full-time employment for your business. These workers may be "free agents" who work for themselves, employees of an organization you are allied with, employees of an outsourcing firm, or even volunteers. In these next three examples the workers are as important in getting the work done as the firm's own employees.

How Free Agents Built the Software for Managing Genomes

The leaders at Ion Torrent had a problem. Managing the huge data files that result from sequencing DNA,[3] even with fast computers, was slow and expensive. The company's IT leader was tasked with finding ways to radically improve compression and decompression of the data. But where to find the right kind of programming talent? The existing employees didn't have the time or expertise, so the leaders at Ion Torrent turned to Topcoder for help. Topcoder, despite its name, does not employ an army of software code-writers. Topcoder reaches out to its pool of 700,000 freelance technologists and sets up a competition with an attractive prize. The challenge this time? Find a great compression solution for Ion Torrent's problem. The result? Many programmers proposed novel ways to tackle the issue, with the best one improving compression by 41 times. Through Topcoder, Ion Torrent leaders found the right talent, and achieved outstanding results quickly and cost effectively.[4]

How might Ion Torrent have gotten this work done without Topcoder? The most traditional way would have been to hire coders as full-time employees. Ion Torrent leaders would need to either motivate and retrain their existing coders to solve the compression problem or hire and construct a team of some of the highest-performing coders in the world. Would the existing in-house employees or the high-performing coders outside the company be available to take the job? Could Ion Torrent bring them on board quickly enough to solve the problem in time? Did Ion Torrent have the internal training and development resources to bring coders up to speed? When you think about it, the "natural" decision to hire or deploy your own regular full-time employees to get work done is actually complex and risky.

As an alternative, Ion Torrent could have used someone else's employees, like hiring a consultancy to do the work. This approach offloads the troubling burdens of employment onto the consultancy. Yet the consultancy must maintain or hire coders on its team of permanent employees, and that cost shows up in the higher price of using consultants to do the work. A consultancy may have employees with skills that Ion Torrent doesn't have, but few consultancies can tap a population of coders as large as the pool accessed by Topcoder. Also, it's still not certain that the best-qualified coders for this particular work would want to work full-time for a consultancy.

Part of the economic argument behind Topcoder is that they can find the very best people to do a particular project. A company might have dozens or hundreds of skilled internal programmers to choose from, but that collection of talent pales compared to the 700,000 free agents in Topcoder's network. The second part of the economic argument is that the Topcoder arrangement is cheaper and less risky because coders compete, and the company pays for only the best end product.

The Ion Torrent case leads us to the inevitable question: Are free agents, when organized by a platform like Topcoder, inherently more efficient and effective than regular full-time employees working inside a company or consultancy? Should you ever get computer coding work done by regular full-time employees? The answer, of course, is that it depends on your situation. The fact that it depends means that leaders must make decisions. As a leader, are you confident that you know when to use free agents via a platform like Topcoder? Why was it the right solution for Ion Torrent? Should you make it your strategy? If software coding is pivotal to your strategic success, the answer may determine whether you can compete at all.

How to Power an Energy Company with Contract Workers

It takes about 180,000 workers to run one of Europe's largest energy companies, but the company does it with far fewer regular full-time employees. More than 100,000 of the workers are not employees. Most of the work there has escaped the employment contract, not to freelance platforms like Topcoder, but to contractors.

This case is a vivid example of shifting work from employees to contingent workers. At one time, contingent work was considered suitable only for low-skill jobs, but today contractors can do the work of professionals and even managers. The contingent arrangement has many advantages for firms: It can be less expensive when one considers the total cost of employment (wages, benefits, etc.), in part because it creates a workforce that can shrink and grow as needed. It also helps a company access the skills it requires and get rid of those it does not with fewer costs than if it were hiring and firing employees.

A workforce consisting mainly of contractors presents its own challenges. Will they be as committed as regular employees? Will they be around long enough to develop the depth of knowledge of the company and the operations needed to handle difficult situations? Will the churn of contractors mean that each new worker will require extensive orientation and training? In the case of this energy company, a "beyond-employment" model based largely on contractors proved best. It figured out how to have significant aspects of its work down through a "plug and play" model that optimizes productivity and knowledge transfer.

Your own organization may well use some free agents such as contractors or contingent workers, so you may feel that you have mastered their use. Yet, consider this question: "Why not use *mostly* free agents the way this company does?" As you lead through the work, are you confident that your organization achieves the right mix of free agents and regular full-time employees?

How to Unravel the Mystery of Folding Proteins with Volunteers

Dr. David Baker, a biochemist at the University of Washington, had a problem. He studies proteins, which, when stretched out in a line, consist of a long sequence of amino acids. What makes things complicated, though, is that they don't *stay* in a straight line. They fold back onto themselves, and predicting how exactly they do so is a famously difficult problem.

If Baker had had an unlimited budget, he could work the problem by hiring a large team of regular full-time employees as researchers. However, most universities can't afford such expenditures, and even if his university could, it would have been tough to find just the right researchers for the job. Indeed, university scientists and R&D scientists at biotech companies had used all sorts of methods, including supercomputers, to try to crack this riddle, with little success.

Working on a tip from Mary Poppins, Baker knew that in every job that must be done, there is an element of fun, so he turned the work into a game. His team created a website and software tools so that enthusiastic amateurs could compete to find the best solution to the folding problem. Over time, the game, called Foldit, attracted a pool of talented volunteers who successfully solved protein-folding problems simply for the fun of it.

Using the Foldit game achieved better and quicker results, with no employees, and with no payment whatsoever. As a leader, should you consider this merely an interesting story, or should volunteers playing games be a component in your arsenal of tools to innovate quickly and efficiently? Are you solving your R&D and other creative riddles by hiring R&D scientists and building laboratories, when a crowdsourcing game could engage the best and brightest workers . . . for free?

The Pressures on Regular Full-Time Employment

As the previous examples have demonstrated, there is an emerging shift in the way companies both large and small are getting work done. In the traditional model for getting work done—such as writing code, solving a research problem, designing products, or creating a TV commercial—you needed regular full-time employees. Traditionally, we organized employees by creating job descriptions, reward structures, systems for recruitment, and so on. It's a bit like building a house out of bricks; it's a lot of effort, but ultimately, you end up with something quite stable and permanent.

The problem with a house of bricks—with all due respect to the fairytale view of these structures—is that they are expensive, slow to build, and hard to change. If you frequently need a bigger or smaller house, or simply a house in a different place, then a brick house is not the way to go.

Emerging approaches allow you to lead through the work, by organizing the work and workers to get exactly the talent you need when you need it. It's like throwing together a high-tech pre-fab structure, snapping the pieces into place for something inexpensive, fast, and disposable.

Yet, it's not as easy as simply shifting away from regular full-time employment as your work model. In a stable environment, the brick house wins. In an environment that is constantly changing, the pre-fab structure can adapt more effectively. As a leader, what environment should you be preparing for? When it comes to getting work done, most organizations are good at building the "brick house" through regular full-time employment. That has its value, but you must also know how to assemble temporary structures suited to a particular need at a particular time.

The Free Agency of the Regular Full-Time Employee

The employees who live in the brick house can see the need to prepare for a future with multiple temporary work structures. Just turn to LinkedIn and see the jobs people have these days. For example, Graham Donald's profile shows he is VP, Insight & Brand Strategy for Day Communications. But wait—he's also listed as president of his own company, the Brainstorm Strategy Group. How can someone be a VP in a leading communications firm and at the same time president of his own business? Donald's case is not that unusual anymore. Alan Burt, the chief technology officer (CTO) of Ricoh Australia, is simultaneously the CTO of PlanDo, a career management software company. The old tidy boxes are breaking down. Like an electron, people can be in more than one place at once.

What we see from Donald and Burt is that people are adapting to a world where regular full-time employment, what we used to call "permanent employment" is not particularly permanent. They have learned to build their individual brand, often while also working as regular full-time employees. A former free agent like Donald has learned it would be risky to jettison the value he built up in his own company, so he keeps it going part-time—a deal made possible by an employer who is enlightened

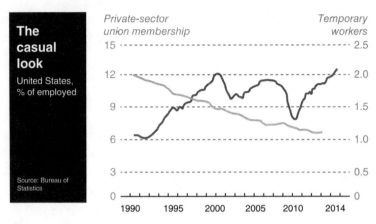

Figure 1.1   The Casual Look: United States, Percentage of Employed

Source: The Economist, 2015; Bureau of Labor Statistics.

enough to see that if you want the best people you need to be flexible in the deal you offer.

As layoffs, downsizing, and rightsizing have become frequent management tools, it's only natural that workers would value arrangements that make their movement between jobs easy. Workers may prefer leaving on their own than being pushed out by their employer. Regular employees now live in a world that bears many similarities to a free agent's life beyond employment. Employment and union trends analyzed by the Bureau of Labor Statistics and presented by the *Economist* validate the shifts we have discussed. Figure 1.1 shows that the proportion of workers protected by union membership has steadily declined by half over the past two decades, while the proportion of temporary workers has doubled.

As leaders, we worry about attracting and retaining employees. As parents, we groom our children, so they can get good jobs. Yet, there are many ways to get work done without having employees, and many ways of being a worker without having a regular full-time job.

Work Is Leaving Organizations

Even when work is done by employees, not free agents, the work need not be done by your employees or in your place of business. Some leaders see the work occurring in an organization with a more permeable boundary, where work—and people—move inside and outside more freely.

Developing Future Leaders by Loaning Out Your Best Talent

In our book *Transformative HR: How Great Companies Use Evidence-Based Change for Sustainable Advantage* (John Wiley & Sons, 2011) we described how Khazanah Nasional, the investment arm of the Malaysian government, recognized that companies did not have sufficiently varied developmental opportunities for leaders. Khazanah Nasional's executives came up with a bold idea: Why not convince the companies in their portfolio of investments to share leaders with one another, with Khazanah acting as the matchmaker? For example, the power company Tenaga Nasional could send a leader with strong operating capabilities to work for several years at Malaysia Airlines in order to acquire skills in turning around a troubled business. And a leader with significant experience in negotiating international energy agreements could move from the national oil company Petronas, to Telekom Malaysia, where she could acquire the skills associated with operating an integrated telecommunications network. The companies embraced the concept. Employees got valuable development experience, the companies got top talent, and Khazanah helped further the nation's ambition of becoming an advanced economy by building a deeper pool of leaders.

At first the idea of loaning out leaders seems bizarre and unworkable, but Khazanah proves it is entirely doable.

Soccer fans will recognize the model: soccer teams have well-established systems for loaning players to other teams where they will have a better chance to develop their skills. A key to these arrangements is a governance structure and agreed rules for making the loans so that the advantages outweigh the costs for each team. For example, in the Premier League, players on loan are not permitted to play against the team loaning them. Loanees are, however, allowed to play against their "owning" clubs in cup competitions, unless they have played for their owning club in the cup during that particular season.

If we can break down the idea that the organizational boundary is an impermeable barrier, it opens up a world of opportunities. Why doesn't Pottery Barn borrow a couple of product designers from Banana Republic to develop next year's products and next year loan their own designers to Banana Republic? Why doesn't American Express swap employees with Geico Insurance to build capabilities related to enhancing cyber security?

Of course, lending your talent carries new risks. Does it matter if one of your best leaders, or best players, is outside the organization giving their heart and soul for another team? Will you reap the benefit when they return? And if you had not created this development opportunity might you have lost them anyway?

Again, it depends, and the difference between success and failure lies in the ability of leaders to make good choices, to lead through the work in a way that optimizes the inherent ambiguity that this kind of talent sharing creates. Leaders must navigate practical issues such as whose benefit plan a loaned employee is on and whether, in a soccer match, we allow the loaned player to play against their original team. What a brave new world, that has such options in it.

How to Sell Kids on Hearing Aids by Borrowing Your Partner's Employees

The engineering and electronics giant Siemens makes hearing aids.[5] Among the end users are kids. How do you make hearing aids attractive to kids? How do you get their classmates to think hearing aids are cool, not weird? For all its immense depth of technical expertise and its world-class employees, these questions were far out of Siemens' comfort zone. Siemens is a great company, but its history, strategy, and culture had never encountered the challenge of marketing technology to kids. The question, "Which of our regular full-time employees can take on this assignment," undoubtedly turned up many remarkable workers, but none with deep expertise in this area.

So, the leaders at Siemens reframed the question to ask, "Who in the world really *gets* kids?" The answer was not hard to find—it was Disney. Rather than trying to build the capability among its own employees to figure out how to market to kids, Siemens took advantage of an alliance with Disney. Disney employees were assigned to the project of marketing the Siemens hearing aid. Their solution: Don't sell the hearing aid. Disney experts packaged the product in a colorful case with a Mickey Mouse stuffed toy and a comic book with a compelling and inspiring story about kids with hearing aids. Disney saw the hearing aid more like a toy than a medical technology.

Children don't buy the wind or gas turbines that are closer to the core of Siemens' business, yet children's hearing aids are a valuable application of Siemens' core capability, an opportunity too valuable to lose. If Siemens tried solving this problem by hiring employees to package and promote hearing aids to children, it would take a long time to hire them, the best of them probably wouldn't consider Siemens an employer of choice, and the new employees wouldn't easily fit into Siemens' core business once they finished work on the hearing aid project. Why build a permanent structure based on employment when Siemens can get the work done faster, with higher quality and less cost, by "borrowing" Disney's employees through an alliance?

Siemens leaders led through the work, by realizing that this project could be constructed with Disney as the employer in alliance with Siemens. Siemens got the benefits of Disney's world-class employees, reward structure, and culture with decades of experience marketing to children, without having to create a similar structure internally. The move was enabled by an existing alliance between Disney and Siemens for building theme park rides; the two had learned the trick of working together, and that set the stage for an unforeseen collaboration on hearing aids.

Does the work of your organization require the talent to reside inside your organization, or do you, like Siemens, simply need a way to access the right talent in another company? If the work you need to do is outside your core value proposition (like marketing to children was to Siemens), might there not be better talent you could borrow from outside? Do you structure your alliances based on optimizing the work, or based simply on financial or technical elements?

Fighting Diabetes through an Alliance between Competitors

How does one develop a comprehensive portfolio of noninsulin diabetes drugs? You might think that giant pharmaceutical firms could take that on, but even for them it is a daunting challenge to perform at world-class levels on all the many elements of drug development. AstraZeneca and

Bristol-Myers Squibb are robust competitors, but their leaders led through the work, realizing that the best way to fight diabetes was to do it together. In 2007, they formed a global diabetes alliance to discover, develop, and commercialize new drugs for type 2 diabetes. Add in Bristol-Myers acquisition of Amylin Pharmaceuticals in 2012 and the alliance had the capability to offer a full spectrum of treatment options.[6]

This is a good example of borrowing and buying capability rather than building it internally. In their book *Build, Borrow, or Buy: Solving the Growth Dilemma*, Laurence Capron and Will Mitchell argue that knowing when to build, when to borrow, and when to buy capability is critical to success.[7] The trouble is most leaders lean too heavily on one tactic instead of applying the appropriate solution to the situation.

AstraZeneca ended up buying the alliance in 2014, essentially incorporating employees who were formerly outside its boundary and bringing them inside. Does that mean the alliance was a mistake? No. It is instead an example of another way to lead through the work: Envision your organization as flexible, constantly changing its shape, rather than as a rigid structure. In 2007 AstraZeneca extended its organizational boundary to overlap with Bristol-Myers Squibb in diabetes research; in 2012 Bristol-Myers engulfed Amylin. In 2014 as Bristol-Myers Squibb began moving in a different direction, it made sense for AstraZeneca to fully absorb the alliance into the main corporate body.

If AstraZeneca thought in terms of fixed structures and rigid organizational boundaries, they would never have achieved their current strength in diabetes treatments. They saw the work of winning the diabetes game as being about moving pieces available somewhere in the world, not just moving the pieces available within the organization.

We are all familiar with outsourcing and the economic value it provides through specialization and its ability to mitigate the impact of product demand fluctuations. Alliances have similar advantages, but they introduce a much fuzzier set of relationships. The alliance between AstraZeneca and Bristol-Myers Squibb on diabetes treatment didn't just share employees, it also shared intellectual property. That fuzziness is important. It is both a challenge and an opportunity. When it comes to leading through the work, the traditional boxes we use to define what is inside and outside an organization are breaking down.

Talent Platforms Optimize Freelancing

Earlier we showed how an organization called Topcoder was a source of freelance computer coders to solve Ion Torrent's compression problem. It illustrates how work is escaping the confines of regular full-time employment. Yet, Topcoder is much more than a source of free agents. It is an example of something called a talent platform that not only provides an alternative source of workers but offers insights about what it fundamentally means to lead through the work. We will deal with talent platforms in depth in Chapter 4. Here, we offer some highlights to show just how fundamentally they change how you think about leading through the work.

Upwork, the leading site for freelance work, was designed to be a marketplace that matches work to free agents. Need a logo? You can find a designer on Upwork. Need a part-time administrative assistant? Upwork can help you find one. Need a brand strategist? The talent you need, for as long as you need it, is a few clicks away. In many ways, Upwork is an Internet-based replacement for a temp agency—at least that is what it was when it started.

Think of it like the consumer buy-and-sell sites Craigslist and Kijiji, but instead of buyers and sellers of used household goods finding each other, work and talent find one another. A leader lists a task that needs to be done and free agents offer their services. Alternatively the leader can search the listings of free agents to see who is available. It is similar to job boards like Monster or CareerBuilder, except regular full-time employment isn't being offered or sought; and it offers services to help overcome barriers that get in the way of working with off-site free agents.

Upwork successfully competes against temp agencies partly because of the efficiencies of being automated, partly because it is useful even if you just have a small task rather than a whole job, and partly because it can tap affordable talent in the developing world. Upwork is important if you are a temp agency competing for market share or a leader looking for some extra help. If a talent platform was just the equivalent of a big room filled with tasks and free agents wandering around to find each other, then it would not be particularly exciting. And if Upwork was the only talent platform out there, it would be interesting, but hardly world-changing. However there is much more to talent platforms than this simple view.

Consider the talent platform Ion Torrent used: Topcoder. Whereas Upwork is usually seen as a way of getting work done more cheaply than using employees, Topcoder intends to tackle programming tasks so difficult that your employees cannot do them.

Topcoder challenges employment on two fronts. As a leader, when does it make sense to get work done with a fixed group of employees (assuming you have an employment brand to attract this highly desirable pool of talent, and they would pick you over Google) versus giving the work to more talented programmers on an as-needed basis? As a talented programmer, when does it make sense to tether yourself to a corporation when you could fly free as a Topcoder? The bigger question has to do with the scale of the change. Are we headed toward a world where most programming work is done via talent platforms?

What Topcoder is to programming, Tongal is to advertising. Tongal strives to be a better way for firms to get advertising videos made. It's a talent platform that enables crowdsourcing of ideas and the production of commercials. It attracts work from top brands like Lego, Anheuser-Busch, and Procter and Gamble. In the old, big-budget world of mass-market TV advertising, traditional advertising agencies may have an advantage, but among the fragmented audiences of the Internet and cable TV, those big budgets are unsustainable. For commercials, talent platforms like Tongal are a big part of the future.

A quite different kind of talent platform is Amazon's Mechanical Turk. Amazon's platform is named for the Mechanical Turk, one of the most notorious machines in the history of artificial intelligence. The Turk was an eighteenth-century chess-playing robot that astounded the intelligentsia of the time. No, your sense of the history of technology is not awry; the Mechanical Turk was a clever fraud. A man was hidden inside the robot and it was he who provided it with the intelligence to play chess.

Even in the modern world of computing there are some things humans do better than machines. Amazon's Mechanical Turk (MTurk) feels like a machine, but it cleverly takes little tasks and farms them out to anonymous human workers hidden behind the interface. Consider image recognition, such as being asked "Is this a picture of a kitchen or a bathroom?" This sort of task is easy for a human but hard for a machine. When leaders at Amazon confronted the problem of handling large numbers of microtasks a computer could not do, they created a talent platform to farm out these tasks to free agents around the world. A free agent working on Amazon's MTurk might only earn 10 cents for a task, but that's okay when a task only takes a few seconds. MTurk worked so well that Amazon turned it from an internal tool to a business.

There are a great many talent platforms. In the video business alone, there are numerous sites competing with Tongal, including MOFILM, UserFarm, Genero, Wooshi, and Vizy. Talent platforms extend to the world of on-premise work with the likes of Wonolo, TaskRabbit, and Gigwalk. These platforms connect managers to local free agents who can do everything from filling in for a cashier, to working on a construction site for the day, to helping your grandmother carry boxes upstairs.

Going down this line of inquiry leads us to ask whether the taxi-like service Uber should count as a talent platform. And if so, how do we classify Uber competitor Car2Go, which doesn't provide any talent at all, but is just a platform for finding the nearest "drive-it-yourself" car? And what about Wikipedia? It isn't really a talent platform, but it does source a vast array of talent on the web and is clever enough to enlist them as volunteers instead of paid free agents. Is Wikipedia part of this story, or something quite different? As is so often the case when the old ways are dissolving and the familiar boxes breaking down, there are more questions than answers.

Seeing a Pattern in the Pieces

If your employees are working for other firms as part of their development, if your programming is done by free agents, if your research is done by volunteers, or if a strategic part of your product line is being handled by an alliance, what does that mean to you as a leader?

You can act as if it is business as usual, and focus on leading your regular full-time employees. What's happening on the outside may not need to be a primary focus . . . not yet.

This "business as usual" approach, grounded in regular full-time employment, has lasted a long time even in the face of massive social and technological changes. The stresses on traditional employment structures were described in 1999 by Peter Cappelli in his book *The New Deal at Work: Managing the Market-Driven Workforce.*[8] The rise of free agents was celebrated in 2001 by Dan Pink in his book *Free Agent Nation: The Future of Working for Yourself.*[9] A few years later, Ellen Ernst Kossek and Brenda Lautsch coined the term CEO of Me to capture the notion that everyone needed to be the CEO of his/her own life and career.[10]

We believe it is time to change your leadership paradigm, from managing your employees to leading through the work. Even if this paradigm shift suggests you will still get work done mostly with regular full-time employees, the very definition of employment has become so seriously eroded that even your regular employees really work for CEO of Me. They are speaking at conferences, maintaining their own side businesses, and leaping for development opportunities outside the firm. A shift toward leading the work is consistent with the evidence that organizations increasingly depend on a web of outsourcers, allies, and free agents. The shift toward leading the work is a way to understand a generation of younger workers that has grown up with no memory of the traditional world of secure regular full-time employment, and no expectation that it will ever return, and the generation of older workers that are working longer, but through arrangements that are different from regular full-time employment.

The leader's job has always been to achieve organization goals by getting work done through others, and for a long time that has been synonymous with managing their own regular full-time employees. Increasingly, that's not enough. Great future leaders will know how to optimize the wide array of options and get the work done across the boundary, at a distance, and with people that may never be your employees. In the extreme, a leader may have no employees at all but may control vast amounts of work done somewhere else. As we shall see, there are already successful companies that operate in just this way.

Having work done by employees is familiar and in some ways simple. Employees do what they are told, more or less. You can keep an eye on them. They are beholden to you because the company is their sole source of income. Having work done outside the organization raises a lot of questions. How do you keep control of intellectual property? How do you ensure continuity? How do you assess the capability of the free agent or outsourcer or alliance to do the work? Do you have enough leverage to make them do what you want—not what *they* want to do?

The solutions to the traditional problems with leading the work exclusively through regular full-time employees are being developed every day. In this book we will bring them together to walk you through the implications.

Figure 1.2 is a graphic representation that contrasts the old way of thinking about work with our new view.

The vast majority of attention in the management literature is on what happens with employees within the organization. If we look at Model 4, it becomes clear that the work done inside the organization is only one element in a much bigger picture. For the leader of today, the question is how to optimize and lead the work across all of these options.

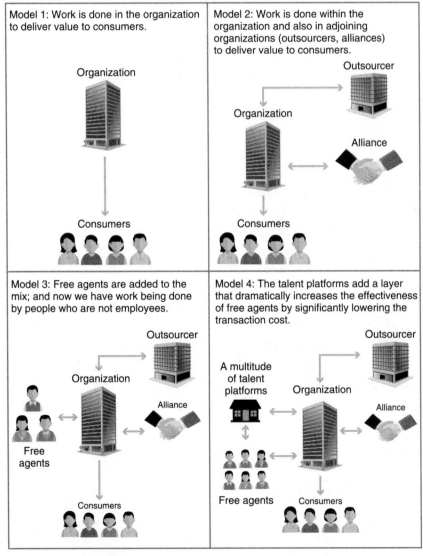

Figure 1.2   Alternative Models For Leading the Work

There are more implications for leaders than just deciding where to get work done. As we have discussed, the rise of the free agent nation and the loss of job security has undermined the solid relationship between employees and employers. What does it means when your "subordinate" is actually CEO of Me? What does it mean when you as a leader are CEO of Me, too?

We have worked with teams where key players offer the excuse that they have only been in the company for a few weeks and are still getting up to speed on what's needed. Sitting beside them the "veteran" turns out to have only a year's tenure with that company, and at the end of the table the technical expert proves not to be an employee at all but is on loan from a consulting firm. The tenuous nature of this group is hammered home when the leader, in a private conversation, mentions she is planning to look for a new job at the end of the fiscal year. That is the reality of organizations today, yet we are still acting as if the team is made up of long-term employees pursuing a career in our firm. We are still pretending that we ourselves are long-term employees, even as we maintain our free-agent credentials and continually scan the market for the next opportunity. How does a long-term project succeed when none of the people involved are there for the long term?

For the individual, the question is where to play. Imagine you are a research scientist. Would you rather be an employee at a consumer products company (where marketing is king) or a free agent going from project to project? Would it be better to work at an outsourcer that specializes in research? To what extent will you be forced to move between the worlds of employment and free agency? What skills would you need to make that possible?

In the first half of our book, we examine the rise of free agents, outsourcers and alliances, and the talent platforms. Once we better understand the dynamics of each area, we set out a framework for managing within this new world.

Leadership Is about the Work, Not Just the Employees

If your business regularly needs to solve some complex problems and you have a staff to do that, what chance do you have against a competitor who has figured out how to use an army of skilled volunteers the way Foldit has?

If your business relies on superior programming solutions and you use a mix of in-house programmers and consultants, will you find yourself continually being second best to a competitor who uses a competition-based platform like Topcoder? Will you always get to market later than everyone else? Will your service never be quite as good? Maybe Ion Torrent's situation was a one-off, or maybe there is a whole class of analogous programming problems where anyone not mastering these new approaches will spend more and achieve less.

In this book we are not trying to highlight unusual stories, we are working to illustrate new ways of getting work done that, in the right conditions, dramatically outperform traditional approaches. In order to make the big leap from a particular success story like Foldit to where the opportunity lies in your own business and in your own life, you need to absorb the stories at a deep enough level so that you see the world in a new way. You need to reach the point where you see your job as a leader being about leading the work, not only managing employees, and recognize that there are a great many ways to get the work done, some of which will dramatically outperform others. The subsequent chapters offer stories, principles, and models to reshape your view of what organizations are, what leaders do, and where the future of work lies in a world beyond employment.

Notes

1. Reed Hastings, Slideshare, posted August 1, 2009, www.slideshare.net/reed2001/culture-1798664 (accessed February 10, 2015).
2. Peter H. Diamondis, XPrize.org, posted March 4, 2013, www.xprize.org/news/ceo-corner/tongal-produced-ad-scores-super-bowl-touchdown (accessed March 12, 2015).
3. Ion Torrent website, Life Technologies, created 2014, www.Topcoder.com/case-studies/ion-torrent (accessed March 17, 2015).
4. Ibid.
5. Ard-Pieter de Man, *Alliances: An Executive Guide to Designing Successful Strategic Partnerships* (Hoboken, NJ: John Wiley & Sons, 2013).
6. Jeanne Whelan, Jessica Hodgson, "AstraZeneca, Bristol-Myers Deepen Diabetes Alliance," Wall Street Journal, published January 31, 2013, www.wsj.com/articles/SB10001424127887323701904578275290772944154 (accessed April 6, 2015).

"AstraZeneca and Bristol-Myers Squibb Diabetes Alliance Provides $5 Million Grant for American Diabetes Association's Pathway to Stop Diabetes Research Initiative," Bristol-Myers Squibb, published January 16, 2014, http://news.bms.com/press-release/astrazeneca-and-bristol-myers-squibb-diabetes-alliance-provides-5-million-grant-americ (accessed April 7, 2015).

Jennifer Fron Mauer, Laura Hortas, Timothy Power, Sarah Lindgreen, James Ward-Lilley, and Karl Hård, FierceBiotech blog, posted January 16, 2014, http://www.fiercebiotech.com/press-releases/bristol-myers-squibb-and-astrazeneca-complete-expansion-diabetes-alliance-t (accessed April 7, 2015).

AstraZeneca press release, posted February 3, 2014, www.astrazeneca.com/Media/Press-releases/Article/20140203-astrazeneca-acquires-bms-share-of-diabetes-alliance (accessed April 9, 2015).

7. Laurence Capron and Will Mitchell, *Build, Borrow, or Buy: Solving the Growth Dilemma* (Harvard Business Review Press, 2012).

8. Peter Cappelli, *The New Deal at Work: Managing the Market-Driven Workforce* (Boston, MA: Harvard Business School Press, 1999).

9. Daniel H. Pink, *Free Agent Nation: The Future of Working for Yourself* (New York: Warner Books, 2001).

10. Brenda A. Lautsch and Ellen Ernst Kossek, *CEO of Me: Creating a Life That Works in the Flexible Job Age* (Upper Saddle River, NJ: Pearson, 2007).

2 | Free Agent World

Having regular full-time employees is not the only way to run an economy. Rather, it's a method that evolved to meet the needs of a particular historical period. That historical period may be reaching its end as we evolve into a new way of getting work done.

In this chapter we describe this evolution, and in particular the emerging work arrangements that do not involve regular full-time employment. As others have done, we'll use the term *free agent* to mean someone who works for themselves. It means the same thing as *freelancer* or *contractor*, but we like the term *free agent* because it emphasizes their sense of self-determination. An individual consultant who works for himself or herself is a free agent, but one who works for a consulting firm is not; when you hire McKinsey or Towers Watson consultants you are contracting with the firm, not individual free agents.

Why Employment Evolved, and What's Evolving Next

Employment has served us well throughout the industrial and information ages. It's not surprising that it dominates our thinking when it comes to leading work. Markets react to small twitches in the unemployment rate. We send our kids to university, so they can become an employee of a great company. Need to get a mortgage to buy a house? The bank wants to know what your job is and how long you've had it. Governments labor mightily to create legislation that protects employees in jobs.

Yet, regular full-time employment for the masses is a relatively new historical phenomenon. For most of the past 2,000 years, economies were built via the labor of independent workers. Being free of the regular full-time employment relationship didn't always mean having lots of discretion. A peasant farmer under the "protection" of a lord was not an employee, but not particularly free either. Something closer to the modern concept of a free agent is the notion of independent crafts people, guilds, and so forth. A blacksmith, for example, would carry out his trade independently, seeking out work, managing his finances, developing his skills, and building his reputation—a CEO of Me.

Why did the industrial world move to the employment model? As industries grew, their leaders needed to have a reliable group of workers gathered in the same place day after day. In the industrial era, most workers really were extensions of the machine, and as a result they needed to be machine-like. The industrial leaders of the day were not hiring talent so much as hiring a pair of hands that needed to be as consistent and standardized as possible. You could buy the other parts of the machine but not the pair of hands. Thus, employment evolved as the next best alternative.

The history of labor in the industrial era is largely a story of a battle for power. Business owners (and hence leaders acting on the owners' behalf) wanted as much work as possible for a given pay outlay. Employees wanted more money, fewer hours, better working conditions, and protection from arbitrary firing. Over many decades, the battle lines shifted back and forth between capital and labor with government setting the rules of engagement. Those battles never ended, but in the 1950s, in the developed economies, there came a sense of reasonable accommodation.

The sense that it was finally working out pretty well for most created an overarching belief that this was the right and natural way to structure work. Blue-collar workers enjoyed the protection of unions and regulations. White-collar workers felt secure as they climbed up the ladder. Businesses had a skilled, committed, and permanent workforce, and they developed elaborate ways of managing their employees.

Leadership and management became big enough subjects to create business schools in universities, whole stand-alone libraries of business books, and a thriving industry of consultants. Brilliant minds put a lot of effort into understanding the work done by regular full-time employees in jobs. An illustration of how seriously companies took jobs as a stable building block of the organization was the effort put into job evaluation. The most famous method, the Hay Job Evaluation system was developed to determine the size of a job, so corporations could better understand who should get bigger pay. The Hay system can help answer questions such as "Is a pastry chef a bigger or smaller job than a carpenter?" Organizations invested significant sums in writing job descriptions and engaging commit- tees of managers to assess the size of each job. Underlying this effort was the belief that the way the organization got work done was through jobs staffed by regular full-time employees. While nothing is permanent, in the 1950s many organizations went so far as to suggest lifetime employment for good workers.

Problems in Job Land

A significant pillar of regular full-time employment was the presumption that the worker, the work, and the organization in which they meet were relatively stable. Even if one of them changed over time, the idea was that the best way to manage that change was to maintain the regular full-time employment relationship, and invest in developing the worker to adapt to the changes. It was a model of spurts of incremental change followed by longer periods of relative stability. However, as Chris Worley and Ed Lawler observed in their book, *Built to Change*, the world was evolving to make change a constant, not an event.[1] That puts strains on all sorts of organiza- tional and leadership assumptions, not the least of which is the assumption that regular full-time employment is the optimal way to get work done.

The sense that the system of permanent jobs was working well for most people began to erode in the 1980s and 1990s. Rather than having work done by employees, businesses discovered that they could use outsourcers who were able to tap a much cheaper pool of talent. Some well-paid manufacturing jobs disappeared in the West and reappeared as low-paid positions in the developing world, particularly China. It was a huge gain for developing economies and a devastating loss for blue-collar workers in the developed world.

Many whose jobs were not easily sent overseas faced a different problem: They were replaced with contingent workers. Contingent work was less secure and lacked benefits. Some of this work was part-time and unpredictable, and stories emerged of workers who were formerly regular full-time employees and now struggled to cobble together enough work to pay the bills.

Professional and managerial workers also had an uncomfortable fate. The story is well told in Peter Cappelli's book *The New Deal at Work: Managing the Market-Driven Workforce.*[2] When the recession of the 1980s hit the developed world, organizations discovered they had too many managers. They had built a process for developing managers based on the presumption of predictable, ongoing growth, but when that growth failed to materialize, they had no need for such a rich talent pipeline. In addition, their management structure had grown bloated with far too many management layers. It was then that we came up with words like "downsizing," "delayering," and "rightsizing." As Cappelli points out, all the downsizing put a big pool of managerial talent in the labor market. Organizations stopped developing so many managers and simply hired the experienced talent they needed on the open market. With that, the concept of lifetime employment had contracted a fatal disease, but the idea persisted that permanent regular full-time employment was still the main way to get work done.

In today's world, even in the best of times, companies are keen to remove layers and cut headcount. As an experienced business development manager said recently, "I'm doing really well, but that doesn't mean I couldn't be whacked tomorrow." In the United States and in many countries, not only has job security disappeared, but managers expect that it is normal for them to eventually be let go. Still, the idea is that they will move from one regular full-time employment gig to the next.

While the illusion of long-term job security is gone, the old "regular full-time employees in stable jobs" model has built up massive inertia that continues to color our thinking. It takes a lot of work to break through to new ways of thinking and to fully appreciate the implications that the new world we occupy is destined to have on organizations, leaders, and individuals.

The Cost of Employment

One significant factor driving work outside of companies is the high cost of getting work done within the confines of the organization. Consider the following shift in the mix of labor cost within America's companies (Figure 2.1); the increase in payroll and benefits costs makes employees more expensive than free agents, which typically only require companies to pay them their cash wages with no requirements for benefits or payroll taxes. This encourages companies to minimize the number of regular employees on their payrolls.

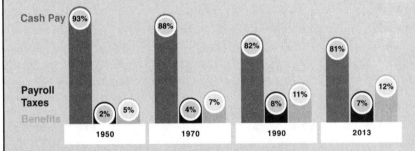

Figure 2.1 Increasing Payroll and Benefits Costs
Source: Bureau of Labor Statistics and Towers Watson Analysis.

The Less "Regular" Full-Time Job

We are in a world where a good deal of work has been pushed outside the organization and the jobs that remain are not secure. When you take security out of the employment relationship, what are you left with? At first, the new deal appears to indicate that people will go through a series of jobs over the course of their career—not just one or two like their parents or grandparents. The analogy to marriage feels unavoidable. Traditionally, marriage was a lifelong commitment: "till death do us part." Divorce allows people to escape that lifelong bond, and it is not uncommon for people to have two or three marriages in a lifetime. But what would happen if the average marriage lasted only a year or two? Is it still marriage in the full sense of the word, or is it better seen as a kind of dating?

That is exactly what seems to be happening to regular jobs. LinkedIn commonly features resumes with long lists of jobs: two years here, three years there, one year somewhere else. Is this still regular full-time employment or an early version of free agency? Yes, people still move from one full-time job to another, but when it happens so quickly can it really be described as "regular" full-time employment any longer? Add to that the feeling of "any day I could get whacked," and the psychological transition to CEO of Me is well on its way, even for those who technically hold regular full-time jobs.

The end of job security loosened some fundamental rigging that held the organization together. The organizational boundaries had been breached, and as a result, people left more readily and work was sent outside the company without much fanfare.

History suggests that the idea of an organization as getting work done with a stable group of regular full-time employees may be just one step in the evolution. Increasingly, leading the work with regular full-time employees is supplemented by things like outsourcers, alliances, and free agents. If more work is done by workers and providers with monikers like outsourcers, alliances, and free agents, then leading the organization requires going beyond employment to optimize how work gets done. Workers that come to you in the form of outsourcers, alliances, free agents, and through other employment alternatives can be just as committed, engaged, and motivated, as regular full-time employees, but it's a different relationship. The leader's job becomes figuring out how to lead the work, not simply managing the regular full-time employees.

The Starbucks Office and the Social Acceptability of Free Agency

The shift to a free agent nation was motivated by economics. However, there is a softer factor accelerating the shift: the growing social acceptability of free agency.

The world of free agency was, and to some extent still is, characterized by an attempt to pretend it doesn't exist. A free agent—for example, a management consultant—may describe herself as "Smith & Associates" when in reality, she is just Smith, a self-employed worker. Smith will list her address as a box office in a downtown office building rather than say she works from home. Her marketing literature will read, "We provide . . ." not "I provide . . ."

This pretense of being part of a bigger organization is often threatened by one of the deep dynamics of free agency: its flexibility. The "associates" of Smith & Associates do not exist in any permanent way, but Smith does join up with other consultants on occasion. When a project is too big for Smith, she will show up with a colleague or two presenting the image of a firm with employees. Likewise, Smith may be invited into projects by another free agent, and she is presented as an associate in Jones & Associates. Free agents may end up with several different business cards fronting different work identities. Showing up at a client and fumbling through a set of different business cards reveals the consultants true identity as a flexible free agent, not a fixed full-time member of a larger firm.

We think the prevalence of free agents means that the need for the pretense of being part of a bigger organization is disappearing. Smith can simply present herself as a free agent, working from home, collaborating with Jones and others as needed. Free agency is becoming respectable.

Smith and Jones may be the people you see sitting in a café with their laptops. They wear a T-shirt most days, but when they have an appointment, appear in formal business attire. Gradually, the free-agent style is becoming accepted as a normal part of business life, professionals are happy to meet in a café in casual dress, and business attire and a fancy office are no longer required to convey seriousness. The question is now, "Is your free-agent career working out for you? How do you do it?" People ask because many employees bound to a corporation long for the freedoms that come with working for yourself. They want to know if the escape route really exists.

One last illustrative scene from the life of a free agent: The conference call with apologies for the dog barking in the background or the child calling for Daddy. The explanation, "I'm working from home today" is getting easier to give, and is often met with the reply, "That's okay—me, too."

The "me too" answer is important because a big part of the acceptance of free agency as a legitimate professional lifestyle is that employees are becoming more like free agents. Organizations removed the most important distinction between employment and free agency by removing job security, in effect making all jobs akin to temporary projects. Also, what was once called "telework" is now just a common alternative work arrangement. Employees are working from home more often, erasing yet another distinction between employees and free agents. Telework has become a normal way of working as more organizations realize the significant employer benefits (lower real estate cost, improved employee engagement, better access to the right talent in a different location) and employee gains (greater flexibility, reduced commuting cost).

We have reached a point where free agency has become a far more mainstream career option. It is now common, attractive, and not as sharply differentiated from corporate life as in the past. Many move back and forth between free agency and employment. A gig as an employee can be attractive for free agents because it offers steady income for a few years. Still, they are unlikely to invest their identity in the corporation, as they are still CEO of Me. Social acceptance sets the stage for a rapid expansion of free agency. No longer a fringe phenomenon, free agency is duking it out with employment for a share of the market in how work is done. In 2001, Dan Pink, author of *Free Agent Nation: The Future of Working for Yourself*, estimated that more than a quarter of the U.S. workforce was made up of free agents.[3] Unfortunately, there it is no standard method for defining or counting free agents and estimates vary widely. In 2011, a survey by Kelly Services found "44 percent of American workers across all industries classify themselves as free agents."[4] whereas research house EMSI reported in 2014 that in the United States fewer than 10 percent of workers were self-employed.[5] There are all kinds of estimates on the prevalence of free agency; however, it is safe to conclude they play a big role in how work gets done, and we believe their impact will grow.

Estimates of the number of free agents may be conservative because new models arise all the time. Consider the rise of microbusinesses (defined as organizations with fewer than 10 employees). In the UK, the number of microbusinesses has increased by 40 percent since 2000.[6] A microbusiness is often a free agent writ large: an individual who has surrounded themselves with a small staff to leverage their free agency. We have entered an economy where free agents and microbusinesses are not fringe players. Individuals will build their careers there; and larger businesses will rely on them to get work done.

The challenges of measuring the prevalence of alternative work arrangements are nicely described in a paper by Cappelli and Keller.[7]

From Free Agent Nation to Free Agent World

Free Agent Nation is becoming Free Agent World. Low Lik Min lives in Kuala Lumpur and wanted to make commercials for big global brands like Lego. Not long ago, that would have been a pipe dream unless he could make the move to a city like London, Tokyo, or Los Angeles, where large advertising companies were located. Tongal changed all that. As advertising projects appeared on the web, it didn't matter where you lived, what school you went to, or who you knew. A free agent like Min could enter the competition and win on merit alone, and he did.

Are there advantages to hiring a free agent who's local? Yes. It can help to meet face-to-face from time to time, and a local is less likely to stumble over cultural differences. However, there is no question that free agents around the world have begun to compete for work. Even when a company prefers to use local talent, if the price or quality differential relative to competitors in another country is too high, then the local talent will not get the work.

We tend to think of labor costs as the driving feature of free agent world. After all, it's possible to get work done by free agents in the developing world at a fraction of what it would cost to have the task done locally. Check on Upwork and you can find some jobs paying just a few dollars an hour—good if you are in a low-wage economy, but not so good otherwise. Sometimes, though, it's not cost but quality that drives the free agent world. For his projects, Min may send work to free agents in the United States or UK. If he needs a voice-over for a commercial, then the quality of the talent is more important than price.

Yet sometimes it's neither cost nor quality that drives the free agent world. Sometimes it's just an accident. The talent platforms are inherently global. If you post tasks on MTurk, you probably won't know and won't care where the work is being done.

From the perspective of leaders, free agent world creates a deeper and more diverse pool of talent. Normally we just ask, "Who can we get to do this here?" but we now have the option of asking "Who is the best person in the world to get this done?" or "Who in the world will do a satisfactory job at an extraordinarily low price?"

Scanning the world takes effort. Leaders of the future need to ask different questions. When should you scan the world for the best or cheapest talent, and when should you rely on the talent that applies for your regular full-time jobs? If you consider the time it takes to hire an employee (90 to 120 days) relative to the time it takes to hire a free agent on Upwork (approximately three days), the economics alone suggest that leaders cannot ignore the alternatives to regular employment. Instead of placing all your bets on finding that one superstar employee, you now get to give three or four highly capable free agents a test run at nominal cost with no continuing obligation.

The Implications of Free Agent World

The implications of free agent world spill out all across our once-familiar landscape:

- Will there be a convergence of labor rates around the world? Will a lawyer in Lagos eventually make as much as one in L.A.? Will a clerk in Calgary make the same wage as one in Chennai?
- What will it be like to compete with people around the world in your specialty? There will always be someone cheaper. There will always be someone better.
- What pressures will this put on languages? Will Pakistani free agents be studying Japanese, so they can serve that market, or will Japanese companies follow Nissan's lead and make English their working language?
- How will governments react to this? Can they control the wild genie of the free agent world where work and payment for that work are oblivious to national boundaries?
- As a leader, how will you navigate the talent platforms that are in a sense the new factories of production? How much should your professional associations lobby governments to enable them?

The Remaining Barriers to World Domination

There are three main barriers standing in the way of free agency coming to dominate the world of work. One is that gathering a community of regular employees committed to jobs as part of a common endeavor is still a potent way to get work done. Leaders sometimes find that the bonds of employment chafe, but that cuts both ways; they may not like labor regulations, but they like the control that comes from being the employer.

However, the second barrier facing free agency is bigger than just competing with a committed team of employees. The second barrier is that being a free agent is hard. The free agent has to have deep expertise in their profession, whether that's plumbing or financial reporting, and also expertise in sales, marketing, office administration, and technology. The oft-repeated advice that free agents should do what they are good at and "hire" people (enlist other free agents) to do the things at which they don't excel is hard to follow for a lone free agent struggling with cash flow. Many people find the current model of free agency too hard to sustain from an income perspective.

The third barrier is legislation. As we have seen in the various legal challenges to the operating models of companies like Uber and Lyft, there is considerable discomfort with the perceived ambiguity between being an employee and a free agent. Do the facts that drivers are integral to their businesses, can be terminated at any time, and are under the direction and control of the company make them employees of Uber or Lyft? Or do the facts that drivers can choose when they work, the customers they pick up, and how they dress for work make them free agents?

This leaves us in a world where free agency has advantages; however, the growth of free agency is constrained by how difficult it can be to succeed. What happens when innovative businesses erode that barrier? As we shall see, talent platforms are revolutionizing the design of work to make it easier and more efficient for free agents and those who engage them. In addition, there is an increase in less dramatic but still important services, making it easy for free agents to get affordable accounting systems, technical support, and administrative help. And, and as we will discuss later, this situation does present an opportunity for other stakeholders (e.g., unions and regulators) who have traditionally been allied to the employment relationship to redefine their role and step in to meet this emerging need of free agents.

The tide is moving in the direction of more and more free agency. The barriers to free agency are crumbling, as are the advantages of employment, and the boundary between free agency and employment is blurring.

Leaders wedded to the traditional view that work is done by regular full-time employees will increasingly miss out on powerful opportunities. An individual chasing a career based on regular full-time employment will be chasing a mirage. Governments counting jobs and tuning legislation around issues such as paternal leave will overlook a vast amount of the work economy. A world beyond employment will be better in some ways and worse in others; however, if the tide is taking us into that world, then the sensible course of action is to learn to swim with the tide.

Notes

1. Chris Worley and Ed Lawler, *Built to Change*, (San Francisco: Jossey-Bass, 2006).
2. Peter Cappelli, *The New Deal at Work: Managing the Market-Driven Workforce* (Harvard Business Review Press, 1999).
3. Dan Pink, *Free Agent Nation: The Future of Working for Yourself* (Warner Books, 2001).
4. Mark Lanfear, KellyOCG.com report, published 2012, http://www.kellyocg .com/uploadedFiles/Content/Knowledge/Ebooks/Free%20Agency%20is %20Here%20-%20A%20Scientific%20Perspective%281%29.pdf (accessed March 17, 2015).
5. R. Senz, "Analyzing Structural LMI and Job Postings to Understand Key Occupations," posted June 24, 2014, http://www.economicmodeling.com/ 2014/06/24/analyzing-structural-lmi-and-job-postings-to-understand-key-occupations/ (accessed April 7, 2015).
6. Benedict Dellot, "Salvation in a Start-Up? The Origins and Nature of the Self-Employment Boom" (London: RSA Action and Research Centre, May 2014).
7. Peter Cappelli and J. R. Keller, "A study of the extent and potential causes of alternative employment arrangements," working paper 18376, http://www.nber.org/papers/w18376.

3

Outsourcing and Alliances

Chapter 2 describes the rise of the Free Agent World. It showed us that getting work done is not just a matter of managing your own employees. When we say "lead the work" (not just employees) we mean leaders should first clearly identify the work to be done and only then decide if it is best done by employees, or by other means such as outsourcing, alliances, free agents, or platforms. It can be difficult to envision these other means, if you are accustomed to thinking only about work done by employees. So, in this chapter and the next, we describe several common ways to lead the work beyond employment.

In this chapter we describe two mechanisms—*outsourcing* and *alliances*—that tap another organization to access workers, who in turn are employees or contractors of that other organization. With outsourcing, a client's work is done by the outsourcers regular full-time employees or their free agents. Alliances are similar but it is being done by the employees (or free agents) of the ally, who is not in the business of providing workers, but has a collaborative relationship. For example, Siemens formed an alliance with Disney to use Disney marketing employees to design a marketing campaign for a Siemens hearing aid for kids. The marketing workers at Disney may be working hand in hand with Siemens as part of the alliance, but they will no doubt identify primarily with the mission of Disney. If Siemens had placed the work with a company that provides marketing solutions as its business, that would be outsourcing.

Decisions about outsourcing and alliances are typically made to optimize costs, processes, or financial market indicators, but not to optimize the work. That's often a mistake, but it's easily made when you think of leadership as ending with your own employees. You can avoid that mistake by focusing leadership on the work. When you do that, you realize that even if the work is done through an external provider through outsourcing or alliances, you must still consider how the provider's decisions about leading the work mesh with your own. At the extreme, you may actually need to require that your partner change their approach, and that they lead the work your way. For example if you have a strong emphasis on process compliance/integrity and specific individual accountability and your alliance partner has a very informal culture with more emphasis on getting the job done regardless of specific protocols, then it is a good idea to agree on how the people you share will be managed. Also, if you need to track worker performance in a certain way, then you may need to ask your ally to use that method to track the performance of their workers assigned to your project. You may need to enforce different rules on knowledge transfer and work documentation for your ally's employees. We will see more examples like this later, when we describe how IBM tackled these problems, and how HR processes must change.

Outsourcing and alliances fall into a broad category economists call *labor market intermediaries*. The term describes a situation where a separate organization takes on a role as go-between connecting the worker to the organization that receives the work. It can be as simple as a job board that does the searching and matching between workers and employers, or a "professional employer organization" which takes on the legal obligations of employment and then provides their legal employees to other organizations. The term *labor market intermediary* thus covers a variety of quite different roles and services, but they have in common that they take on some aspects of a relationship with workers that had previously been handled through an employment contract, or directly by the employer. We will return to this idea in Chapter 7 when we describe how you can detach elements of the work from the employment relationship.

For now, leaders should simply realize that outsourcing and alliances are two of many ways to engage with workers. It is not simply a choice between regular full-time employment and outsourcing or alliances. You will probably need to create hybrid approaches that fall somewhere in between. Yet, understanding how outsourcing and alliances work today, can help you think more creatively about how you lead the work.

The Rise of Outsourcing

The story of outsourcing is well known, and came into its own in the late 1980s. Robert Handfield described it in "A Brief History of Outsourcing":

> Outsourcing was not formally identified as a business strategy until 1989. However, most organizations were not totally self-sufficient; they outsourced those functions for which they had no competency internally. Publishers, for example, have often purchased composition, printing, and fulfillment services. The use of external suppliers for these essential but ancillary services might be termed the baseline stage in the evolution of outsourcing. Outsourcing support services is the next stage. In the 1990s, as organizations began to focus more on cost-saving measures, they started to outsource those functions necessary to run a company but not related specifically to the core business. Managers contracted with emerging service companies to deliver accounting, human resources, data processing, internal mail distribution, security, plant maintenance, and the like as a matter of "good housekeeping."[1]

Manufacturing moved out of organizations to capture the wage differential between the developed and developing world for low-skill work. Call centers moved to India—thanks to cheap and reliable international phone networks that made it practical to locate call centers far away from customers. In India companies found not only an inexpensive English-speaking workforce but a highly educated one as well. The point where companies were actually in touch with their customers, something that one might think would have to stay within the organization, was happily handed over to a third party.

Not all outsourcing was about moving jobs to other countries. Companies have long been outsourcing functions like payroll to specialist providers. Payroll is particularly suited to outsourcing because it can be cleanly disconnected from other activities in the organization; in essence, the interaction between a company and a payroll outsourcer can be limited to the exchange of a data file once a month. Furthermore payroll processes are very similar from one company to another, allowing an outsourcer to develop economies of scale.

And there is no reason to think that innovation in outsourcing services has stopped. For almost any function, methods currently exist or are being invented to do it outside the firm, and this changes the job of a leader. If you use an outsourcer, you are leading the work through that outsourcer, which means new decisions. Will you treat the outsourcer simply as an arms-length vendor, with little concern about how they lead their employees? Many global companies have learned the dangers of treating their outsourced factories that way, when labor conflicts, fatal fires, or safety issues in some factories affected the client company. It obviously is not possible to say, "please don't hold that against us because those are only our outsourcers, and not our employees." So, leading through the work means understanding the work practices of the outsourcer, to ensure that they approach the work and workers in ways that support your leadership mission. Issues such as training, safety and identification of pivotal talent may extend far beyond your own employees.

The Rise of Alliances

Alliances shine a spotlight on a potentially radical change in what an organization is. Most broadly, they show how the boundaries are breaking down and it's becoming more natural for organizations to be interlinked and collaborative. In many cases, alliances are also a means of moving big chunks of mission-critical work outside the organization.

One of the age-old decisions in management is "build or buy." If you need a computer application, do you build your own program or buy a program already on the market? Alliances change that decision to "build versus buy versus collaborate," and often collaboration is the way to get the best of both worlds.

Consider the research of Dr. Ard-Pieter de Man, a professor at the VU University, Amsterdam. He argues that alliances have gone from a fringe phenomenon in the 1970s to a massive engine of value creation today.[2] How massive? In 2009, the Association of Strategic Alliance Professionals surveyed its member companies, asking about the impact of alliances on market capitalization.[3] More than half of the 431 organizations that responded (mostly U.S. and European firms with more than 1,000 employees) forecast that by 2013 (four years from the time they were surveyed), alliances would generate more than 40 percent of their company's market value. And to illustrate how big and successful alliances can be, the Sky Team Alliance—which includes Air France/KLM, Delta Airlines, and Alitalia, among others—yields gross revenues of $10 billion, which is then shared between its partners.

Alliances came to the world's attention in the 1980s thanks to the success of joint ventures, particularly in research and development. Joint ventures, though, are relatively inflexible. The 1990s saw the emergence of contractual alliances, which can be designed to be more flexible and to serve an enormous range of purposes. For example, the coffee machine manufacturer Philips partnered with Sara Lee/DL, which sells coffee, to create the Senseo product line. Senseo offers single-cup coffee makers that use a pod containing both ground coffee and a filter. The capabilities of both companies were needed to launch the product, but there was no need to create a stand-alone joint venture; they simply created a contract with an appropriate governance structure to enable collaboration.

The phrase "simply created a contract with an appropriate governance structure" actually underplays the difficulty of the task. The management of alliances is complex, especially since there are so many possible forms. A glimpse into that complexity comes from the Australian government's Department of Infrastructure and Transport "Guide to Alliance Contracting" (2011); it's a whopping 168 pages long and addresses the many issues—from governance to risk to key roles—needed to make alliances work.

The success rate of alliances seems to be on the rise. In the aforementioned 2009 survey conducted by the Association of Strategic Alliance Professionals, 57 percent of member respondents rated their alliance as successful, up from 50 percent of respondents who answered the same question in 2007. They also reported that management investment in alliances was strong and steady. Alliances have arrived as a major force in management and are continuing to get stronger as companies learn how to handle these arrangements.

Alliances are a means for handling undertakings that would be risky, difficult, or impossible for a single company to do on their own. For example, the aforementioned airline alliance creates a set of global routes in a way the individual airlines could never have done. Senseo would have been difficult for Philips to pull off on its own. ASML Holdings certainly has the know-how to make the equipment that makes computer chips, but the risk of funding research and development on its own would give the board sleepless nights. The solution was to embed ASML in an alliance with Intel, Samsung, and TSMC.

Put simply, alliances are often just a better avenue of bringing specific concepts to fruition. A good example is the Dutch government-owned railway company ProRail, which creates alliances with construction firms. This motivates the firms to find creative ways to minimize delays and cost overruns in rail construction.

According to the 2009 survey by the Association of Strategic Alliance Professionals, alliances break down into five basic types:

- Comarketing alliances (45 percent of all alliances). For example, for eight years Cisco and HP ran an alliance that helped them sell each other's products.
- Research alliances (16 percent). A good case study is TransCelerate BioPharma, an alliance of leading pharmaceutical firms collaborating to improve the very expensive process of clinical trials.
- Distribution alliances (13 percent). Rolls Royce has created an important alliance with three logistics companies to transport expensive and urgently needed jet engine parts around the world quickly.
- Supplier alliances (11 percent). The classic example is Toyota, which has long-running collaborative relationships with suppliers, working together to improve productivity and share gains. The suppliers almost feel like a part of Toyota. This is quite a contrast to a focus simply on the lowest price.
- Coproduction alliance (10 percent). The oil industry majors will often ally on drilling projects and even refineries.
- Other (5 percent).

Of all the different forms of alliances, we are most interested in the ones involving firms that might have done the work in house with their own regular full-time employees, but decided instead that the work was optimally done through an alliance.

One particularly bold alliance was started by Metro AG, the world's fifth largest retailer. In 2002, the company launched an ambitious effort to invent the store of the future. The "Future Store" was set up as a real, functioning supermarket where the alliance could try out new processes and technologies, set standards, and resolve integration issues. The best minds would get to work on it, it would have a substantial budget, and fantastic discoveries could be made along the way. It would be a big endeavor, but Metro is a big company.

Yet, even with Metro's size and scale, questions arise: Are Metro's employees always the best talent for every piece of work? Even if they are, can Metro afford to pull them all away from their regular work onto the project? With so many things to learn to keep pace with technological innovation, could Metro learn fast enough, relying only on its own employees?

Metro decided the best way—maybe the only way—for the Future Store Initiative to achieve its potential was to open up, interlink, and collaborate with a broad alliance of partners from the retailing, consumer goods, IT, and service sectors. The alliance included 75 partners including well-known giants like SAP, Visa, IBM, Intel, and smaller specialists running across the alphabet from ADT Sensormatics (security) to XPlace (retail self-service). Many of the innovations developed at the Future Store have already been implemented at other stores. The Future Store itself returned to its role as a normal Metro supermarket in December 2012.

Metro does not own all the knowledge and information that flowed from the Future Store Initiative the way it would if the company had kept everything behind the walls of the corporation. But Metro is on the field playing with the best in the world and is now in a better position to stay at the cutting edge of retail.

We pointed out that Metro is large enough to build a Future Store on its own. Doing everything on your own is the sort of approach that an organization takes when it thinks about leading the work only as managing its own regular employees. Instead, Metro's alliance blends the work of workers that are regular employees of 75 partners. Certainly, the partnership encompasses information, products, and processes. Yet, at its heart, it is an alliance of workers. Metro's leaders can no longer presume their leadership of work stops with their employees, or even the free agents with whom they directly engage. In a very real sense, Metro's leaders are now in partnership with the leaders of the Future Store partners, to lead the combined work of all of their workers. It is that combined set of work and workers that must be considered when Metro and its partners craft their vision, establish their culture, and design the work, organization, and rewards that affect those combined workers.

De Man says that most alliances are full of ambiguity. To be successful, it's necessary to develop trust and to take risks. How best to make the alliance successful? That needs to be discovered over time, and the areas of opportunity may not be what the leaders originally foresaw. This takes a different kind of manager and a different culture from one that emphasizes control.

An Ecosystem for Augmenting Reality

Meta is a startup that is developing the technology for augmented reality glasses, display devices worn on the head offering a small, computer-generated display in front of the eyes. We can probably expect it soon to be quite normal to walk around and see computer images imposed on the real world.

Meta's ambitions to change the world are stunning. Their goal is to replace the hardware you use today (desktop, laptop, phone) with Meta glasses that enable you to layer digital content on the world so that people can interact with the real world and computers simultaneously. How can a 70 employee company change the world? Certainly not on their own, they need allies.

In Meta's case the most important allies are those software developers who have the vision to see how augmented reality computing could work and the skill to make it happen. One such ally is SimX (simxar.com) which is working to revolutionize how doctors are trained. In today's hospitals an important training tool is the physical simulation mannequin; these are expensive and typically modelled after a fit white male. SimX replaces the physical mannequins with a customizable, high-definition, 3D virtual patient. Doctors won't need a million dollar simulation room; they will be able to practice on a virtual patient on any empty bed or gurney.

Alliances are not easy to manage. Todd Revolt, director of strategic alliances for Meta, says he looks for companies that share the same mindset. His role is to evangelize Meta to the developer community, help support them to develop apps, and showcase their successes. The *capabilities* of an ally matter, however what Meta really needs is to find developers who can *imagine* how to layer content into a 3D world in a way that will change how we interact with computing. A leader who is skilled in managing the relationships brings an immense amount of power to an organization. An organization without leaders who can manage these relationships is hobbled because they miss out on one of the most powerful ways to get work done.

In the case of SimX, Meta has helped by giving their ally early access to technology and marketing support. Meta and SimX attend conferences together and share useful contacts. Generally no money changes hands.

We refer to the relationship in terms of "allies" and "an ecosystem"; however Revolt talks about "a part of the family" and "a community." Meta and its allies are independent firms, but as a community they share a mission and a culture that may be more coherent than that found in most large firms. The relationship between Meta and its allies may be more cooperative than two divisions in a typical multinational.

Meta's leaders cannot look inward and think of their organization as an isolated unit. It is one node in a dynamic ecosystem that they think will change the world. Success will come from surfing through that ecosystem, interlinking with other players, and collaborating with skilled developers. They can't succeed unless the ecosystem succeeds, and they can't succeed if they don't continually evolve their own niche in that ecosystem.

What does leading the work mean for Meta's leaders? Obviously, it doesn't end with leading Meta's regular full-time employees. Everyone working in the community matters to Meta, and Meta's leaders will do everything in their power to ensure the right people are attracted to that community, that they are developed, supported with the right tools, and motivated. Their resources are limited, but the passion in the community is one of their greatest assets.

Microbusinesses

It gets even more interesting when we look at alliances of small businesses. De Man discusses how a number of Dutch tomato farmers, who ran small family businesses, were facing a crisis because the quality of the tomatoes had become so poor. As a single family, already working long hours to run the farm, how can you possibly deal with the R&D, production, and marketing demands involved in trying to orchestrate a turnaround? You cannot do it on your own, but you can if you ally with other small farms. That's exactly what the farmers did. Six of them created a cooperative in 1994 that had, by 2013, grown to 23 members owning 206 hectares of tomato greenhouses. The cooperative has working groups that look at common issues like marketing, purchasing, and all the other noncore activities (that is: everything other than growing tomatoes). The mechanisms for successfully running this cooperative are many, and that is a discipline in itself. The alliance developed new means of efficiently growing high-quality tomatoes and in doing so rescued their businesses.

For the Dutch farmers, leading the work means leading the workers within the microbusiness ecosystem. If each farmer defines leadership to apply only to their own employees, the entire idea collapses. Alliances of free agents and microbusinesses are potentially more flexible and efficient than hierarchies of employees. This economic form brings to mind an analogy from the world of nature: coral. A single coral organism is insignificant as an individual, but corals collaborate to build a reef that becomes the dominant structure in an ecosystem. The Dutch farmers with their collective of small farms managed to become a powerful entity in their ecosystem, dramatically improve tomato quality, and save their businesses. However, it required that they redefine what it means to lead, leading means getting work done by whatever talent can do it best, not presuming it must be done by your own employees.

Bharti Airtel: A Demonstration of the Market-Moving Power of Alliances

Bharti Airtel's rapid growth to become the second-largest telecommunications provider in the world in a short 15 years has made the company very interesting to study. In fact, eight *Harvard Business Review* (HBR) cases have been written about it. Akhil Gupta, Bharti's vice chairman who orchestrated its alliances with IBM, Siemens, Nokia, and Ericsson, laughs when he recalls the *Wall Street Journal* front-page article with its "reverse outsourcing" article. "These were actually alliances where we shared the risk associated with growing our business with strategic partners," he explained. It might have sold more newspapers to tell the story as one of an Indian company achieving market dominance by outsourcing its operations to Western multinationals, but the fact remains that Bharti achieved its exponential growth by wisely tapping the mission-critical capabilities, talent, and scale of a select group of world-class partners—not by merely shipping off a series of ancillary processes and activities to be executed at a lower cost somewhere else in the world.

In Gupta's mind, the deals were done out of sheer necessity, as there was no other way for them to grow. Bharti had acquired the numerous telecom licenses to provide coverage all across India but recognized that it did not have the human or financial capital needed to fully deliver on its vision. It had two choices: Give up the licenses, or curb its ambitions. The company chose neither. By moving to share its stake in the rapid growth of the Indian telecom market with partners who provided them with the infrastructure needed to power their growth, the company also shared the risk associated with that growth.

"In the case of our IT infrastructure," he continues, "IBM could do it all. IBM's legacy in technology, its global scale, and its ability to attract the best talent made them a logical choice. With all four of our partners, we chose organizations who could not afford to fail us. The sense of shared destiny was essential to the success of the alliances."

The trick was structuring an agreement that worked for both parties. Bharti and IBM struck a 10-year agreement covering hardware, software, and services. IBM would ensure that all three elements were in place, so the Bharti enterprise could run seamlessly. In return, it was paid a percentage of Bharti's revenue. The relationship involved trust and shared risk and was predicated on the two parties' shared belief in the continued growth of the telecom sector in India.

"We allied on the activity—not the strategy," Gupta says. "You can have a permeable organization when it comes to activities, but not strategy. Nor did we give up accountability for the results. We asked ourselves three questions in deciding whether we should partner or keep an activity in-house: 'Who has better domain knowledge? Who has better economies of scale? Who can attract better human capital?'" Bharti had 220 people in its IT department prior to forging the relationship. All this staff was transferred to IBM with the promise that anyone who wanted to come back within two years would be able to do so.

Thus, for both IBM and Bharti, leading the work went well beyond each organization managing its own employees. True leadership meant a nuanced combination and interaction between the workers involved from both organizations. It meant deconstructing the work so that the alliance could be based on activities without compromising the strategy. It meant designing the performance and rewards of the integrated workers from each company so that accountability was properly assigned. It meant deciding exactly where the work would flow across organizational boundaries and where it would stay within boundaries. It meant deciding who could attract better human capital when considering each organization's unique advantages, and then optimizing their combination.

The Future of Alliances

Alliances are potentially important anywhere your organization is not the best in the world at what it does. Just as it makes sense to engage a Topcoder to handle a specialist programming language that your own staff is not familiar with, it makes sense to engage allies for parts of the business that are not strong. In Chapter 1, we mentioned the case of Siemens partnering with Disney to reach children. An early step for organizations is to look around at where they truly are world class and where they are not, then start identifying potential allies.

A second step is to look inside and see what alliance-building skills the company already has. Leaders are often surprised to discover how many alliances of one form or another already exist within their firm. After that, one has to develop various capabilities, from selecting partners, to setting up systems that measure progress, and from a focus on internal hierarchy, budgets, and power, to looking outward.

De Man says he believes the next generation of open alliances is being born now, and that this generation is steeped in the idea of flexibility and relationships, rather than contracts that try to nail down every eventual possibility. Alliances work best when they are designed to evolve, and that means creating means for developing and maintaining trust. Another aspect of this next generation is a perspective that looks beyond the alliance itself to the broader ecosystem. For example, there are application development companies with no relationship to Google that nevertheless play a role in supporting the Android ecosystem. Google needs to keep these companies in mind as they develop Android. A significant factor is how the work of this ecosystem of companies fits with the work and the goals of Google.

As alliances move forward, all kinds of interesting questions arise. For example, we think of the CEO as responsible for resources in the company, but what is the CEO responsible for when half the resources are outside the company? And, how do you articulate the value of alliances to shareholders? And, to what extent will alliance management be an essential part of any leader's career path? Thinking in ecosystem terms is a natural next step for organizations committed to open alliances, and when the ecosystem must change rapidly, that means relationships based on trust. Trust is built through relationships, worker to worker. Thus, the new world of alliances will be built as much upon leading the work as on leading technology and information.

Leveraging the Power of Alliances to Rapidly Capture Growth: Towers Watson

Towers Watson (TW) is one of the largest consulting companies in the world. Yet despite its many resources, it has chosen to leverage the power of alliances to both capture growth in emerging areas and mitigate the risk associated with such growth. The reasons for the two alliances described below are unique—one combines the market presence of TW with the technological capabilities of Jiff, while the other leverages the intellectual property of TW with the distribution capabilities of Verizon.

Towers Watson and Jiff

In 2013, Towers Watson and Jiff, a digital health technology company, formed a strategic alliance to provide employers with a new digital health solution to measure and improve various health outcomes while educating employees and their family members on how to make better lifestyle choices.

Under the alliance, Jiff and Towers Watson plan to work together to test and market a new digital health offering. Built on the Jiff platform, the Health Outcomes Marketplace is a scalable solution featuring digital health tools and applications that allow employers to deploy health and wellness programs. The combination of Jiff's technology and Towers Watson's health and wellness consulting expertise will help employers implement wellness incentive programs more successfully, thereby helping them to more effectively manage health care costs. While Jiff's mobile platform helps connect consumers with employers, health plans, and health providers, TW leverages its scale and relationships in health and wellness consulting to employers to introduce Jiff.

The relationship greatly mitigates the risk associated with TW participating in this space (versus attempting to build such a capability for its clients).

Says Paul Matthews, alliance leader for TW, "The partnership with Jiff has allowed us to access the best platform available while sticking to our core strengths. TW is educating Jiff on what other apps and solutions to include in their platform based on insights we have about what employers value."

As we have seen in multiple other industries where the sheer velocity of change requires new and creative approaches for capturing market share, the speed of change in the wellness sector (changing client needs, a changing competitive set, changing market requirements) makes alliances like this a viable way of mitigating risk while capturing emerging opportunity. It makes the "build and sell" option redundant.

Towers Watson and Hughes (now Verizon) Telematics

In 2012, Towers Watson and Hughes Telematics, a Verizon company, formed a strategic alliance to provide personal line U.S. auto insurers with comprehensive data services for usage-based insurance (UBI) programs. Usage-based insurance involves variable pricing structures that vary based on specific measurable driving behaviors instead of a fixed premium. Under the terms of the alliance, Towers Watson's DriveAbility service offering will be powered by Hughes' In-Drive solution. DriveAbility helps insurers convert driving data into industry-applicable metrics, which enables the development of new insurance products and services for consumers.

TW had been working in the area of usage-based insurance for the six years prior to the relationship, advising its many insurance industry clients on how to design products and analyze them leveraging TW's proprietary analytics. Says Robin Harbage, alliance leader for TW, "We never contemplated providing telematics solutions, as we did not want to get involved with the technology." Hughes (which was subsequently bought by Verizon) had the technology but lacked the analytics. This created all the necessary conditions for a marriage made in heaven.

Whatever data is gathered from a vehicle, TW would create the algorithm and analytics to enable the creation of new usage-based insurance products. TW would have access to data that could be sold to insurers while Verizon and other telecommunication providers would provide the technology to gather and transmit the data. As a result of this strategy, TW is now embedding such analytical capabilities in the devices of other mobile providers (beyond Verizon).

According to Harbage, "The whole relationship has morphed. We used to just provide referrals to Hughes for the technology. When the Verizon relationship was established, it became a true strategic alliance. As a result of the success of this relationship in the United States, we now have something similar with Vodafone in Europe."

Notes

1. Robert Handfield, "A Brief History of Outsourcing," SCRC, NC State University, http://scm.ncsu.edu/scm-articles/article/a-brief-history-of-outsourcing.
2. Ard-Pieter de Man, *Alliances: An Executive Guide to Designing Successful Strategic Partnerships* (Hoboken, NJ: John Wiley & Sons, 2013).
3. Association of Strategic Alliance Professionals, The Third State of Alliance Management Study, 2009.

4 | The Talent Platforms

The largest employer in the world is Walmart with 2.2 million employees.[1] There are only three companies with more than 700,000 employees (Sinopec and Hon Hai Precision Industry round out the list)...if you only count regular full-time employees. Appirio (the parent company of Topcoder), is a company with 700 employees worldwide, yet it boasts more than 700,000 "community members" working on more than 1,500 projects, through "cloud solutions." It was lauded in 2014 as a best place to work by ITPRO in the United Kingdom, based on a survey of its 700 employees.[2] Yet, does "working" at Appirio mean being one of its 700 regular full-time employees, or does it mean participating in Topcoder's cloud-based design projects? What's more important to Appirio, being the best place to work for 700 employees, or the best place to work for 700,000 nonemployees that Appirio's Topcoder platform connects with its clients?

You may think, "That's Apprio's problem, but it doesn't affect me. I will focus on being the best place to work for my regular full-time employees and just leave the cloud-based work and free agents to Appirio."

Suppose you tap Topcoder's network to develop vital software applications for your company. Does it matter to you if those workers find your company and its projects attractive and motivating? Does it benefit you to try to be a best place to work for those workers, not only for your regular full-time employees? Some of the world's top programmers do all their work through Topcoder, and they can choose what projects to work on. These workers communicate with each other about how interesting your projects are, and how your regular employees relate to them when they work on virtual teams together. Topcoder's talent chooses your company just as much as you choose them.

Leading the work increasingly means leading in cooperation with platforms like Topcoder. If you focus on leading only your employees, you not only overlook a potentially significant part of your workforce, but you also will miss seeing the laboratories where advances in the workplace happen first. Even if you are not a client of Topcoder or another platform, your workers will eventually be affected by what such platforms are learning and executing when it comes to work, organization, and rewards.

As talent platforms like Appirio's Topcoder perfect cloud-based work solutions, they offer alternatives to regular full-time employment not just for you but for the workers you need. Your organization starts to look like a mix of regular full-time employees and platform-provided workers that are not employees of anyone. Your ratio may not be as high as Appirio's, where there are 100 times the number of cloud-based nonemployee workers to regular full-time employees, but your ratio will very likely be much higher in the future than it is now.

In part, that's because platforms are ever more sophisticated marketplaces for you to find and employ free agents to do work that might previously have required regular employees. As disruptive as this marketplace evolution will be, there is a more subtle, but potentially even more significant, development for leaders getting work done. Talent platforms are evolving from only offering you a marketplace to find free agents for a specific task like coding or logo design, to increasingly providing a platform to organize and optimize the work of a complete project like application development or a web-based marketing campaign, and they increasingly solve issues such as worker rewards, development, evaluation, trust, and governance.

Talent platforms are evolving to be much more than marketplaces, and that means they will disrupt and redefine a much larger domain of work in all sorts of organizations. Increasingly, your job as a leader will be to optimize not just the mix of free agents and your regular employees to do tasks, but to optimize how you design the work itself. Being the best place to work for free agents will increasingly mean not just finding them and assigning them a task, but designing the work itself to optimize their role.

In this chapter, we describe several leading talent platforms: Upwork, Tongal, Topcoder, and MTurk. Much has been written about these platforms, but here we focus on a particular goal: to illustrate what they can teach you about leading through the work, beyond regular full-time employees. We do that through five questions that you can also ask about your organization:

1. What is the offering to our customers?
2. What is the work?
3. Who are the workers?
4. How do we engage the workers?
5. What's the future?

As a leader, pay close attention, because these platforms have long faced the issues that you will soon face in your own organization. The platforms have the advantage of learning from the work experience of hundreds of thousands of workers, millions of work transactions, and thousands of projects that often involve subtle and clever ways to optimally combine free agents and regular full-time employees. These platforms have a learning laboratory that is far larger and more diverse than any organization's cadre of regular full-time employees. They offer important object lessons for leaders in all organizations, who will increasingly get work done through just such optimal combinations.

Upwork

The Offering and Clients

Upwork is currently the largest freelance talent platform in the volume of work (i.e. the number of jobs completed). Launched in 1999, Elance originally focused on software helping companies manage their contractor workforce. It then evolved into a kind of job board for free-agent work that also facilitated payment and other services. oDesk launched in 2003, aimed at matching freelancers to projects. In 2014, Elance and oDesk merged, bringing their combined revenue to $941 million. As the Upwork website describes it: "Elance is where businesses go to find, hire, collaborate with and pay leading free agents from more than 180 countries. . . . With a community of over 9.7 million free agents and 3.8 million businesses." While the original Upwork clients were small businesses with limited in-house resources and a tight budget, more recent Upwork clients are Fortune 500 companies. The platform's popularity with big firms likely started blossoming when adventurous, tech-savvy managers within companies used Upwork for projects done on a limited budget and got good results. Then word spread, and over time, the idea of using Upwork became a normal, accepted option for any kind of work that can happen via the Internet.

The Upwork site includes a video from client Chris Clegg of Portland Marketing Analytics.[3] He says when he started using oDesk, he would look for one free agent who possessed a mix of the skills needed for his project—say, a programmer who could do coding, design, and also know something about search engine optimization (SEO), or an entry-level analyst who knew Word, Excel, and PowerPoint. But this didn't turn out to be the most effective way to approach matters. Instead, Clegg says he learned it was better to deconstruct the work and hire specialists for each part.

Embracing the concept of deconstructing work and hiring specialists, like Clegg now does, shows how the talent platforms are not just a way to fill temporary jobs cheaply and easily. The real payoff of these platforms comes when you rethink the work itself, with an expanded perspective that doesn't assume you must use regular full-time employees, and that the work must be embedded within a job.

When Clegg limited himself to thinking about hiring a regular full-time employee for an existing job, he looked for someone who could do all the different tasks within that job. When you realize there are alternatives such as free agents and talent platforms, you can engage workers for elements of the job. You can get a designer to lay out the look of the site and choose fonts and images, engage a programmer to do the coding, then engage a search engine optimization specialist so that the site can be found.

The Work

At its core, Upwork is the Monster.com of freelance work. There are a vast number and a great variety of tasks offered there, and a large population of free agents available to do the work. The work that flows from Upwork is almost all done virtually. The most common types of work offered via the site are programming projects and creative tasks such as writing, graphic design, and website design. However, part of the beauty of Upwork is that it's big and diverse enough to find talent for almost any task. Upwork senior vice president Rich Pearson tells the story of a relative who dreaded composing a speech for a wedding. The solution turned out to be straightforward: Find someone on the talent platform who could write wedding speeches.

For programming work, there are two typical use scenarios. For projects involving new programming languages, leaders may have no in-house employees with relevant experience, so it makes sense to go to Upwork looking for that fresher skill set. The opposite use case occurs when your in-house programmers only want to do work on the newest platforms, and you won't be able to retain them if you keep them working on old languages. In this situation, the talent platform can be used to find free agents to do the work your in-house team considers mundane.

The process starts with a client posting a task and their budget (either fixed price or hourly). Free agents review the posted tasks and apply for work they would like. Clients can also search the database of available free agents and invite people to submit a proposal. The platform will also automatically recommend free agents who match the client's requirements. The system controls the number of people who can apply for a task; each post is limited to 30 invitations. This is an important control feature so that a client doesn't get hundreds of applications for one task, and free agents have a reasonable chance of winning the proposal.

The client then selects a free agent for the work in much the same way they would hire any other worker. They scrutinize resumes, portfolios, test scores, and reputation ratings to create a short list, then interview those on the list to make a decision.

The most straightforward type of project seen on Upwork is a small one, like the wedding-speech example, that can be done in a few days.

However, clients also use the platform for large projects requiring multiple free agents over a period of months. Some go further, using Upwork for on-going staff augmentation where a free agent works perhaps 15 hours a week for an indefinite period of time.

The Workers

Put very simply, Upwork provides a place for free agents to find work, and this is key, as many free agents are good at their core skill—writing, designing, coding—but lacking when it comes to other parts of running a business, particularly sales and marketing. Talent platforms take away some of the need to market and sell yourself. The other major upside for free agents using talent platforms is the ability to work from anywhere in the world, at any time, for as long as one wants. There is a huge population of people who, for whatever reason, cannot or do not want to work nine to five at an office.

Free agents who use Upwork routinely make a couple of points about the experience. One is that you need to learn how to find work that is suitable for you and that pays decently. Navigating your way through the platform is not technically difficult, however efficiently navigating to the right work is a skill. Because many of the tasks are posted by small businesses that don't have much experience in that particular task, they may have unclear or unrealistic expectations. The free agent will have to be ready to deal with that. Free agents also say it can be hard to make a living entirely on Upwork. That is by no means universally true, and it may be even less true in the future if more work migrates to the platform.

The Engagement Model

Upwork provides a variety of tools to structure the communication between the two parties. "We are trying to build trust between the free agent and client," says SVP Pearson.

The ways Upwork builds trust provide an interesting contrast to regular full-time employment. Yes, workers are paid, their work is evaluated, and there is a grievance system, but it typically takes place outside the employment relationship, often with far greater flexibility, quality, and lower cost. There are lessons here for you and your leaders, about how you could get these things done beyond employment.

Like employee performance management systems, there is an optional feature in which an Upwork tool takes random screen shots of the free agent's screen while they work on a client's project so that both the worker and the client can see when the worker is working on the client's task. There's also a free code review, so clients without technical expertise can be sure their programming work was professionally done.

Like an employee project management system that coordinates and tracks progress, Upwork has tools for organizing projects by milestones with ongoing status reports. To manage relevant files, there is a consolidated "work room," a feature particularly useful for projects involving multiple free agents.

Like an employee sourcing and selection system, Upwork offers clients best practices, such as, "Do at least a brief interview by phone before you select a free agent" and, "Be very clear about your expectations, including whether the work is suitable for a novice, journeyman, or expert." Like a recruitment and selection system for employees, the platform educates both clients and free agents in how to successfully deal with each other.

Like an employee grievance and dispute resolution system, Upwork monitors client feedback during the course of a project. If problems arise, they'll offer help and if necessary guide the client on how to begin a dispute-resolution process. If the dispute resolution isn't successful, Upwork will absorb the loss itself, paying the free agent for the work done, and letting the client use the funds to hire another free agent. This process is reassuring, however it is rarely needed; disputes occur in only 0.1 percent of projects.

Like an employee training system, free agents take tests on Upwork to get certifications that prove to clients they have the necessary skills, and to assess their own abilities and see what they need to learn. Upwork offers online training, some of it free. Free agents must take the initiative in learning, but Upwork makes appropriate training available.

Like an employee career and development system, the talent platform points free agents toward the kind of work they might want to pursue. The platform provides a transparent and real-time window into the demand for work, how well it pays, and what skills are required. They can match that to their skill to see how they fit into the competitive field for each type of work. The platform provides the tools, but the free agent does their own career planning.

Like an employee-reward system, the platform provides an escrow service that holds the money from the agreed budget for the work, releasing it according to an agreed-upon schedule, and on the approval of the client. Trying new things is also an important reward. In a traditional employment relationship, an accountant will seldom get the opportunity to try their hand as a speechwriter, but a talent platform gives them that chance.

For companies using a large number of free agents, Upwork provides a Private Talent Cloud that represents a central place for a company to control and track all work done via free agents. The clients can route all payments through the Private Talent Cloud, evaluate the reputation of free agents who have worked for them, track who's performing tasks for the organization, check who is currently available for other projects, and be alerted when coveted talent will become available. Upwork can even act as the employer of record for compliance purposes. The Private Talent Cloud is an example of a category of software called Freelance Management Systems (FMS). Others are Field Nation, OnForce, and Work Market.

If you think only of regular full-time employment as the way to accomplish sourcing, performance review, rewards, and dispute resolution, you miss these evolving new options. When these things are done through a platform, you can disperse the work beyond your organization, you can tap a pool of workers beyond those that are willing and available to be your employees, you can tailor your rewards to fit each worker and their contribution, and if your best worker leaves you have the arrangements in place to bring in a replacement without going through a hiring process. If using free agents carries practical difficulties, you can be sure that Upwork and the other talent platforms are working hard to overcome the problem.

What This Means for Your Future As a Leader of the Work: A Hybrid Model of Organization

Could Upwork itself be the model for the organization of the future? It's a hybrid firm of 225 employees and 500 free agents. Most of its employees do not have any direct reports, but each one is in fact a manager (and needs managerial skills) because they oversee free agents. A look at the organization chart of employees tells you little about what is going on since free agents outnumber employees two to one.

Upwork Pearson says the hybrid model is particularly useful for growing firms that are not ready to be locked into a static structure of jobs and employees. He personally uses free agents to get to those items lower down on his to-do list, the ones that otherwise might not ever get done.

It's fascinating, too, to see the birth and evolution of roles like "the free-agent wrangler." These are free agents who help organizations pull together a team of other free agents for a project as more and more elements of an organization are being recreated within the talent-platform space. A free-agent wrangler is a manager who exists beyond the walls of an organization and beyond employment.

Of course, regular full-time employment does and will always have advantages, but the optimal way to get work done will increasingly blend platform-based work with regular employment, because the line between them is blurring. Your leadership framework needs to master that optimization.

Tongal

The Offering and Clients

Tongal, a successful talent platform for creating video content, commercials, and similar products—perhaps eventually even feature films—is an excellent example of the new world of work, one unconstrained by the employment relationship. It delivers value to its clients, its talent community, and of course to Tongal itself. Its founders are James De Julio, Mark Burrell, and Rob Salvatore. De Julio's story starts right after college, on Wall Street, where he learned that he didn't fit in with that particular business culture. Instead of making a career there, he headed west to seek creative work in the movie business. He eventually landed a job at Paramount Pictures. De Julio noted that even though the business revolved entirely around creative talent (screenwriters, producers, cinematographers, etc.), the breadth of talent being considered for work was stunningly limited.

The industry had backed itself into a corner where everything was extraordinarily expensive; they would spend millions just to develop a story line. That was fine for a big blockbuster, but with the increasing fragmentation of the industry, this model was no longer working. People now are more likely to see what's available on Netflix than follow Hollywood's plan that they spend Friday and Saturday night at the cinema. Advertising faced a similar challenge: When you're preparing a commercial to be seen by millions sitting down to watch *Modern Family*, high costs are not a problem. But in the new world of audiences fragmented across multiple platforms—broadcast TV, cable, Hulu, Amazon—that cost structure would kill the business. De Julio says, "In 1986 you could reach 35 percent of the U.S. audience by advertising on a hit show; today no audience is like that. Adjusted for inflation it costs three times as much to reach an audience without even considering the fact they may be skipping your ads by using a DVR or tuning-out during your ad by doing something on their smartphone. The industry has transformed and models for creating advertising need to transform too."

Tongal has attracted clients like Lego, Anheuser-Busch, and Microsoft. These firms are experienced in working with the best creative agencies, yet they use Tongal for some of their projects, presumably because Tongal does it better, faster, and cheaper. Yet it's no longer about cost cutting. Tongal has partnered with a movie production company to produce a full-length feature documentary. Nigel Sinclair, the production company's CEO and co-chairman, told the *Los Angeles Times* (September 17, 2013) that "Filmmaking is no longer elite. It's now a populist activity. . . . What Tongal is doing is creating a way to find these new filmmakers and bring them across." As online platforms like Hulu, Amazon, and Netflix start producing their own movies and television shows, can more such crowdsourced production be far behind?

The Work

The Tongal model is best understood in the context of the traditional ways of matching talent to work. A company that wants to make a TV commercial typically goes to its advertising agency, whose employees then brainstorm ideas for the commercial. After numerous meetings, presentations, and approvals, the agency begins to shoot the commercial, often drawing from its own small roster of free agents. This process is not all that different from a company having its own in-house creative department.

The Tongal process has three stages that use a familiar crowdsourcing contest model with a twist: First is the idea stage, where anyone from a creative agent to a consumer is encouraged to submit an idea for the commercial using no more than 140 characters (you can even submit your ideas as you fly across the United States on Virgin America airlines). The simplest way to do the next step is for the client to cull through the mass of ideas, choose the top three, and award the top three submitters a payment. The second phase is a video pitch stage. Using the three best ideas from the first stage, a new group of workers who can make a video pitch how they'd execute each chosen idea. Again, the top three are chosen, and all three win the cash needed to make a video. The third phase is when the best of those three videos receives the contract to make the commercial.

We state that the simplest way of choosing which ideas to develop is to have the client pick them. Tongal can also harness the power of its large community of creatives to assess ideas; and since it has demographic data on its community it can tell you not only which ideas the community thinks are best, but which ideas different demographic segments think are best. This "complication" is important because it shows what an amazing creative resource Tongal is sitting on, and how much more innovation is potentially possible.

The three phases Tongal uses in its process offer an important insight into creative work: There are many people who can come up with ideas but are not able to produce a video and many others with the skills to create a video who are not able to generate great ideas. It just makes sense to deconstruct the work so that idea creation and video production are separated. Tongal's entrepreneurial insight was understanding the work behind the industry and the creative process, and deconstructing and reconstructing that work into a process that can engage workers in ways other than employment. That new process looks very different from the typical studio approach, which structures the engagement as regular full-time employment or employment contracts. The Tongal process deconstructed the work and then reconstructed it into contests, iteration, idea formation, idea refinement, and execution. Thus, Tongal borrowed the work structures and tasks of a traditional employed manager in an advertising firm and morphed them to fit a world of nonemployees.

"We don't want to call it a marketplace; it's really a new alternative workforce model," De Julio says. Yes, this is technically crowdsourcing, but it's not just a matter of casting a task or a problem onto the web and waiting for the crowd to provide the solution. Tongal shows that structure matters, and that structure reflects how Tongal figured out how to help clients lead through the work—not simply manage employees—by thinking beyond employment.

You can learn a lot by recognizing how Tongal deconstructed and reconstructed the work, reengineered its organization's boundaries to be more permeable, and adopted more customized and imaginative rewards. The same principles can help you to recognize when this kind of reengineering can produce breakthrough results for your work.

The Workers

There are a vast number of screenwriters in the world, but for any given project, in the traditional model, the studio only looked at a list of about 10 names. The same thing applied to other roles like producer or cinematographer. Why? Because when you approach the work through a traditional model of regular full-time employment, or even employment contracts, you tend to consider only those people whom you know well and who can perform all the elements of the defined "job." The risk is simply too great to work with an unknown given that it costs on average $200 million just to market a new film globally, and there are few economical ways to evaluate talent before you hire them. This did not serve the clients for the work well, and it did not serve the workers well, many of whom were waiting tables while awaiting their chance to break into the industry.

Tongal has only 48 employees but sees itself as having 70,000 workers. That's a very different type of organization from the ones we've grown up with. Tongal cares about their workers, and while it structures the work, it looks nothing at all like a company with 70,000 employees.

These three profiles of actual Tongalers in the sidebar illustrate the types of workers that Tongal engages.

A Tale of Three Tongalers

We have focused on the talent platforms themselves and wanted to take a moment to look at some of the talent working on the platform. Here is the tale of three Tongalers. You will notice that Tongal is not their whole life but has played an important role in their careers.

Tyler Funk

The talented Tyler Funk graduated from film school in Canada and while he did get some contract work making films his main job was disappointing: he made most of his income as a waiter. Looking at the oversaturated film scene in Vancouver was depressing; he could not see himself spending his life as a production assistant. Then he found Tongal, and that allowed him to launch his North of Now business.

Funk has had a lot of success with Tongal, winning more than 30 projects. Winning takes time and talent. Developing the pitch can take anywhere from two days to a week and there is never a guarantee you will win. When he does win he needs to be creative in finding ways to pull off a great video on a tight budget. It can require calling in a lot of favors. When casting agencies hear the project is for a big brand the dollar signs light up in their eyes and they are disappointed when they discover the budget is much smaller than for a traditional TV commercial. For Funk there is a lot of negotiating, including having talent do multiple jobs and being creative in finding ways to get the work done, such as using Airbnb to find locations.

Funk likes the way Tongal structures the work, separating out the idea phase from the production phase. It means that when he is making the pitch he knows the client is already happy with the idea, which takes some of the pressure off.

There are various other sources of income for a free agent like Funk. There are grants from the federal and provincial governments, and work for the major TV channels such as the Canadian Broadcasting Corporation. He knows some Tongalers who also do corporate videos and some who find local work like wedding videos.

Funk says there is a long list of talent platforms that offer video work including TalentHouse, UserFarm, Genero, Wooshi, and Vizy, but some video contest sites have a poor reputation and the work experience can often leave a lot to be desired.

Don Broida

Don Broida pursued the traditional path of a creative professional in the world of film. He lives in Los Angeles, got a job right out of high school as an intern editor, and then spent more than a decade working his way up the ladder. Along the way he has worked with all the major studios and even did some script writing.

When a friend pointed him to Tongal he saw it as a chance to take a break from doing editorial work and try directing. He submitted some wildcard projects, won, and that launched him into the world of being a Tongaler.

Over the years Broida has had considerable success with Tongal—and the rewards stretch beyond the monetary. He points out that Tongal gives filmmakers the opportunities to build their reels and hone their skills, which gives them the tools needed to be successful in a very competitive industry. Furthermore, the creative freedom offered at Tongal is unparalleled. They encourage filmmakers to do what they feel is creatively the best.

Broida has now transitioned into working mainly in the traditional advertising agency model where bigger budgets broaden the scope for major league projects. Broida represents an example of someone who has had success both with Tongal and in the traditional world of filmmaking.

Low Lik Min

Low Lik Min, based in Kuala Lumpur, started doing animation for a variety of studios in Malaysia, working on TV series for Disney and other clients. He tried Tongal just for fun. A national drink brand had a contest for a commercial, and he wanted to know how his work would stand up against international competition. He did not win, but he was in the top three and learned how to make a strong pitch. The next contest was for an even bigger brand, Lego™. Min won that contest and became a regular Tongaler.

Can you earn a full-time living on Tongal? Some do, but for Min it is just one avenue for work. His work on Tongal has built his reputation and visibility; now clients come to him.

One of the things that makes Tongal special is that it brings in projects from big brands, and those brands are actually going to use the resulting video. Min says that on some of the other video contest sites the project seems to be a bit of sideshow for the client, and that attitude does not make for satisfying work for a creative professional.

Min made an interesting comment about a studio he set up earlier in his career. He found that, using the employment model, he was pretty much bound to the people he hired, and he was limited by the talent he happened to have on staff. Now he staffs his projects with free agents; if he needs voice-over talent he might use an American free agent or pick up a technical specialist in Egypt or the UK. He is fully immersed in the free agent world, both in supplying his own skills and getting the skills from the global free-agent marketplace.

The Engagement Model

De Julio says "We have 70,000 people who have no obligation to do any work whatsoever." They do the work because they are passionate about it.

Like an employee recruitment system, the Tongal contests are in essence a sales pitch. When you think about it, everyone makes a sales pitch to get a job or a work assignment. In many traditional employment systems, and particularly with creative media talent, that process can be very uncertain and time consuming for the worker, and it limits the number of candidates that an employer can consider. Tongal protects the interests of workers and clients by making sure the pitches don't demand an inappropriate amount of work. In the idea stage, the submission can be limited to 140 characters. That length is useful for clients who can now go through hundreds of entries in the time it might have taken them to meet just a few candidates in the traditional system. It also ensures that the workers ("creatives") don't spend too much time on a pitch at the early stage when they are unlikely to win. A creative does not get into the heavy work of production until after they are awarded the contract.

Like an employee selection system, the Tongal second-stage pitch contest whittles a large number of applicants for the work down to three superior candidates. It also provides a focused and relevant set of information to help the client make the best choice among the top three worker candidates. Unlike employee selection all of the top three are "winners" and get funding to make a video.

Interestingly, Tongal even has a sort of "appeals" system if a worker thinks they were unfairly overlooked in the pitch stage. A "wildcard" creative can produce and submit a full commercial to the client if they want to invest the time and energy, and it will be considered along with the final product of the winning entry. It's a risky proposition for the free agent, who must produce the commercial at their own expense, but it provides a means to address the concerns of workers who feel they were unfairly passed over. The wildcard process has turned out to be quite important: one in six top prizes actually goes to a wildcard, to a creative person who was so sure they had the right stuff that they rolled the dice and made a video even though the client hadn't liked their pitch.

Like an employee pay process that aligns rewards with contribution, the Tongal talent community has the opportunity to earn a competitive wage. Forty of them earned more than $100,000 in 2014, and a great many more earn a substantial part of their income through the platform. Because its workers are not employees, Tongal knows that if the platform doesn't work for them, the best creatives won't come back. So, Tongal tracks the work and pay progress of its workers to make sure the system is getting the right work to the right workers at the right price. This is a common aspiration of employment reward processes, too, but traditional systems are often much less transparent and effective than Tongal.

Tongal also sets aside a pool of money so that workers who do well on multiple projects get a bonus. It is called Tongal Seasons, with a season being 20 eligible projects. For each project people finishing in the top five get points and at the end of each season the pool is split among the top 20 performers. It shows how some traditional reward elements can be brought into this distinctly nontraditional means of getting work done.

But the rewards don't stop there. Tongal imagines rewards beyond money. Similar to an employee engagement system, Tongal also has a big annual awards event: the Tongies. It's basically an award ceremony to recognize and celebrate the greatest accomplishments of the whole Tongal community. It blends competition, excitement, camaraderie, and mutual appreciation. Tongal flies in the top nominees from around the world, and the Tongal community sit nervously as they hear the words, "And the Tongie goes to..." If you thought of Tongal as merely a marketplace where free agents can pick up some creative work on the web, consider how different it is to be a Tongaler participating in the Tongies. Tongal is building organizational culture among workers who are not employees of any organization. Incidentally, Tongal is considering offering health insurance to Tongalers.

Like any employee total rewards system, the Tongal system has attractive and less attractive elements.

The Attractions

- The pay (which in some cases will exceed all but the very highest paid agency workers)
- The opportunity to build one's reel (samples of your work), which is often a precursor to getting work through traditional channels
- A chance to learn through competition
- The freedom to work on what you want, where you want, when you want
- The thrill of working with internationally known brands
- A chance to try directing
- Access to work that free agents would typically have little chance of landing because they don't have the relationships or live in the wrong location
- Protection from clients (Tongal sets out clear rules so that brands don't take advantage of creative talent; for example, by asking for multiple revisions of the film).
- A sense of community

The Challenges

- The lack of income security
- The expense of preparing for the competitions
- In most cases lower pay than what a director makes working for an agency on traditional television advertising
- Loss of money while working on a project for the sake of building one's reel and reputation

Notice how similar some of these attractions and challenges are to those of regular full-time employees of an ad agency or production studio.

Notice as well that by organizing the work to fit a world beyond employment, Tongal can amplify many of the attractions. As a leader, you must ask yourself whether your system of regular full-time employment can compete in a talent market where Tongal and their peers are constantly honing their value proposition. If it cannot, then you need a framework to understand where you can dial up some things that Tongal does well (e.g., reconstructed work, imaginative rewards, community culture, etc.) without dialing down the elements that give employment an advantage (income security, benefits, etc.).

What This Means for Your Future as a Leader of the Work

At the moment, nearly half of all advertising spend is still on old-style TV commercials. As more and more of that budget shifts to digital and web-based platforms, the industry will be looking for more cost-effective approaches, and that will drive work to Tongal. Tongal is not limited to advertisements; the leaders' original inspiration was movies. One day we may see Tongal produce a feature film, it has already produced a winner of the Sundance Institute Short Film Challenge: the film, which you can find on Vimeo.com, is called *175 Grams*, and it documents Ultimate Frisbee competitions in India. Tongal also has a partnership with Lionsgate on Stephenie Meyer's Twilight franchise. This project aims to create a series of short films based in the Twilight universe. Tongal has drawn on its vast community of creatives, which contains no small number of Twilight fans, to decide which characters to feature, and then goes on to create the films. The point is that Tongal is already spilling over the edges of the simple "we can make a commercial" model and using its potent talent community in creative ways. Perhaps one day a Tongal-like platform will assemble and coordinate talent for projects like designing a satellite, where assembling talent for a project has many of the same elements as assembling talent for a movie.

The future is a competitive game on an unstable landscape. For big-budget advertisements, traditional agencies with employees and contractors are currently the typical choice. In the world of Internet advertising, though, Tongal has the advantage, and agencies will scramble to adjust their model to stay competitive. Tongal will find ways to mimic the structures that give agencies their power; just as the agencies will be drawing lessons from the Tongal model. Talent marketplace evolution means that the less agile agencies and talent platforms will fail, as the agile ones find their unique niche—no doubt combining features of the old and new worlds.

Topcoder

We met Topcoder (now a part of Appirio) in Chapter 1 with the example of Ion Torrent, which illustrated the classic Topcoder model: a corporation—in this case, Ion Torrent—has a difficult programming problem, Topcoder runs a contest with a prize appealing to talented programmers and from that contest emerges the best solution.

Topcoder began in 2001 as an online Java platform for running timed coding competitions. Each month, Topcoder ran several competitions and through these were able to identify great programmers. The problems put to coders were just tests, an inexpensive, effective, and fun way to find out who was the best computer coder. Topcoder's founders quickly realized that they could run competitions using real problems that real clients would pay to have solved: writing actual code, finding a real bug, or architecting an actual system. They were deconstructing the work, creating an alternative software-development method: break a problem into small pieces, set up a contest, get the best solution to each discrete piece, award the winners, and deliver the best solutions to the client.

The Clients and the Offering

Topcoder's clients are typically fairly large organizations and include famous names like NASA, Comcast, Honeywell, Salesforce.com, Harvard, and JDRF. The Topcoder model works best for larger organizations because there is an initially high cost to build the skills and processes to interface with the Topcoder talent platform. Once built, it's easy and not very costly to scale usage up and down.

While Topcoder case studies often lead with a statement like "project accomplished at half the usual price," the real value is often superior quality rather than price. Their pitch is that Topcoder can get you a Google-like engineer at a fraction of the cost you would usually pay (presuming you could even convince them to work for you). For run-of-the-mill programming that doesn't require regularly and quickly scaling up and down resources, though, a traditional IT outsourcer is the more obvious choice.

The Work

Topcoder originally focused on only programming projects. The reason for this laser focus can help you understand the elements of work that make it highly suitable for talent platforms and the elements that may offer an advantage to other engagement models such as regular full-time employment. The project that works best for Topcoder, says Narinder Singh, chief strategy officer at Appirio (who acquired Topcoder), uses cloud-based computing. If the work requires a large application stored within the client's organization, like a traditional enterprise resource planning (ERP) system, it is much harder to deconstruct the work into pieces and disperse those pieces to the best talent, wherever and whenever they can do the work. When the work can be done with cloud-based applications, then the worker (usually a software coder) can access the tools and data they need from any location at any time without the client having to provide them special access. The work must be able to be deconstructed so that it can be dispersed. Singh observes that a single individual running an IT consultancy based on cloud-based applications can access the capabilities that previously might have required a 100-plus-person firm.

If you're the leader of one of those 100-employee organizations, understanding how Topcoder competes by systematically deconstructing and dispersing the work may be a key to your own survival. But there's more to understand.

The particular niche that Topcoder chose, software development and coding, also presented a unique talent pool that was already accustomed to a system of organization and rewards that suited cloud-based work design: programmers are accustomed to working on projects as contractors. Software and applications change so quickly that the clients for the work already realize they can't count on regular full-time employees to keep up. Both clients and workers had long experience using the cloud as the organization and location for the work.

As a leader, your job is to lead the work to achieve your mission. The Topcoder case shows how creative leaders saw a way to lead differently by deconstructing and dispersing work, creating rewards and an engagement model that fit the necessary niche of workers, and using the cloud as a more permeable and malleable organization. Does this work only for software programming? We get a hint of the broader future of talent platforms by looking at where Topcoder is heading: beyond narrow coding problems and into work in design, development, and data science. Having conquered one programming niche, they have begun to spread outward. As we will see in later chapters, you can also use these dimensions to more clearly see creative ways to lead through the work. You may not have a choice, as Topcoder may be heading your way.

The Workers

The Topcoder worker community is diverse and interacts with Topcoder in different ways. We dropped by the Museum Tavern in Toronto and ran into a couple of Topcoders. In a way, it is not too surprising. There are more than 700,000 Topcoders in the world. You could run into one almost anywhere. The ones we met at the tavern had studied programming, but their primary employment is bartending, a job they love that pays well. Participating in Topcoder from time to time is a way to keep their hand in programming and earn a little extra cash.

Another interesting case shared by Singh is about a programmer, who has a traditional full-time job in the Midwestern United States, yet earns 30 to 50 percent of his income on Topcoder. This is not secret moonlighting; his boss encourages him to do this because it's the only way to retain him. In fact, this programmer turned down a tasty job at Twitter because he found he had plenty of interesting work where he was and there was no professional need to move to San Francisco.

Some Topcoders are extremely active on the platform and use it as their sole source of income. Others use it simply as one source of free-agent work. Part of the strength of the platform is that it can appeal to a broad range of programmers.

Are Competitions Ethical?

Many people are concerned that competitions may exploit workers. For example if 20 designers put in the effort to create a logo, and only the winner of the competition gets paid, then the other 19 may feel mistreated. On the one hand, in every business you need to compete for sales; when responding to a request for proposal companies may put in a great deal of effort and yet only one wins the work. Seen this way competitions are par for the course in business. On the other hand, it is rare to need to submit a completed project, as with the logo design example, to get a chance to win the sale. Ultimately if competitions require more work than they are worth, then skilled workers simply won't enter and the talent platform will fail. Good talent platforms take this issue seriously and make sure there competitions are attractive to the best workers—Tongal and Topcoder prove competitions can be good for workers.

The Less "Regular" Full-Time Job

The Engagement Model

Both Upwork and Tongal work in part because they can tap fresh and less expensive talent pools. In Topcoder's world, the economic driver is less about saving money and more about finding the very best person to do the work. Singh explains, "The most productive person in the world for a particular task is the person who has the skills required and who performed virtually the same task last week. The delta in productivity between that person and a smart engineer new to the problem is massive."

How can you engage workers and work to take advantage of this massive productivity potential? If you think in terms of traditional organizations and regular full-time employment, you look within your organization and choose the best person out of 10 or 100 or perhaps 500 employees, and hope they are available. By deconstructing and dispersing work to the cloud, and engaging nonemployees, Topcoder can use a pool of hundreds of thousands of programmers. Remember Ion Torrent's need for a star programmer who worked on a particularly tough data-compression problem last week? The likelihood that this person sits among the employees of any one organization are remote. The chance they exist somewhere in the Topcoder universe is much higher. Further, because you can focus that person on the task they are best suited for, their performance advantage is magnified.

Like a piecework pay system for employees, Topcoder does not pay for time worked, but rather for a unit of output. The pay-by-unit-of-output model is clean and easy to manage; however, it presumes you can deconstruct the work into appropriate chunks. Singh says that deciphering that enigma is one of the critical capabilities that Topcoder brings to projects. Indeed, the inability to properly deconstruct work into meaningful activities is often the downfall of traditional piecework systems applied to traditional employees. A significant element of value to clients is that Topcoder helps them deconstruct and reconstruct a project into parts that can be accomplished and rewarded via the talent platform. The step of breaking apart the work can be handled in various ways. Companies can have one of their own IT employees act as the disintegrator and integrator. Another approach is to use the Topcoder platform to tap its worker community for the best copilot to assist with the project.

Like an employee learning and development system, the Topcoder platform offers a powerful way for programmers to develop their skills. With thousands of software projects available to the community, Topcoder allows programmers to do real work on interesting problems and have it reviewed by peers. It's that side of Topcoder that keeps bartender-programmers engaged. In a traditional job, that bartender might have only a small fraction of the experiences they can have on Topcoder.

Like a performance evaluation process for employees, Topcoder workers get visibility based on the quality of their work. That work quality is measured very precisely, because Topcoder deconstructed the work to make the activities, output, and their quality highly visible. Coders' output can be evaluated not only for its functionality, but also for whether the code itself is elegant. Coders are rated red, yellow, and blue. Those with a red rating can step to the front of the line for corporate jobs. The yellow- and blue-rated programmers are also very skilled, and that rating helps them get good work. In a cloud-based system, your reputation carries far more weight than a performance rating in a single employer's database.

Similar to a culture-building celebration for employees, Topcoder holds the Topcoder Open, an annual gathering that brings 100 top programmers from around the world to participate in a tournament. Videos at the Topcoder website show a participant who said, "It's a chance to see the very best people solve some brutally hard problems really fast." The passion and enthusiasm of computer coders to show who's the best rivals gatherings of spectators to watch stars play interactive web games like League of Legends. Talent-platform workers do not share an office or a company logo; however, they are a community with a culture. There is more to life than CEO of Me and no doubt in the midst of an event like the Topcoder Open, the contestants will describe themselves first and foremost as Topcoders.

Why would Topcoder have any regular full-time employees? The engagement model for their employees provides you with a clue as to how best to optimize the combination of work done through employment and work done beyond employment. An employee handling demanding projects may have no employees reporting to him but have dozens of people working for him—all free agents engaging through the Topcoder platform. On the typical organization chart, this employee looks like an individual contributor with no subordinates. In reality, his span of authority is more similar to a high-level manager or director. His value is a unique ability to take the work that clients bring to Topcoder and deconstruct and reconstruct it to fit the population of workers that he can tap in the cloud. That kind of unique capability resides in an employee of Topcoder, because it cannot easily be deconstructed and farmed out to the cloud and because Topcoder leaders anticipate a steady need for that capability across virtually every cloud-based project they receive. Appirio has 1,000 employees whose value is multiplied severalfold by the company's capability to engage cloud-based workers and cloud-based work in ways that are beyond employment. The company can have a lean internal structure, with all the benefits of the simplicity that come from having a manageable number of employees, but still punch far above its weight because it has the know-how to tap the skills of thousands of free-agent workers. Even here, for common projects like developing a mobile app, Topcoder can set out standard guidelines on breaking the work apart. It seems inevitable that one day Topcoder will have "wizards," interactive programs that will guide an IT manager on how to parse the work into various common projects.

What This Means for Your Future as a Leader of the Work

Can you bring the Topcoder model in-house to your regular full-time employees? Some CIOs use Topcoder to peer into the quality of their employees. Traditional employment systems often cannot tell a CIO if the best team of Java programmers is in their Singapore office or in Poland, or laboring away in obscurity in Milwaukee. A Topcoder contest for employees provides an X-ray for assessing regular employee talent. Topcoder already has benchmarks and programming challenges developed by analyzing millions of coding assignments and outcomes, so why try to invent them yourself? As a bonus, the Topcoder database already spans thousands of workers, so you can see how your internal staff matches up to the rest of the world.

As a leader, should you use contests to measure and find the skills among your employees? It's a good example of a hybrid model that takes one of the best elements from the world beyond employment, and combines it with the world of employment. Yet, if you suggest to most HR departments that you're going to pay your employees through contests, they will correctly tell you that this might strain your existing employment systems to the breaking point. Because your systems are based on a traditional model of regular full-time employment, you'll run into the inertia of compliance, established HR processes, and deeply rooted notions of the meaning of pay equity. As a leader, your most important task may be to oppose that inertia, or to hire HR leaders that are prepared to break tradition.

NASA is working with Topcoder to run competitions called Single Round Matches (SRMs) to assess their employees' skills. Topcoder has good benchmarks on SRM performance, such as how many people solved a particular problem, how well they solved it, and how quickly; these benchmarks allow NASA to get a great handle on how good their internal programming team is. One large bank is even using this benchmarked internal-only Topcoder competition to allow their strongest performing employees to show off their skills and pick their "dream job" based on winning.

Topcoder is continuing to hone its model. For example, leaders there looked at whether it's best to let programmers work on problems independently or to get them to share ideas as they go. Topcoder found that having programmers work independently creates a great diversity of ideas, while sharing ideas enhances collective learning. This gives the company a process for structuring work, starting with independent work to create a diversity of ideas, hitting a checkpoint where leaders bring people together to share and create convergence, and then opening it up again to independent work. This sort of sophisticated process improvement makes Topcoder and platforms like it ever more effective alternatives to traditional methods of getting work done.

MTurk

Upwork, Tongal, and Topcoder all have quite distinct models, but there is an even more exotic beast in the talent-platform jungle. Amazon's Mechanical Turk (MTurk) was originally built to solve Amazon's own internal data-processing problems.

The Offering and the Clients

Some conundrums, such as identifying duplicate web pages, are simple for humans, but too hard for computers. Amazon created a platform where this kind of work could be broken up into tiny pieces and distributed to a low-cost workforce. Amazon calls it "artificial intelligence." One feeds a problem into the MTurk engine and back comes an answer; behind the scene are humans, nearly invisible to the user.

MTurk has a wide range of clients including AOL, the U.S. Army Research Laboratory, Statera (an Internet media metrics company), and university researchers. It takes a certain amount of sophistication for a client to use MTurk, but it's a natural tool for anyone handing large amounts of data.

Amazon liked MTurk so much that its leaders launched it as a subsidiary in 2005, and it has grown into a sizeable business with access to half a million workers in almost 200 countries.

The Work

The work generally requires no special skills, and clients really only care to distinguish between people who do work of adequate quality and those who do not. There may be significant skill differences in various tasks. For example, some workers may be much faster than others in transcribing grocery receipts. However, that skill difference doesn't matter to the client who is paying a piece rate.

Some examples of work to be found on MTurk include

- Record a word or phrase in your own voice (pays $0.02).
- Transcribe all of the purchased items and total from a shopping receipt ($0.09).
- Find the headquarters of a particular company ($0.10).

Typically, there are thousands of cases for each task, so a Turker (as the workers are called) might do 500 cases of "recording a word or phrase" and earn 500 × $0.02 for a total of $10.00. Amazon charges the client 10 percent of the amount earned.

Amazon calls the units of work Human Intelligence Tasks (HITs). These are microtasks, far smaller units of work than most managers are used to seeing. Microtasks are quite a common feature in the information age. Main categories of work are

- Photo and video processing (such as tagging images)
- Data verification and clean-up (such as verification of a store's hours of operation)
- Information gathering (such as filling in a survey)
- Data processing (such as podcast editing)

This work can be done virtually and usually requires no special skills.

Tagging photos is the classic example of a task that is easy for people and hard for computers. That is changing. Research by University of Toronto assistant professor Ruslan Salakhutdinov and others on "deep learning" have, in the past few years, led to stunning advances in creating algorithms to enable computers to accurately tag photos. Ironically those smart computers are being trained, as you probably have guessed, by Turkers.

The Workers

Panos Ipeirotis, a New York University business professor, has researched the demographics of the MTurk talent community. In a 2010 survey he found that 46.8 percent of MTurk's labor force was American, 34 percent was Indian, and 19.2 was "other."[4] The workforce will likely become increasingly global as more people discover the platform. In the United States, Turkers are often stay-at-home parents and younger unemployed and underemployed workers, with women Turkers about twice as common as men. In India, male Turkers are about twice as common as females, and the platform is more likely to be an important or even sole source of income. Even though HITs are low-skill work, most Turkers have a university education, which is likely reflective of the fact that educated, computer-literate people are most likely to discover MTurk. Average earnings are about $2 per hour, according to Ipeirotis. For developed-country workers the platform can serves as a way to earn a little extra money using time that might otherwise be spent surfing Facebook or watching videos.

The Engagement Model

The MTurk model is far different from platforms like Tongal, Upwork and Topcoder. It relies far more on the contractual relationship between the client and the worker, providing far fewer connections between MTurkers as a community and far less infrastructure in support of its workers. That's not necessarily a bad thing, as both clients and workers are fully aware of the arrangements when they undertake the engagement.

There are several ways clients can be sure the Turkers taking up a task are qualified to do good work. One way is to require Turkers to take a test before being allowed to work on the task. The test becomes the first task the Turker does for the client, and if they pass, they can move on. Another method is for the client to restrict their work only to experienced Turkers. A Turker's forum noted that to get most of the better-paying requesters (i.e., clients) requires between 5,000 and 10,000 approved HITs to be completed before you can work on theirs. Perhaps the most mechanical way to insure quality is to give multiple workers the same task. If two workers give the same answer (e.g. add up a receipt to the same total), then the answer can be deemed to be correct. This last method is particularly suited to a platform that can quickly access workers to do standard tasks at low cost. A traditional employment model probably carries too much overhead to consider giving two employees the same task very often.

Unlike Topcoder, the MTurk talent isn't celebrated in contests on YouTube and isn't visible to most clients. While Upwork has a dispute-resolution mechanism, MTurk clients simply don't pay for work they don't like, and are not required to give a reason. In the absence of the sort of loving care Tongal provides its community, third-party groups have sprung up to support Turkers such as Turkoptican, which can alert workers to shady employers, and CloudMeBaby, which provides a forum for people using MTurk and other platforms.

What This Means for Your Future as a Leader of the Work

MTurk illustrates how talent platforms can span a wide range of work and workers, in this case creating a model uniquely honed to work that can not only be deconstructed into small parts but can be done with widely available capabilities. It also illustrates that talent platforms need not be devoted to only highly qualified talent where the objective is to find the best and pay them highly. Indeed, many writers lament the possibility that a world beyond employment will look more like MTurk and less like Topcoder or Tongal, with a race to exploit workers as commodities.

As a leader, this diversity has an important message for you. Your future task of leading through the work will require that you segment the work and the workers at least as precisely as you segment your customers and your product offerings. Regular full-time employment is only one option, but even when you recognize the possibility of using talent platforms, the diversity is stunning. MTurk shows the diversity of niches that are open to talent platforms, and that diversity will only grow, creating more opportunities for leaders to tap free agent world.

The changes in the way we work and the way we buy appear to be moving quickly, but pull back and you'll see that such evolutions do take time, even when the Internet is involved. As Gary Swart, former CEO of oDesk points out, after 20 years of ecommerce, still only 7 percent of all sales take place online. We started by buying books on the web and then progressively moved to electronics, financial products, cars, and even groceries. But even so, this accounts for only a small percentage of current consumer spend.

Similarly, companies will dip their toes in this new space by segmenting the work and testing the effectiveness of these platforms. There will be early adopters who push many different types of work onto these platforms, while others will sit back and watch. As we move up the maturity curve, we'll get more comfortable as we better understand the nuances of work and how best to get it done. Talent platforms are like the first fish crawling out of the sea hundreds of millions of years ago. They do not look that impressive right now, but what will they look like with time and evolution? Will they become giants striding across the earth, filling a thousand ecological niches?

Getting Started in the Talent-Platform World

There are hundreds of different talent platforms, each with their own strengths. Leaders need to be alert as to which ones are most relevant for their work; and stay up-to-date as this is a dynamic, ever-changing world. Also, as with any tool, there is a learning curve. Upwork and Tongal are pretty straightforward, Topcoder requires more effort to learn, and Amazon's Mechanical Turk requires some programming skill to set up a job. These requirements to using talent platforms should not deter you; however you should create time to try them out, so you have the capability when you need to get the work done.

Notes

1. http://en.wikipedia.org/wiki/List_of_largest_employers
2. www.itpro.co.uk/strategy/21840/the-best-companies-to-work-for-in-it
3. Chris Clegg, YouTube video for oDesk, posted August 15, 2013, https://www.youtube.com/watch?v=hTEx2sFiN8Y (accessed February 18, 2015).
4. G. Paolacci, J. Chandler, and P. G. Ipeirotis, "Running Experiments on Amazon Mechanical Turk." *Judgment and Decision Making* 5, no. 5 (2010): 411–419.

PART TWO

The Model

5

Leading the Work Beyond Employment: A Decision Framework

The first few chapters suggest a tantalizing new world beyond employment, and one that many leaders have glimpsed. Leaders and managers have heard about outsourcing, free agent nation, Upwork, alliances, CEO of Me, the end of job security, crowdsourcing, and so on. Some leaders may even have experience with a few of these emerging work arrangements.

Yet, these examples and trends often appear isolated and unique: the stories may be intriguing, but they don't give you a way to make logical, evidence-based, and optimal decisions. What you need is a decision framework that isolates the most important dimensions and choices, and offers you a way to optimize them. That means defining your choices not simply as "regular full-time employment versus some shiny new alternative," but as "creatively combining key elements to achieve my goals in the most optimal way."

A decision framework defines the dimensions of the fundamental changes in organizations, work and workers signaled by these examples. It helps you as a leader make better decisions. This chapter describes just such a framework. A leader's job is to lead through the work. In our framework, we show how that means making optimal choices about how to design the *assignment*, the *organization*, and the *rewards*.

The previous chapters showed that as a leader you face some important decisions such as

- Should you break formerly intact jobs into smaller pieces that can easily be handled by skilled and inexpensive free agents?
- Should you see if your clients are taking work they formerly gave to you, and getting it done through a talent platform (exactly what is happening to ad agencies, thanks to Tongal)?
- Should you reinvent your "employment" brand so that it attracts not merely the best employees but the best free agents—and you might want to stop calling it an *employment* brand.
- Should you borrow talent from one of your organizational partners, when it is too hard to hire?
- Should you loan out your own talent to give them the experiences they need or desire, while staying loyal to your organization?
- Should you create internal rewards that mimic talent platforms and crowdsourcers, such as using contests to give your workers imaginative rewards, measure their capabilities, and let them compare themselves to the population of free agents?

The array of choices is expanding constantly. Even when your work is mostly or completely accomplished with regular full-time employees, their expectations and your options will be influenced by developments in the world beyond employment. When combining employment with things like contests, talent loans, and moonlighting on talent platforms, it's apparent that even useful ideas like *free agent*, *CEO of Me*, and others don't effectively capture all the possibilities, nor do they offer enough guidance on how to decide.

The possibilities are never binary. For example, today many firms outsource compensation design but manage compensation administration internally for confidentiality reasons. It is about constructing a solution from the many possible configurations. Perhaps a useful analogy is that of a purchasing agent. A purchasing agent scours the world for the best sources of goods; leaders will have to scour the world for the best ways to get work done.

The right choices depend on the particular leader and organization, and they require more than just a list of tantalizing examples and stories. Leaders need a framework to pull the pieces together and make more informed, logical, and optimal decisions. Today, they have lots of "shiny objects" to draw their attention, but it's difficult to see the underlying pattern behind them. It's like trying to understand astronomy when you see only a few bright shiny stars.

This chapter describes our framework. Think of it as a map and a set of dials that let you navigate to your optimum place on the map. We will use this framework as a language to make sense of the examples we described in earlier chapters, and as to guide a deeper analysis in later chapters. We hope you will use this framework as you map your own journey toward a more systematic approach to leading in a world beyond employment. This book will show you how to use this framework to create combinations of new work arrangements to optimize your objectives and achieve your mission. You're not limited to the work arrangements that exist today, nor are you limited to stark choices between things like regular full-time employment versus free agents. The work evolution we've described offers you exponentially increasing options, as you can dial up or dial down any of the individual elements.

You need a way to map these alternatives so that you can see their relationships, using dimensions like the lines of longitude and latitude that let you map locations on the globe. That map also helps you make navigation decisions just as longitude and latitude help you decide on the direction and speed to a location. When it comes to leading through the work, seeing the various dimensions and how they interact allows you to better navigate the fundamental building blocks of work and put them together in new ways that better fit your strategies, goals, and needs.

Our framework consists of two closely related tools. The first is a map that can be used to locate the work on three fundamental dimensions: Assignment, Organization, and Rewards. The second is a decision framework that describes the choices leaders can make on each of these dimensions. Dialing some dimensions up and others down not only maps and deciphers the bewildering array of work alternatives we see today but offers insights about new hybrid work designs that may better fit your strategic needs.

The three major elements of the framework are the Assignment, the Organization, and the Rewards.

1. Assignment refers to the deliverables that the worker produces and the client receives, such as coding software, driving a car, creating a logo,

evaluating an X-ray, or figuring out the optimal folding pattern of a protein needed to treat the AIDS virus.

2. Organization refers to the relationship between the work, the workers, and the clients. Is there more than one legal entity such as an alliance partner, a talent platform or outsourcer? If there is more than one entity how much do they share information, risk, decision authority, and accountability?

3. Rewards refer to the outcomes that the workers receive, such as money, learning, experience, sense of pride, bragging rights, or membership in a desirable group.

The "Lead the Work" Map

The diagram below shows three scales, Assignment, Organization, and Rewards, with the traditional regular full-time "employment" version of each dimension on the left, and the most extreme "beyond employment" version on the right (see Figure 5.1).

On the left, we see traditional employment. The *Assignment* is constructed into jobs, collected in fixed times and places, and engaged through a regular full-time employment relationship. The *Organization* is self-contained, unlinked, exclusive, and has a stable shape. The *Rewards* are based on a long-term connection, are collectively consistent, and use traditional elements (money, hours, working conditions, etc.).

On the right, we see the most nontraditional elements beyond employment. The *Assignment* is deconstructed into tasks, dispersed in

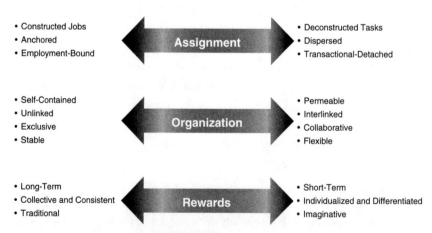

• Constructed Jobs
• Anchored
• Employment-Bound
Assignment
• Deconstructed Tasks
• Dispersed
• Transactional-Detached

• Self-Contained
• Unlinked
• Exclusive
• Stable
Organization
• Permeable
• Interlinked
• Collaborative
• Flexible

• Long-Term
• Collective and Consistent
• Traditional
Rewards
• Short-Term
• Individualized and Differentiated
• Imaginative

Figure 5.1   "Lead the Work" Map

time and place, and engaged through transactions that are detached from regular full-time employment. The *Organization* is permeable, interlinked, collaborative, and flexible. The *Rewards* are short-term, individualized, and differentiated, and use imaginative nontraditional elements (game points, reputation, mission, etc.).

Unlocking the "Lead the Work" Code

Each of the three dimensions implies fundamental choices. It's very much like using the dimensions of the map to dial up or down each dimension to find your optimum combination or code. That code unlocks your strategic success. Figure 5.2 below poses the questions that define the choices for each element.

The Assignment has three major choice categories:

1. **Deconstruct?** When this is dialed far to the left, work is contained in traditional jobs. When it is dialed far to the right, work is parceled into smaller units such as projects, tasks, and microtasks.
2. **Disperse?** When this is dialed far to the left, the work exists in fixed locations at predefined times (such as major surgery). When it is dialed

Assignment
- How Small to **Deconstruct**?
- How Widely to **Disperse**?
- How Far from Employment to **Detach**?

Organization
- How Easily to **Permeate**?
- How Strongly to **Interlink**?
- How Deeply to **Collaborate**?
- How Extensively to **Flex**?

Rewards
- How Small the Time Frame to **Shorten**?
- How Specifically to **Individualize**?
- How Creatively to **Imagine**?

Figure 5.2   Unlocking the "Lead the Work" Code

Source: Wikipedia. Image used with permission under the GNU Free Documentation License. http://commons.wikimedia.org/wiki/Commons: Welcome.

far to the right, the work can be done in any location and at any time (such as web-based microtasks that can be completed wherever and whenever the worker has access to a cell phone).

3. **Detach?** When this is dialed far to the left, the work conditions, rewards, and rules are attached to and contained in a traditional employment relationship. When dialed far to the right, the work is detached from regular employment using alternative relationships, virtual markets, alliances, talent platforms, or volunteer crowdsourcing.

The Organization has four major choice categories:

1. **Permeable?** When this is dialed far to the left, the work resides only inside an organization boundary. When this is dialed far to the right, the work resides inside and outside and flows freely across the permeable organizational boundary.

2. **Interlinked?** When this is dialed far to the left, the organization is unlinked to the outside, relying on internal relationships and processes. When this is dialed far to the right, the organization is interlinked with the outside at many levels and with many connections.

3. **Collaborative?** When this is dialed far to the left, the organization is exclusive, operating only through formal and protective arms-length relationships with outsiders. When this is dialed far to the right, the organization is collaborative, with outside relationships based on mutual trust and shared norms and values.

4. **Flexible?** When this is dialed far to the left, the organization is stable, never changing its shape or what is included and excluded. When this is dialed far to the right, the organization is flexible, constantly reshaping, stretching and contracting in ways such as acquiring and divesting other organizations, outsourcing or insourcing processes, and forming alliances.

The Rewards has three major choice categories:

1. **Shortened?** When this is dialed far to the left, work rewards are provided over a long time, such as single-organization careers, retirement pensions, or equity that vests many years hence. When this is dialed far to the right, work rewards are provided in a very short time, such as immediate electronic payment after a task is finished, or an immediate ranking on a virtual scoreboard.

2. **Individualized?** When this is dialed far to the left, work rewards are consistently applied to all workers, such as a negotiated contract for all production workers in a factory. When this is dialed far to the right, work rewards are different for different individuals or subgroups.
3. **Imaginative?** When this is dialed far to the left, work rewards are drawn from traditional elements such as pay, benefits, conditions, and security. When this is dialed far to the right, work rewards are drawn from less traditional elements such as prestige, purpose, spirituality, fun, and reputation.

How the Framework Deciphers the Work beyond Employment: The Case of Upwork

This framework can help explain what has happened across the landscape of work and workers, and can help you as a leader to describe how to turn the dials to achieve your goals. Recall our examples in the earlier chapters.

Upwork dials the first two of the Assignment elements far to the right, creating work that is dispersed in time and place, and deconstructed into specific tasks. The third Assignment element is not dialed fully to the right because the workers of Upwork are attached, but not to an employment agreement. They are nonemployees attached to a platform. Indeed, the insight that the work should be attached not to employment but to a platform is what has allowed Upwork to build that platform to become much more than a meeting place for detached free agents doing microtasks, but instead to become a place to organize larger projects, and that allows Upwork to command additional revenue. Upwork dials the first three of the Organization elements far to the right, with work and workers flowing into and out of the permeable platform, and with increasingly strong interlinkages and even collaborations with its clients. The fourth Organization element is in the middle, because Upwork does not acquire and divest smaller organizations at will, but it does extend its platform to include outside organizations when it runs contests inside them. Finally, Upwork dials all three Rewards elements pretty far to the right. Its rewards are almost instantaneous as payments are made virtually, but there are also rewards such as reputation that occur only if workers have been on the platform for some time. Rewards are extremely individualized, with top performers getting far greater rewards than middle or low performers, but the system through which the rewards are calculated is the same for everyone. Upwork gets some attention for its imaginative rewards such as reputation, but that dial is not all the way to the right, because they also rely heavily on a traditional reward element—money.

The framework allows you to see developments like Upwork, Uber, Tongal, and Khazanah as more than bright shiny objects that pundits use to demonstrate how much the world is changing. It allows you to look inside, map their location, and see more clearly how the decisions they made fit their particular strategic challenges.

More important, the framework allows you to use these examples to decide how you will lead through the work. Understanding them through these dimensions allows you to better perceive and then to choose the elements that are right for you. You may decide to disperse your work while regaining it within jobs that are filled with regular full-time employees. You may decide to retain the work inside your organization among employees, but to implement elements of talent platforms like Topcoder, which more transparently and publicly track performance and accountability, and add a sense of fun and recognition to the work. You might look at an intact job such as controller, and decide to keep it intact and a relatively permanent part of your organization, but to outsource it to a consultant employed by a contractor or consulting firm. You may decide that the job of software manager can be deconstructed so that the coding part of it is sent outside your organization boundary and managed through a platform like Topcoder, but that the rest of this job (managing projects and teams) should remain within a traditional employment relationship.

The framework is also useful for workers, navigating a world beyond employment. An individual worker can decide where in this new world he or she wants to play. A whole range of options exist. Some will want relatively permanent jobs in protective organizations and be willing to accept the risks and rewards that come with that "Company Man" approach. Others will opt instead to work as independent individuals doing microtasks with no employment relationship, perhaps operating completely independently through their own websites and apps, or perhaps joining a global talent platform that preserves much of their freedom, but organizes work and workers. Thus, workers can use this framework to map their preferences and to understand how the marketplace for work and workers in their field is changing.

Our position is that leaders, workers, and of course governments need to understand this framework and use it to actively manage their decisions. Some configurations of the work, the organization, and the reward will be much more effective than others. People who are conscious of the options are in a better position to find the best configurations.

6

How IBM Leads the Work

Our Lead the Work framework suggests leaders should consider how Assignments can be deconstructed, dispersed, and detached; how their Organization should manage its boundary in terms of permeability, interlinkages, collaboration and flexibility; and finally how much Rewards should be shortened and individualized and make use of imaginative elements (Figure 6.1).

IBM has tackled the opportunities shown in the Lead the Work framework very comprehensively, and often by building a talent ecosystem within the organization that rivals or even anticipates the future developments we have seen occurring outside. IBM's approaches range from extreme deconstruction and dispersion of the assignment (where IBMers can choose to work on short-term projects) to those that retain tasks in a job but create permeable internal and external boundaries, such as exchanging employees to clients or partners for short-term assignments. IBM can draw on a range of these approaches by housing many of them in a single unit whose purpose is to optimize the work by choosing and combining the best approaches. The company sees tangible business and client results and enhanced development opportunities for employees. While not every organization will create

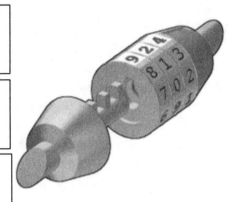

Assignment
- How Small to **Deconstruct**?
- How Widely to **Disperse**?
- How Far from Employment to **Detach**?

Organization
- How Easily to **Permeate**?
- How Strongly to **Interlink**?
- How Deeply to **Collaborate**?
- How Extensively to **Flex**?

Rewards
- How Small the Time Frame to **Shorten**?
- How Specifically to **Individualize**?
- How Creatively to **Imagine?**

Figure 6.1 Unlocking the "Lead the Work" Code (Reprise)

such an extensive internal platform to optimize the work ecosystem, IBM's experience holds important lessons and a glimpse into a potential future.

In this chapter we look at three examples of how IBM leads the work:

1. Open Talent Marketplace: An internal talent platform.
2. The IBMer Assignment Agency: A sophisticated department that manages a variety of programs for creatively matching talent to assignments.
3. The IBM-Apple Alliance: An example of how flexing the organizational boundary accesses talent that would otherwise be unavailable.

IBM's Open Talent Marketplace

IBM has developed an internal talent platform that gamifies some of the work activity in software development projects. It's called the Open Talent Marketplace (OTM).

The Open Talent Marketplace makes it possible to tap the skills of IBM's workforce employees with the time, interest, and skills to do stand-alone chunks of software development projects. Pilot experiments began in 2009, the system was scaled up in 2011, and since then IBM has been conducting 12 to 15 thousand work events per year.

OTM assignments begin when a project manager deconstructs a software development project into short-cycle events, typically 0.5 to 7 days in duration. Project managers post specifications describing the required outcome on the OTM website, where people can find and register for events that interest them. Events can be multisourced, where multiple players submit their work and the best submission wins, or single-sourced, where players submit a proposal for how they will do the work and the project manager (PM) selects one player to deliver the outcome. On the site, OTM events are also segregated by player channel, with some events earmarked for internal employees and others directed toward a contingent workforce of freelancers who have been certified to deliver via the marketplace. To encourage continuity on projects, PMs will sometimes "market" their events by reaching out to players they've worked with in the past and notifying them of upcoming events, but all participation is voluntary. IBM depicted the OTM process as shown in Figure 6.2.

Why Did IBM Develop the Open Talent Marketplace?

The Open Talent Marketplace offers IBM project teams a flexible, on-demand talent channel that increases agility in delivering software solutions. Before OTM, IBM generally staffed projects with dedicated project teams—employees who were assigned to work solely on a specific project. So, a complete project plan required assigning a sufficient number of people to all required roles on an ongoing basis. The work was contained in jobs and collected into one project team. While this provided dedicated staff, it meant that every project incurred the entire cost of each person, including additional costs associated with discontinuous work assignments, idle time, attrition, and retraining. During the project lifecycle, development workload fluctuates, but the cost of the dedicated team members remains the same regardless of output. When OTM is engaged for certain types of work on the project, the equivalent outcomes are developed at a fixed price and billed only when delivered successfully. No other costs are incurred for engaging teams. Project costs align directly with deliverable work output, and therefore talent costs do not accrue between development work cycles, resulting in "up to 50 percent lower cost of delivery for equivalent outcomes."

Prepare for Event	Engage OTM Engine	Deliver Outcomes	Award Results
Project Team	**Platform**	**Players**	**Outcomes**

• Constructs technical work plans with short cycle outcomes using component, based work planning • Identifies which components will be procured through Open Talent Marketplace • Develops encapsulated outcome-based work packets to launch event • Sets outcome prize based on work level	• Dispatches contest events to the OTM website • Recommends events to players using analytics • Provides players facility to consider scope, prize, and schedule to determine how to respond • Tracks player registration and participation in events	• Submit solutions that meet the event requirements within event time frames—from 0.5 to 7 days • May participate in player forums to build community ties and gain insights • May reuse assets from internal or external catalogs at their discretion or when prescribed by the event	• Project team scores player submissions and determines winner(s) according to the scorecard set for the event • Prizes awarded when outcomes are accepted (final fixes may be required) • Successful players earn points and enhanced digital reputation

Figure 6.2 IBM's Open Talent Marketplace Process

When IBM needs talent for a project, OTM can often get exactly the talent they need, with costs incurred to the project only for the work performed. The project manager doesn't need to know who in the vast IBM organization has the skills to do the job and the time to do it; the OTM platform lets the person find the work.

OTM has enabled and inspired IBM leaders to approach the work very differently while still taking into account local and regional requirements. Eric Bokelberg, IBM senior product manager, Smarter Workforce, said,

> One IBM team needed to convert their enterprise application and information warehouse to a new product stack and framework. This complex application would normally have taken 12 months or more to complete with existing traditional employment. Instead, they built a "loyalty pool" of OTM players. The project team first marketed the opportunity to see which players were interested. They then ran a series of training events to get players up to speed with the application and validate their expertise. Within one month, the leaders had 11 players trained and engaged in the project—much faster than the traditional staffing process. The team built commitments from the players to stay engaged by providing a steady stream of events and distributing the work equitably across trained players. By running multiple parallel work streams staffed by workers with the right skills continually available, the team completed the conversion more than five months ahead of schedule and at a lower cost.[1]

The benefits of OTM are not limited to IBM's internal work. IBM clients benefit directly by tapping the IBM talent platform. Eric Bokelberg said,

> An insurance industry customer came to us with an urgent need for website testing. Their financial advisors relied on a "portfolio optimizer" web application built and supported by a local development company (not IBM). A new release was approaching, and they had no one to test it. The customer didn't know exactly when the test effort would be required but had no funding in their budget to keep a test team on standby. IBM offered the Open Talent Marketplace—running events on demand to first create the test cases and then execute them. The cost was so low that it was almost insignificant to the client and yet they were able to engage qualified skills right when they needed, ensure a quality release, and get the function out to their financial advisors with no delay.[2]

The Assignment: How Do IBM Managers Optimally Deconstruct and Combine Regular Work Outcomes with the Open Talent Marketplace?

OTM requires that project leaders at IBM become adept at deconstructing the assignment, properly distributing the right kind of work to the platform, and then reconstructing the work that remains so that it can be assigned to the regular employees on the team. As Eric Bokelberg said, "To effectively leverage this new model, project managers have to adapt, decomposing the project work into more discrete units and adopting corresponding planning and management strategies."

It also requires creative and diligent attention to the internal boundaries between units, projects, and managers. As Eric Bokelberg described it, "The standard policy is that an employee's assigned responsibilities always take priority. Any time an employee registers for an event, his or her manager is notified. OTM events are—by design—very short in duration so that employees can accurately forecast their free cycles over the next week and determine if they have the bandwidth to participate." In essence, IBM employees take the initiative to fill up any slow periods in their own unit by taking on a small project from some other unit, quite possibly for a client on the other side of the world. Managers become participants in leading the work that now falls outside the boundaries of their own unit and the regular employment relationships of their own workers.

IBM managers and HR leaders have developed a good sense of what kinds of assignments can be deconstructed. For example, on the one hand, the work of migrating an application from one technology to another is well suited to deconstruction because the requirements are well defined and it is easy to judge a successful outcome (i.e., the application now works on the new technology). On the other hand, where an assignment's success depends on a close-up understanding of a client's unique circumstances, it is better not to deconstruct or disperse that work.

Eric Bokelberg put it this way:

Alignment of demand forecasting and resource management is the key to success, and we've developed sophisticated models to achieve that. Most important is the ability to decompose work into defined, short-cycle outcomes coupled with the discipline to manage a project via delivery of

those outcomes. Not all projects lend themselves to this model. Where it
has been most successful is where project teams have actually architected
their solutions to take advantage of OTM benefits—using widely known
technologies to ensure resource availability, and developing templates for
repeatable work that make it very easy to run large numbers of events.
We think that this is a model that can be applied within other large enterprises, and we are exploring engagements where IBM helps client make
it happen.[3]

IBM is a technology company, so it's not surprising that it first applied
OTM to technology development work. However, IBM is finding that they
can extend this expertise to other types of work with similar characteristics, such as graphic design, data entry, and document enhancement and
translation.

The Reward: What Does the Open Talent Marketplace Do for IBM Employees?

An employee who participates in an OTM event does so in addition to
his or her existing job responsibilities. Why would anyone take on extra
work? Perhaps the most compelling reason is the chance to develop (and
publicly demonstrate) new skills. IBM surveyed its participating employees and found that this was the highest-rated motivation for participating.
This is not just for the pleasure of learning; skills are the currency of the
IT world and having spent many years working in an area that has become
technically obsolete is worth next to nothing. Digital reputation and recognition are essential elements for making this type of model work within
the enterprise. Employees (and their managers) track their OTM digital
reputation using "Blue Card," a web application that is analogous to a base-
ball card. It includes a comprehensive history of outcomes delivered, skills
demonstrated, points earned, and levels of achievement. In fact, even if an
IBMer doesn't win a project (or doesn't bother to bid) OTM supports their
development by giving them valuable insight on what skills are in demand.

OTM also provides an opportunity for employees to receive additional
cash compensation as awards are distributed to top players (based on points
earned) on a regular basis. However, an even greater motivation is the chance
to work on interesting projects. Maybe an IBMer grew up in Indonesia and

is eager to work on a project that is applicable to that country. Maybe he or she is interested in the future of cities and is keen to work on a smarter cities project. OTM challenges employees with the opportunity to challenge themselves and work on projects far beyond their daily job responsibilities.

The Organization: Optimizing across IBM's Permeable Boundary

The traditional view of organization has permeability dialed down, creating a distinct barrier between employees and outsiders. With OTM, IBM has dialed permeability up by extending the platform to free agents. It extends the opportunity to optimally lead the work by drawing on external workers when internal ones are not available. This is not done in a haphazard way: IBM has developed protocols for when and how to use OTM to engage internal versus external free agents. These include considerations of security, careful domain access, talent selection, and the type of work for which internal versus external workers are eligible.

The Assignment Agency: Optimizing Work in a Single Unit

OTM is just one of many examples of how IBM optimizes work and engages its employees. OTM focuses on highly deconstructed projects, but IBM's other arrangements include

- Blue Talent Cloud: A cloud platform that matches remote workers to short-term assignments.
- External temporary redeployment: Temporarily assigns IBMers to an opening with external partners or clients.

All the arrangements are managed by a special unit called the IBMer Assignment Agency. This agency creates a sophisticated internal ecosystem for matching projects to talent that rivals (perhaps even surpasses) the external work ecosystem we discuss in this book. Andreas Hasse, the director of the IBMer Assignment Agency, says, "We aim to be the trusted partner for internal talent sourcing and placement. It is *the* integration point for the hiring manager, the people manager, and all the employees. It is not just about getting assignments done by finding the right talent. We provide the opportunities for employees to develop skills and expertise and grow their careers. Our goal is to scale this to include not only all of IBM but also the ecosystem of IBM partners and clients."

By creating a host of different programs for matching assignments to talent, IBM has built a kind of laboratory for new work arrangements. The assignment agency is constantly thinking about innovative ways to overcome the constraints of geography and organizational structure to find opportunities to match people to projects. Of course, IBM is so big that there are a great many opportunities, but size creates its own challenges in that it is hard to find just the right person—creating the mechanisms to do so is one of the IBMer Assignment Agency's key tasks.

There are many advantages to having such a sophisticated range of programs:

- The range of options helps retain talent IBM might otherwise lose to attractive opportunities outside of the organization.
- Hiring managers get IBMers who come up to speed faster than an external hire would.
- Both leaders and employees learn how to manage in a world of remote working and break the habit of assuming workers must be onsite.
- The investment IBM has made in creating these systems shows employees how committed it is to developing talent and offering interesting work.

The agency is a new kind of organizational unit that may become more common, particularly in very large organizations with thousands of jobs and hundreds of thousands of employees. At that scale, it becomes feasible to create internal systems that rival those that are evolving outside the organization, bringing the advantages of work optimization and imaginative rewards and development to regular employees. Not every organization will need to create such extensive internal agencies, but IBM's approach offers lessons for those who do and offers insights about how external platforms and permeable boundaries between internal and external workers will evolve.

Blue Talent Cloud: Temporary Jobs inside IBM

Blue Talent Cloud assigns IBMers from his or her existing country to another unit on a temporary basis (typically 2 to 12 months). The person doesn't relocate, although they may make visits to the other unit. A typical example would be where an IBM unit in emerging markets needs a specific kind of work performed for a limited time and doesn't have the skills required, but another unit in the major markets has extra capacity and an employee who does. The work remains constructed as a job, but it's possible to dial up dispersion and collaboration between business units to create work arrangements that provide unique experiences for employees and optimization opportunities for leaders.

For IBM, the Blue Talent Cloud creates efficiencies by matching excess demand for talent in one part of the organization with excess supply in another. As Andreas Hasse described it, "We leverage IBMers' experience to cover peaks and valleys in the need for talent. This is a particular advantage in growth markets, where high turnover in the IT industry is common or the time to develop needed expertise can take months or years. When you have an urgent need to provide certain expertise to the client, an experienced IBMer from another region can take on the job for a few months. This is often the difference between missing the opportunity and delivering it well. We can bring the latest technology to our clients without waiting for the developing region to be able to hire a regular full-time employee for the long term." For IBM employees, the idea of actually moving to a new region might be daunting, but providing services on a short-term basis to other parts of the business allows them to understand the broader IBM business and specific local cultures. It provides some of the same development benefits an employee would from expatriate work without as much disruption.

Such assignments don't just happen; they require cross-boundary coordination and collaboration that the IBMer Assignment Agency provides. For example, when an employee in the Shanghai office unexpectedly took a short-term leave of absence, the Agency found an IBMer in Spain with the key skills needed. With few changes to working hours, their work-life preferences were met. Indeed, the assignment was so successful that, at the end of the quarter, the Spanish employee went to Shanghai to do the quarter-end accounting.

Relocating Workers: Dispersion with a Bit of Deconstruction

IBM's value proposition is to deliver great solutions from anywhere in the world to anywhere in the world. That can mean relocating workers temporarily or permanently. Bringing in an IBMer is usually preferable to hiring a newcomer because the IBMer already knows the IBM culture, they have satisfied all the IBM entry requirements, and they have honed their capabilities within IBM's system. In many organizations, relocation can be difficult and unsystematic, because the two units may not have an easy way to see each other's workers, they may describe similar jobs differently, or there may be no available "broker" to help optimize the desires of the employee and needs of the units that move the employee. In IBM, relocation is housed in the IBMer Assignment Agency because it can take lessons learned from its other programs to make relocation a better tool for optimizing the work. The IBMer Assignment Agency offers a database of talent where a leader can search for the skills needed in other IBM units. The Agency helps optimize a balance between development for the employee and capacity help for the units involved. With Agency coordination, the boundaries of the two units become more permeable and interlinked, imaginative development rewards are enhanced, and the assignment is understood in a common language for both units. The Assignment Agency not only maintains the database and tools to expedite relocation, it helps leaders make optimal decisions. For example, the manager providing the talent loses a valued worker, but the organization benefits by sending the worker to a role where he or she can add more value or have essential development experiences. The IBMer Assignment Agency helps with these trade-offs, smoothing the paths between organizational unit boundaries.

Temporarily Assigning IBM Employees to Clients (Zenith) and Business Partners (Champions for Growth)

In other chapters we described a number of alliances that allow organizations to exchange their employees, such as the partnership between Siemens and Disney or Khazanah trading of leaders between the companies in its investment portfolio. The IBMer Assignment Agency includes two programs to assign IBM employees temporarily to other organizations. One program focuses on clients (called Zenith) and the other on business partners (called Champions for Growth). Both programs make IBM's work boundary more permeable, interlinked and collaborative. They allow IBMers to tap into imaginative rewards such as experiences with clients or business partners that IBM might not be able to offer, and the chance to build relationships and even future career paths to other organizations. For IBM, its employees gain unique experience working directly with an outside client or partner so that when they return they are even better ambassadors to those valued clients and partners.

For example, a client may say, "We know that your financial professionals in IBM have profound knowledge about how finance should be executed in an organization that relies on technology, cloud computing, and solution development. Our strategy is evolving in that direction, and we need a CFO who has deep experience in those areas." A traditional organization might think of this only in terms of regular full-time employment; with that model, the only way to satisfy the request is to lose a great employee, so most organizations would discourage it. That's a lost opportunity, especially when there may be financial professionals between assignments who would love the chance to take a temporary stint with a client or a business partner. A temporary talent exchange can be a win for IBM, the client, and the IBMer.

The IBMer Assignment Agency enables such opportunities by making IBM's boundary more collaborative, in part by deconstructing the work into a language that both the outside organization and IBM can use to accurately match workers to the work. It maintains the work as collected in a job and attached to employment, but it disperses it outside IBM's boundary to its client and partner organizations. That requires providing a governance structure that can figure out issues of accountability, protecting intellectual property, and how to translate performance assessments between the two organizations. The outside organization pays IBM for the worker, so the outside organization has a tangible economic incentive to put the person in a significant role.

IBM's goal is to bring the workers back, now armed with their new experiences, but if the worker and the outside company want them to stay, the Agency works out the transition. As Andreas Hasse said, "The majority of these folks work at the other company for two or three years, and they wear that company's employment badge while they work there. We always assume they will return, but if they choose to join the other company permanently, then we know we have placed in that client or partner a person that will help them grow in ways that make IBM's services more valuable and relevant, so it can make a significant improvement in the amount and duration of business IBM does with them."

An example of imaginative rewards involved Deloitte, the global consulting organization. Deloitte saw an opportunity to expand its software sales in Belgium. The best workers with the capability to expand those sales were employed by IBM. Deloitte is an IBM business partner, so the IBMer Assignment Agency worked out the secondment. The IBMer, now working at Deloitte, developed ways to use deeper business analytics to support Deloitte's endeavors, coincidentally extending Deloitte's use of IBM software and services.

Creating Synergy and Optimization: The Lessons of Governance and Coordination

IBM enables its managers to lead the work by creating an internal ecosystem that reaches beyond regular full-time employment. The IBMer Assignment Agency has faced challenges and developed solutions to some thorny issues. We have seen in other chapters that those issues have already started to arise in the outside world, as organizations tap the broader external ecosystem of platforms, alliances, partners, and free agents. Because the agency operates internally within IBM, it has a good deal of experience with challenges that are still just emerging in the external ecosystem. Certainly, solving those issues within one company is different from solving them in an external ecosystem of independent entities, but the techniques used by the IBMer Assignment Agency are valuable examples for organizations navigating the broader ecosystem beyond employment. Not everyone who applies gets an assignment, and not every assignment gets filled. It requires skill at matching work opportunities to the best of the programs, and skill at recruiting and assigning workers to the right opportunities.

One of the most important tools of the IBMer Assignment Agency is a single database where opportunities from a system called the Global Opportunity Marketplace and information from a registration site for IBMers are stored. Workers can actively search the Marketplace for opportunities, but often busy IBMers prefer to register their profile on the system so that it can present appropriate opportunities to them as they arise. As registered IBMers go through cycles of considering and accepting or rejecting opportunities, the Agency learns their preferences by analyzing their clients' transactions. Over time the Agency offers IBMers opportunities that are more exact matches, based on what the system has learned about their choices.

The matching, as one might expect from IBM, uses sophisticated algorithms and fuzzy logic. However, there is a crucial human element. Human analysts in the IBMer Assignment Agency examine the matches that are returned by the system to check whether they are a good-quality match. It's a constant endeavor to improve the matching process, to minimize offering workers something they reject, or offering clients a person they don't accept. IBM draws upon its own tools of artificial intelligence and a vast library of skills and competencies. As the scale of the Agency grows, it automates processes such as communication with candidates and managers, but again it's an artful combination of using machine learning to assist the human capability. Christiane Schuetz is an IBM communications leader whose job is to humanize the communication and matching process, to get the advantages of automation and predictive analytics, but avoid the "cold feel" of an exclusively computer-based mathematical algorithm.

Finally, because almost all of the Agency's assignments are undertaken with the assumption that the person will return to IBM, or return within IBM to their original role, the Agency has developed a system of after-care for its assignees. That means that employees' performance on their assignments are tracked in a language that can be understood and compared to past and future assignments. It means keeping them in touch with IBM, particularly on long assignments with clients or partners so that they stay connected to IBM culture, strategy, challenges, and networks. The Agency leaders want to make sure that no IBMer is left behind, so they make sure to include them in team meetings, career fairs, and other bonding experiences.

Found in Translation: A Common Language of Work

"What we've got here is a failure to communicate," is the classic line from the movie *Cool Hand Luke*, where Paul Newman is working on the chain gang. A failure to communicate about the work people do may not be as dramatic as in the movies, but it can be an increasingly important barrier to achieving your organization's mission. It's relatively easy to understand the skills of the regular full-time employees in your own department. But what if you are using services like the IBMer Assignment Agency to tap talent from across the IBM world and beyond? How can you accurately communicate which skills you need, and how can you accurately assess what skills other people have?

Just as accounting and finance provide a common language about money that allows it to move between organizations, a world beyond employment increasingly requires a common language so that work can move efficiently between organizations, or even between positions within a single organization.

Perhaps the most vivid example of the limitations of today's language of work is the challenge facing organizations from Walmart to Starbucks who wish to hire military veterans. The military language of work doesn't map well onto private-sector jobs. To help address the issue, the U.S. Department of Labor provides a "crosswalk" to translate between military occupational specialties (MOS) and civilian language. Search the word "analyst" in the Air Force and you get a long list of "interpreters and translators." Search the word "leader" and you get a list of jobs called "architectural and engineering managers." When organizations borrow talent, as Siemens did when it allied with Disney employees to market its children's hearing aid, they rely largely on the partner organizations' language of their workers' qualifications and capabilities. When you get workers from an agency or consulting firm, you rely on their language to describe what the workers can do. Often, these organizations have a very different language for the same work, just like the different military branches. If there is a failure to communicate, then the match of task to talent will be poor.

Clients feel pretty sure IBM must have a solution to their technical problems. Clients say, "You have a vast network of employees and contractors; you must be able to find someone among them to solve my problem." The clients are not wrong, but it is a significant challenge to identify the right person. IBM has made it possible to find the right person by creating a five-layer taxonomy of 20,000 distinct skills, as well as introducing more advanced methods (a folksonomy) to keep up-to-date information on who has what skills.

You might think the size of the taxonomy, not to mention the folksonomy (which we discuss further in a moment), would make it difficult to navigate. Surprisingly, Andreas Hasse says, "It's pretty simple: I just tap into the database of the IBMer Assignment Agency that contains all the requisitions and all the candidates. An interface prompts managers who have work needs to answer a set of relevant questions. It prompts IBM employees to answer a set of questions about what they can do, what they want to do, and when they are available. We need to ask them only a few questions because we can pull everything else from the human resource information warehouse (HRIW). I don't need a complex set of commands or database queries; I just use natural language to ask for what I need."

The value of a sophisticated and ever-evolving language system for work is an important lesson for leaders who hope to get more creative in matching assignments to talent within their own organization, but perhaps even more significant for workers, managers, and citizens who will need to navigate a world of work beyond traditional employment. Building and maintaining the taxonomy is not a small or a one-time project: IBM's Expertise Taxonomy is built, maintained, and developed with 75 employees. Anne Lake, who heads the Expertise Taxonomy, expressed the big idea: "as we perfect the system, a business leader will tell the system what they want done in their own words, and the system tells the leader who can do it, it tells IBMers what they need to develop to be qualified, and if IBM doesn't have a matching skill, it can help the manager locate a freelancer or outside employee."

The limitation of a taxonomy is that new skills are constantly being created (e.g., skills around a brand-new programming language), and people are constantly acquiring new skills. How do you keep everything up to date? To address this problem, IBM leverages an interactive mobile app codeveloped with the IBM software and research teams called the IBM Expertise Locator. The system is increasingly using data-mining techniques to analyze the data that naturally occurs as people do their work, and it infers the skills and expertise depth of the employees through advanced algorithms. This app captures the expertise of every employee through their digital footprint to highlight their skills, knowledge, experience, network, and contributions to other employees. It further differentiates experts by using social business capabilities based on those who share and surface their expertise to connect with others, which fuels innovation, decreases response times, and delivers a differentiated client experience. Thousands of global IBMers searching for expertise via the app creates a folksonomy that empowers the organization to gain visibility of current and up-and-coming market skill needs and trends, ultimately informing updates to the taxonomy.

The IBM Expertise Locator solution, available to clients as part of the Expertise 360 Talent Suite, provides a new level of access to experts and expertise within one's organization. Features and functions include

- Rapid access of the vast, collective knowledge of experts through a mobile app (iOS and Android) or web search
- Search for subject matter experts based on their expertise
- Browse keyword categories
- Select from a list of popular keywords
- Easy to use, fast, and efficient
- Experts prioritize and redirect to another expert when needed

The Lesson of IBM

IBM shows that optimizing the array of work options described by the Lead the Work framework is no longer speculation, because it is actually happening at IBM. IBM shows the value of not merely using different existing alternatives like platforms, outsourcing, or alliances, but of instead creating hybrid work arrangements that dial some elements up and others down. That offers a wide set of options for getting the work done: from sending a piece of work to a free agent, to assigning a temporary job to an IBMer, to seconding employees to an alliance. IBM isn't simply using a variety of alternative approaches; it has built integrated systems to enable the framework, such as OTM, the IBMer Assignment Agency, and the IBM Expertise Locator. IBM shows how the ecosystem of talent platforms and labor market intermediaries is rapidly evolving, not only when it comes to workers outside its boundary but also when it comes to its internal workers, who increasingly have the chance to get all the benefits of IBM employment as well as the benefits of being a free agent. It shows how leading the work applies to employees just as it does to outside workers.

IBM–Apple Alliance

In 2014 IBM got a call from Apple. It turns out that Apple, for all its skills, needed help to crack the corporate market. It had visionary ideas, but not the contacts, not the understanding of how the big corporations work, not the insight into the enterprise IT. There was work to be done, but it couldn't be done by Apple's own employees; the organization boundary had to stretch out, become more permeable, and find the talent they needed through IBM.

Making the alliance work depended, more than anything else, on being sensitive to the cultural issues. For example, you don't walk into the Apple campus with a Samsung phone.

The mix of the two cultures could sometimes lead to odd events. One day the IBM leader of the Apple/IBM alliance, Fred Balboni, now appropriately attired in ultracasual style, got a call to attend an urgent meeting. Next thing he knew he was in a meeting with the top 10 IT people from one of America's biggest banks—dressed like he was at the cottage, not representing corporate IBM.

Not deterred by fashion issues, in the alliance, Apple and IBM employees work side by side. Most of Balboni's team works in the Apple headquarters and in the design studio with seven to nine IBM designers who work directly with the Apple designers. Apple has also provided a facility where the alliance can bring in clients who cycle in and out on projects, finding new ways to do things in business. There are Apple development centers in Toronto, Chicago, and Atlanta with both IBM and Apple employees, and a big IT center in India with over 1,000 employees—mostly IBMers. In field sales the size difference between the companies is evident: Apple fields 100–150 people and IBM has 10,000 sellers/consultants around the world.

We asked Balboni if this size difference created any problems and the answer was "not at all," which leads back to Balboni's insistence that it's all about trust. To him, one indicator that the relationship is working is that the team has reached the point where they can finish one another's sentences. There is a contract—it's an inch thick—and IBM and Apple spent months working on it, but trust came first and once the contract was agreed upon it could sit in a drawer gathering dust. When it comes to potential governance, concerns such as stealing one another's employee is a nonissue; if an employee wants to move, no one is going to stop him or her, and it would not be perceived as stealing—just a normal flow of talent across a permeable boundary. Not every employee can fit into the alliance; three or four times people have been "voted off the island"—maintaining an atmosphere of trust and collaboration is all-important.

As IBM had hoped, the alliance is doing important and innovative work that will have a large business impact on its corporate clients; or as Apple would say, "What we're doing is insanely great." For example, a large bank is transforming the whole customer service around a mobile experience. You'll deposit money with your iPhone, get a loan through your iPad, and take money out of your account with your AppleWatch.

IBM and Apple are driving changes in how banking works in a way neither of these proud and capable organizations could have done on their own. The leadership had to see past the organizations' boundaries, look out into the world, and ask, what's the best possible way to organize to get this done? Where can we get the talent, the capabilities? And once it was clear that overlapping their boundaries was the way to do it, the two organizations had to really crank up collaboration for the alliance to be a success.

Notes

1. Interview with Eric Bokelberg, April 3, 2015.
2. Interview with Eric Bokelberg, April 3, 2015.
3. Interview with Eric Bokelberg, April 3, 2015.

7

The Assignment: How Much to Deconstruct, Disperse, and Detach?

Topcoder and Upwork are impressive platforms, but they are not for everything. When we asked the leaders of these companies what makes their platforms work, they talk about how the assignment given to a worker is structured. An assignment needs to be packaged in a way suitable for the platform and some assignments are more easily packaged than others. Even the leaders of these platforms don't try to do all of their work with free agents. Why does an assignment such as computer coding, logo design and Internet video production work well on these platforms, while an assignment such as leading a team, or project management, may be better done with regular full-time employees? The leaders use different language, but a recurring theme is that such platforms work best when the assignment can be broken down to a tangible result. This principle shows up throughout the sharing economy. For example, Uber can optimize ride sharing because a ride is tangible and specific. Topcoder can optimize computer coding because the code can be easily captured as the result. In both cases, the assignment's quality can easily be observed, and you can objectively decide if it was delivered on time.

The insight that platforms work best if assignments have a clear tangible result does not necessarily mean that an assignment can just be packaged, tossed over to a platform, and forgotten until the result comes back. Tongal explicitly builds in back-and-forth between the client and Tongaler—it is a necessary part of the creative process. Also Upwork has built in tools that make it possible to manage assignments that are not so easily packaged and need to be paid by the hour.

To understand how assignments can be packaged into suitable chunks for a talent platform it is useful to consider how a mix of assignments ends up together in a traditional job. Consider how computer coding work has evolved. The first jobs might have consisted exclusively of computer coding. Yet, when the work is part of regular full-time employment, it may be hard to attract and keep talented people if that's their only work. So, leaders add project management and software design into roles like this to give them more variety and significance, and then perhaps also toss in elements of team leadership and management because that allows them to offer employees a career path upward through company hierarchy. On many levels, it all makes sense to mix coding with employment and organizational membership. However, what gets tossed into the job is often not a carefully engineered collection of intertwined work, but instead what was convenient, and assumed to be done by regular full-time employees. Sometimes work is combined to fit a particular person, such as creating the job of supervising software engineer because a great software coder wanted more managerial experience. That's fine, but it's not unusual for that job to remain, long after the particular person has moved on.

Now, with modern technology and virtual marketplaces, Topcoder can offer attractive beyond-employment arrangements that focus exclusively on being a great coder. If your organization persists in embedding coding into jobs that contain other work, you may be outperformed by companies that rely on Topcoder. Or, the coding quality you need may become impossible to get with regular employees, in part because they have so many other things to do. Topcoder, by deconstructing the assignment and building a platform devoted to it, can provide that quality.

The evolution of work continually changes these decision points. To take advantage of Topcoder, you must question the assumption that coding is part of a "job" structure. To take advantage of outsourcers or alliances, you must be prepared to question whether or not a particular set of activities is best served by being connected to other processes inside your organization.

Only by such deconstruction can you see the emerging opportunities. Complete deconstruction of all of your work assignments won't always be the best way to lead the work, but failing even to consider deconstruction will increasingly lead to missed opportunities. Indeed, deconstructing and reconstructing assignments is becoming a vital capability. Optimization requires not only knowing what to break apart and what to keep together, but how to reconstruct or bring back together all those parts. There is an important natural relationship between deconstruction, recombination, and coordination.

Leading the work in a world beyond employment means more than simply copying what Topcoder does, or engaging Upwork. It requires that you use principles to match the assignment to the appropriate work arrangement. Think of assignments as being packaged as jobs done by regular employees in a specific location and time, and it is very hard to see how you can use freelance talent platforms. We need to shake up that traditional thinking. As we have seen, history has led to the domination of jobs as the way to get work done. Most organizations define assignments not as one result, but as jobs that combine a set of capabilities, activities, and results, and often occurring at a certain time and place, done by regular employees.

This chapter shows you how to think beyond this traditional approach so that you can better perceive when the traditional approach is optimum, when you should fully switch to one of the new approaches (such as a platform for free agents or contractors), and when you should design the assignment as a hybrid of these things. The work in a world beyond employment is enabled by technology, globalization, social acceptance, and business innovation. However, making decisions about how to lead through the work requires more than recognizing the change and its causes. In order to engage with this evolution, you need to decide how to manage it and design for it. A first step is to consider how to design the work assignment.

Unlocking the code of the assignment involves three dimensions of optimization: How small to deconstruct? How widely to disperse? How far from employment to detach?

How Small to Deconstruct?

Deconstruction means breaking the whole into its parts. For example, jobs can be deconstructed into projects, tasks, or microtasks. Many writers have suggested the new world of work will be a "project-based" economy. That's an example of deconstruction, though only one way to think about it. Platforms like Topcoder and Upwork have figured out that if you deconstruct jobs or assignments, you can identify the parts that define a tangible result. When you do, free agents become an option because you don't need to monitor skills, effort, diligence, or even activity. You need only decide if the assignment is completed at acceptable quality and on time. That's why assignments such as data compression algorithms, Internet or TV commercials, and entering figures from receipts work so well on platforms like these. If the job is "being a good marketing analyst," then judging the assignment simply by a result is less optimal. Deconstruction doesn't just apply to individual assignments, it also applies to larger organizational units like functions. For example, many functions within pharmaceutical companies, such as basic science, research and development (R&D), regulatory approval, manufacturing, and sales, were traditionally held internally within the same organization. Yet, if you deconstruct that value chain, you see that R&D need not be yoked with the other elements, and it may best be accomplished by pooling resources across several companies within an alliance. The classic argument for outsourcing draws on deconstruction. You may be able to outsource processes such as payroll more cheaply and effectively to an outside organization for which they are its sole occupation. However, if such processes are closely intertwined with other processes that are vital to your goals, deconstructing them may not be optimal.

How do you decide? Our map and decision framework suggest that optimal deconstruction depends on the goals and situation. Leaders should consider deconstruction rather than assume that assignments must be contained within traditional jobs. Whenever a leader confronts a decision about getting work done, they can think about this: "If I break this work into its parts, does that reveal any options for getting it done that are not available if I keep it together as a job or process?" The answer may sometimes be to use a traditional job and sometimes to break the work apart.

Why is mastering deconstruction important to leadership? Because in the world beyond employment there are rapid innovations that make optimal deconstruction more vital to achieving efficiency, quality, and performance. Before Tongal, running your own contest for commercials would be unthinkable, and without the Foldit platform and community you could never tackle hard biochemistry problems with volunteers.

When Tongal and Foldit exist, failing to consider deconstruction means missing opportunities.

We naturally start with the question, "What elements can we pull out of a job?" However, it may be more productive to ask, "What elements absolutely must be together in a job?" Many jobs are not designed because work elements must stay together, but are remnants of a time when regular full-time jobs were the only way to structure the assignment. Jobs become buckets of tasks designed to add up to a full-time employment role. If jobs were already carefully engineered collections of intertwined assignments, then deconstructing them might be impractical. However, in many cases the question, "Can we deconstruct this assignment?" has never been asked.

Goals and Limits of Deconstruction

Deconstructing the assignment can offer several advantages. Understanding them provides the rationale that helps you decide how small to deconstruct.

First, deconstruction can better allow you to give the assignment to the most qualified person. For example, the assignment of search engine optimization might be embedded in the job of web marketing designer, but might be better done by someone who specializes in such optimization. Second, deconstruction allows you to give the assignment to the least-cost worker. If a highly paid engineer is doing a few hours of administrative work each week we should see if there is some way to deconstruct the job and send that administrative work to a low-cost freelancer. Third, deconstruction allows you to better adjust assignments to reflect volatile workloads.

Retailers like Gap, Inc., Starbucks, and Target may have vast variations in customer traffic in their stores throughout the day, so it makes sense to have workers come in for short shifts. Many of those workers don't use their retail job to fill up their workweek. Rather, their retail job supplements other work they do. If a retailer were to conceive of their associates' work simply as a 40-hour-a-week job, they would miss the chance to engage workers willing and able to work fewer and more volatile hours. For Starbucks, this can actually be a competitive advantage. Starbucks endeavors to be a place where folks kick back and linger, relax, laugh and converse. Starbucks wants customers to hang out and feel a bond with their barista. The workers (known as "partners") who want to work odd hours at Starbucks often do so because their other work is to be performers who rehearse during the day, or writers and graphic artists who prefer to paint or write during a large portion of their day, and do their Starbucks job at other times. In this case, Starbucks' partners are employees, not freelancers, but the work is optimally deconstructed into time periods that fit the right worker population.

Deconstruction raises the question of what we must forever keep together and what we may render asunder. At some point, elements of the work must be connected and happen together. You cannot write a poem by contracting out each stanza to a different free agent. If you use independent programmers to write a piece of code, it must eventually interface properly with all the other code in the system. The nuances of striking the proper balance are a part of the new work of leaders. How far should you break work apart?

The discipline of deconstruction will undoubtedly develop, but these questions seem likely to prove useful in breaking the assumption that assignments must always be grouped into jobs:

- Can we break the assignment into pieces that have tangible outcomes?
- Can we break off low-value added assignments from high-value added assignments and send each to the best person to do it?
- Can we isolate the pivotal element of the assignment, where doing that one piece really well will have a huge impact on the end result, and assign it to the very best talent in the world?
- Can some assignments that a talent platform specializes in (Tongal for commercials, Topcoder for programming) be deconstructed based on what that platform has learned about packaging assignments after seeing hundreds or thousands of similar projects?

Here are some reasons to deconstruct assignments less:

- **The gain is too trivial:** There is an upfront cost to deconstruction. Maybe specialists could do pieces of the work faster and cheaper, but if the gain is small, they won't compensate for the upfront cost.
- **The elements of the assignment are too intricately connected:** In many cases, how task A needs to be done depends on how tasks B and C are unfolding, and vice versa. For example, renowned architect, author, and innovator Christopher Alexander talks about the constant trade-offs he made in building the Eishin high school campus just outside Tokyo,

saying he could not have one person making decisions on the construction of classroom building while another made decisions about the gym because they all had to fit in a harmonious whole. At a less esoteric level, cost overruns in one building would have to be compensated by savings in another.[1]

Here are some reasons to deconstruct assignments more:

- **A specialist can do a piece of the assignment far better than a "generalist":** Any paralegal could check a trademark for you, but they are unlikely to do it as well or as quickly as someone who specializes in trademarks. Talent platforms redefine the meaning of a specialist. At the global scale of a talent platform, you can find not just any trademark agent, but one who has recent experience in exactly the trademark issue you need to resolve. This super-specialist will provide better quality. They will also do the work faster, which means they will probably be cheaper.
- **Engaging a large number of workers makes your regular employees more productive:** Deconstructing assignments can make it easier to engage a very large workforce. If a large number of blueprints need to be checked for certain factors, you might deconstruct the work into a routine check, done by regular clerks, and more advanced analysis, which can only be done by engineers. An army of clerks can quickly do the bulk of work, saving the scarce engineers for only the work that needs them.
- **To disperse the assignment:** Deconstruction is often necessary to disperse work in time and space. For example, if you have work that could be done well by people who work from home, then you first need to break it into manageable chunks before you can disperse it to this workforce.
- **To gain agility:** In *Built to Change: How to Achieve Sustained Organizational Effectiveness*, Ed Lawler and Chris Worley argue that structuring by jobs makes the presumption that the organization is static.[2] If assignments can be deconstructed, then the organization is more likely to take change in stride.

Deconstruction Driven by Growth

Organizations have been addressing the issues of deconstruction, recombination, and coordination since they began. Consider the example of the

HR department of a small business as it grows. Imagine a business with about 100 employees. They have an HR manager who's responsible for recruiting, training, compensation, and employee relations, among other things. The HR assignments feel tightly bound together. She knows what training is needed because she recruited the employees. In her work in recruiting, training and employee relations, she develops such deep insight into the jobs and people that she can develop and manage a fair and effective rewards system. Everything fits together.

Then the company grows to 200 people, and she just doesn't have the time to "know" the talent anymore. The first deconstruction involves an assistant to do the administrative aspects of the job, such as scheduling interviews and assembling training material, hoping that she can pass down enough work to fit 40 hours a week.

The next deconstruction occurs when the company gets bigger still and requires one manager to handle just recruiting. Earlier, the HR leader believed this function was too closely bound to the overall assignments of people management to be pulled out, but now the volume of the recruiting assignment and of her own other work makes it a logical choice. However, to work well, deconstruction must avoid creating silos, or situations in which the recruiter only hears about hiring needs at the last minute or after getting to know the new hire well, fails to pass that information on to her colleagues.

As the firm grows, assignments that were formerly part of the self-contained job of the HR leader continue to be deconstructed and parsed out. Soon, the job of HR leader becomes one of integration, with separate functions for training, compensation, employee relations, and so on. At each stage of deconstruction, we can divide work on the basis of a functional area (for example, all the tasks in recruiting fit together) or by level of work (for example, all clerical tasks are put together).

Thus, deconstruction is not completely new, but the world beyond employment creates new opportunities to deconstruct and coordinate assignments that are increasingly smaller and dispersed. Leaders must bring more rigor and discipline to a deconstruction process that traditionally might simply happen organically as a byproduct of growth.

Deconstructing and Reconstructing by Necessity:
The Lean Entrepreneur

Lean entrepreneurs often are reluctant to add employees. A lean entrepreneur recognizes that as soon as he hires an employee, he has a mouth to feed, a set of legal obligations to fulfill, a junior to direct and mentor, and potentially a long-term commitment that will be expensive to break. Lean entrepreneurs avoid the employment contract as long as possible. Some who have successfully grown a business once with employees, and have the opportunity to do so again, say, "Why on earth would I want to take that burden on?" Fortunately, the choice is not as stark as give up on growth versus hire employees; there are options such as outsourcing, alliances, and free agents to help drive growth and profits.

Lean entrepreneurs may farm out clerical or specialist work, either by outsourcing or contracting with free agents. They may get a free-agent bookkeeper to do the accounting for just for a few hours a month, and hire a virtual assistant, perhaps one they found on Upwork to handle clerical work. They may form alliances with professionals in closely related fields so that they can handle bigger projects. Chapter 2 described Smith & Associates, where the associates were simply people Smith could call on when needed to help with bigger assignments. Smith may consider these associates friends, allies or subcontractors, but they are certainly not employees or partners.

At what point does pushing work outside the organization fail? There is no obvious upper limit. Certainly a 1:1 ratio of employees to free agents is manageable, but why not 1:2 or 1:4? How could Instagram, with only 13 employees, be sold for $1 billion? With Instagram, almost all the work is done by the unpaid users of the service. The same could be said for Google, whose vast wealth depends on hundreds of millions of content creators the company neither pays nor manages, or Apple, with its vast network of applications developers.

Compared to the "deconstruction driven by growth" case, the lean entrepreneur case is one of systematic *recombination* of elements, but only when necessary to the coordination requirements. If successful, lean entrepreneurs find the right balance of deconstructed and combined work, and just enough coordination to tie them all together.

Deconstruction through Projects

An alternative way to approach deconstruction is to look at work as a series of projects. In an article in the *Harvard Business Review*, Roger Martin argues that knowledge work never belonged in jobs in any case. He feels companies took the model of industrial-age work, where stable well-defined jobs made sense, and misapplied that structure to knowledge work.[3] Martin argues that knowledge work is naturally organized into projects and you see this embodied in how a professional services firm works. This perspective of "project work" is a special case of deconstruction. Just as with tasks and microtasks, organizing the assignments as projects will be much easier in a world of free agents, alliances, and talent platforms.

Projects have a finite time span, and often sit uncomfortably within the world of jobs, but very comfortably in the world of deconstructed assignments. An ideal project uses just the right mix of talent for just the right period of time. As we have seen, trying to achieve this with regular full-time employees can be risky, and raises the question of what those employees will be doing after the project ends. Hollywood, of course, is all about projects and a whole set of standard procedures have evolved in the industry so that it's relatively easy to pull the right people together and negotiate the work arrangements such as pay and accountability. Each sub-specialty on a movie set knows where they fit into the project, making coordination easier. Leaders should take notice: It is possible to run an entire industry with surprisingly few regular full-time jobs and employers, when the organizing principle is the project. Also, the Hollywood model works because it sits upon an ecosystem of structures such as the Screen Actors Guild that provides insurance, pensions, matching services, and so forth. Equivalent structures may not yet exist in your industry, but they are evolving quickly.

Final Thoughts on Deconstruction

For the leader, envying the lean entrepreneur who can build a project-based/deconstructed company from scratch, the question is whether she should run the process in reverse. An existing organization with hundreds or thousands of employees obviously can't just start over, and organically grow by deconstructing, dispersing, and detaching the work assignments. The leader may recognize that her business is burdened with high overheads and rigid structures to the point that the talent platforms are stealing their customers. Survival may depend on deconstruction.

Deconstructing your organization could occur through several steps. You might outsource whole departments. You might use contingent workers rather than employees for some assignments. You might encourage your managers to deconstruct individual jobs a piece at a time, tapping the talent platforms and free agent world. As more elements of work are pulled out of jobs, a department will begin to collapse inward. The work that took 20 people can now be done by 10, and perhaps one day that will become five. The ideal speed of execution will depend on the unique dynamics of the particular business. As a leader, are you sufficiently aware of those dynamics, so you can take the organization exactly where it needs to go?

How Widely to Disperse?

Dispersing the assignment means asking, "Can this assignment be done at any other place or time?" As with deconstruction, that question can reveal opportunities that are obscured by assuming regular full-time employment. As a leader, you already disperse assignments when you use teleconferencing, remotely controlled production processes, and global outsourcing. The new world beyond employment will offer you even greater opportunities.

The original reason for bringing work together in one place and at the same time was to gain efficiency and coordination. A factory is a good example. While you might get production accomplished by allowing all the elements to be done by individuals in separate locations working at their own pace, placing all the elements of production and coordination in one place and having them occur at the same time achieved economies of scale and easier coordination. In the field of medicine, the hospital was the factory, so for serious illness, doctors, nurses, technicians, and support staff all congregated there. In education, the factory became the school building.

Collecting work in a factory was driven by the constraint of the machine. It would not go to you, so you went to it. Today, if workers operate robotic machines, then it's easy to imagine them doing so from anywhere, using personal technology. The pilot of a passenger aircraft is onboard, but the pilot of a drone can be located away from the action. Collecting work in an office was traditionally driven by the limitations of communications technology. Paper files existed in a certain location, and most person-to-person communication had to be done face to face. Aggregating in an office became an assumption, a habit, a way of doing work that got embedded in the social fabric of organizations. Today, much work can be done through conference calls, web links, cloud-based file sharing, and so forth.

Recognizing dispersal as a dimension of leading the work doesn't mean that all work should be dispersed. Pixar, which has made animated films such as *Toy Story* and *Finding Nemo*, could disperse all its work remotely. Yet Pixar has employees, and those employees routinely brave California traffic to congregate in a single place. Why? The intensity of the creative process requires a team that gets the emotional and communication benefits of working shoulder to shoulder, at the same time and place.

Of course dispersion is not a binary all-or-nothing decision. A team of workers can be dispersed most of the time but come together face to face at specific phases of a project. There are many different services to facilitate occasional face-to-face meetings from technology platforms like Webex to the ever-popular café meetings, to renting a meeting room in a hotel. WhyWeWork provides a variety of hybrid services and spaces to optimize the balance between remote and face-to-face work.

Here are reasons to disperse work *less*:

- **High-bandwidth communication:** No technology-mediated communication yet comes close to the bandwidth of face-to-face communication. Creative teams building something out of nothing need that high-bandwidth communication. Pixar's CEO Edwin Catmull talks about how all films go through the ugly-baby stage.[4] The early versions of *Toy Story*, *A Bug's Life*, and others were awkward, disjointed, unattractive, and not funny. It's tough for the creative team to look at this kind of mess and believe they can make it something brilliant via a conference call. For an ugly baby to grow up into a beautiful person, Pixar believes the creative team needs high-bandwidth, face-to-face communication.

- **Collaboration:** In 2013, Marisa Mayer, the CEO of Yahoo! raised controversy when an internal memo leaked, in which she ordered Yahoo! workers to come to work, rather than work at home. Two months later, Mayer addressed the Great Place to Work conference and said that "people are more productive when they're alone, but they are more collaborative and innovative when they're together." She cited a new Yahoo! weather app for IOS that was originated by two software engineers working in the same office.[5]

- **Informal knowledge exchange:** Many knowledge-based companies have embraced the idea that random interactions are important for knowledge sharing. The Toronto-based risk analysis firm Algorithmics built stairwells with landings designed to encourage people to bump into one another and start conversations. A Silicon Valley firm connected its coffee pot to the Internet, so it could inform people when a fresh pot was ready, thus drawing a random set of people to the coffee room where they could chat. A slightly more formal idea discussed in John Seely Brown's *The Social Life of Information* is to put experienced call-center reps next to less experienced ones, and install long phone cords.[6] When a less experienced rep had a problem, the mentor could wheel her chair over to help while still staying on her own call. One can't always recreate this kind of informal face-to-face exchange electronically, though a whole category of software called collaboration platforms is trying.

Here are some reasons to disperse work *more*:

- **Labor costs:** Dispersing assignments allows leaders to reach into countries or regions with less expensive labor markets. Leaders can also reach into corners of their home-country labor market, finding, for example, someone who's happy to do the work, but unwilling to move or unwilling to commute.

- **Overhead costs:** Office and factory space is an expensive fixed cost. Many organizations have saved millions of dollars by selling their offices and encouraging their employees to come together only when needed, in shared offices.

- **Finding the best talent:** Dispersing assignments creates an opportunity to send it to the best person regardless of where they are located and when they want to work. In our introduction we alluded to millennial-generation workers who prefer to live on the beach and complete their work at night, or those who prefer to travel the world and complete their work from wherever and whenever they can find a web connection. Some of the best coders, designers, and artists may soon prefer to work this way. The only way to reach them will be to disperse the assignment.

- **Offering a better deal:** When workers prefer or need the flexibility of working remotely, that opportunity can be a valuable element of the reward package. Later in this chapter we describe how JetBlue Airways's innovative approach to creating a call center through a dispersed network of people working from their own homes was a welcome reward for many working mothers.

In most organizations, particularly large ones, we believe the bias is to congregate the work rather than to disperse it. The easy habit is to create jobs and locations where people work together at the same time. Even Google—an iconic modern organization built on dispersed networks, customers, and data—has been building multiacre campuses all across the Bay Area of San Francisco, California. Why create locations where people go to work when so much of Google's work could be done from anywhere thanks to technology? Google has concluded that the value of colocating the work exceeds the value of dispersing it. Leaders there may well be right if the aforementioned reasons not to disperse hold sway. Still, will the Google campuses look like dinosaurs in a few years as lean entrepreneurs create platforms that make dispersed work even more viable?

To lead the work you must avoid the habitual assumption that the assignment must occur at one place or time. Even if you decide to disperse less, it should be for good reasons, and not simply because you have never dispersed work before, or your existing system of jobs doesn't make it easy.

How Far from Employment to Detach?

A brick-and-mortar store used to be the typical intermediary between the maker of a product and the person buying it. In the same way, an "employer" is the typical intermediary between the person doing the work and the person who receives and pays for it. Amazon, PayPal, iTunes, and other market innovations "disintermediated" the brick-and-mortar store. Basically, they detached the purchase from the store and created new ways to connect purchasers with products. In the same way, while employment can be a very effective way to connect workers with assignments, the world beyond employment is constantly detaching assignments from the traditional employment relationship.

Detachment often involves mixed loyalties. A worker employed by a supplier of Boeing, who is working at the Boeing plant side by side with Boeing employees on a 787 may feel attached to some extent both to their employer and to Boeing; or they may actually feel more attached to the 787 *project* than either company.

To lead the work requires that you make good decisions about just how much you attach assignments to the traditional regular full-time employment relationship. If you were to start with a clean slate, would the work that you currently tuck within an employment relationship stay there? Increasingly, you have lots of options, but they require that you break the habit of attaching work to employment as the preferred relationship.

The Role of Intermediaries in Detaching Assignments from Employment

A significant factor driving work to be detached from employment is the emergence of what some have called "labor market intermediaries."[7] Intermediaries stand between the individual worker and the client organization that needs the work.

"Intermediary" is an umbrella term and includes a disparate array of organizations.[8] They include membership-based organizations such as professional societies and guilds, public-sector organizations, and educational institutions that educate and place workers, as well as an expanding class of organizations that offer services for a fee, such as information exchanges (job boards), search firms, temporary help agencies, outplacement services, and professional employer organizations (that act as the employer of record). We would also include the Talent Platforms as one of the most important intermediaries.

They are important because they take over some of the tasks traditionally handled within the employment relationship. For example, an executive may look to a search firm to navigate their career, rather than the HR department of their current employer. Similarly, a free agent may look to a Freelancers Union for health benefits rather than seek employment to provide them.

In the example of the search firm, that executive is not quite as firmly attached to her current employer because the intermediary is doing the important work of planning her career. In the case of a Talent Platform like Upwork the employment relationship between the free agent and client organization is completely severed, so Upwork meets many of the needs of the free agent including learning, career planning, and getting assignments.

Intermediaries make it easier to dial up detachment because services that were formerly only available through employment are now available via the intermediary. Some free agents look with puzzlement on employment offers that offer little compared to what they can get on their own via one or more intermediaries.

Rethinking the Purpose of the Employment Relationship

Whenever the need arises in a small company to get more work done, the first instinct is to ask, "Where can we get this done?" rather than, "Should we hire more employees?"

AppMakr is a company that builds smartphone apps, and they have taken detaching work from employment to the extreme: they have no employees. We asked AppMakr cofounder Jay Shapiro how many workers they have, and he said, "We have around 60 active contractors working with us at the moment, but that could just as easily be 200 people at another time. Unlike traditional headcount where you hire a person for a permanent full-time role, we have lots of people we have hired for a particular skill, to work on a particular project for a couple of hours/weeks/months, and then we both move on. It's one of the joys of being task-oriented, rather than role-oriented, in your HR approach."

AppMakr shows that you can turn the "detach from employment" dial to the maximum to create a successful small company. Indeed, we should say that the company is successful *precisely because* they turned the dial to the extreme. Shapiro notes that a fully detached model may be easier to manage than a traditional model that attaches the assignment to employment. That's because if you try to mix the models, with some of the workers being employees and others being detached, then detached workers can feel left out. If everyone is detached from employment, then the whole culture adjusts to fit detached assignments.

One reason detaching the assignment seems natural for small companies but hard to imagine for big ones is that when a company is built on an employment model, all structures and processes are designed to work with employees. For example, an established firm may have a specific way it handles performance management, and until you have worked for the company for several years, you won't be good at it. A company built on a "detach wherever possible" model probably needs a simpler, more generic performance management system that's easier to use with free agents, contractors, or platform-based freelancers. Indeed, it may need no performance management system at all, if the intermediary provides performance management.

To lead the work requires some interesting decisions. A retailer could decide that they want to design the work in a way that draws on long-term learning by store managers and employees, with lasting relationships with the customers that patronize the store. That design fits a model where the work is not detached from employment. Often, this happens not because of a decision to attach the assignment, but due to an assumption that the work must be done by employees, because it always has. What if the retailer detached the work from employment? If they wanted to use a pool of free agents to staff the stores, they would design the assignments so that shop assistants don't need as much product or customer knowledge. The role of a store manager (that might well be embedded in a traditional employment relationship) is to manage that pool of detached free agents.

Even if you need work done by people who act much like employees, they need not be your own employees. Often, with recruitment process outsourcing, the recruiters are on-site, exactly like a regular full-time employee. However, the company does not need to manage the person, worry about their career, or provide the tools they need to do the job—that is all handled by the outsourcer.

One argument posed against detachment is that some roles require long-tenured employees to develop firm-specific knowledge. Yet, even here, can you assume that regular full-time employees will stay longer than free agents or other nonemployees? In a world of increasing job mobility, retaining workers may actually be more effectively done through an ongoing relationship with a free agent or outsourcer. That ongoing relationship may simply mean that the free agent or outsourcer is given a project from time to time, but such a relationship stretching over years or decades creates the continuity and firm-specific know-how that the organization would normally have created through employment.

When to Detach and When Not to Detach

So, there are good reasons for leaders not to assume that work must be attached to an employment relationship, and they should at least consider the options. Sometimes the employment relationship is a good option, sometimes other relationships are a better option. Leaders need to be sufficiently clear about the pros and cons, so they can make the right choice.

Here are some reasons to detach less:

- **A stable core:** Organizations may feel they need a core of people fully committed to the organization, and that attaching the work to employment best facilitates that commitment. Even talent platforms like Upwork have employees, and within that group some will be the core who stabilizes the company. One might even say the core employees *are* the company.
- **Lower transaction costs:** It may be easier to assign tasks as needed to a team of employees, rather than incur the cost of packaging assignments that can be detached and the price negotiated. In fact, the British economist Ronald Coase argued that these transaction costs were the original reason organizations existed. Coase pointed out that having to negotiate every transaction was expensive, and employment is a kind of blanket agreement whereby the employee agrees to do the work the manager assigns, day by day.
- **Careers:** Careers can be development tools. When organizations require specific expertise that takes years to build, and can't be purchased outside, internal careers may be the best answer. Attaching the work to an employment relationship is often the most effective way to give both the worker and the client confidence that their investments in that specific expertise will eventually pay off.
- **Community:** Some organizations strive to operate as a community, such as some family firms where workers are seen as part of the

extended family, co-ops where employees are also owners, and others. Attaching work to employment relationships may best capture that community spirit.

- **Societal laws and regulations:** In many countries, regulations require companies to make employment relationships with workers who work a certain number of hours, are under the authority of the organization, and so forth. Until such laws evolve to provide protections to arrangements that are detached from traditional employment, organizations may be wise simply to embed the work within an employment relationship.

Here are some reasons to detach more:

- **Workers of higher quality, or lower costs.** As we have seen, the workers that can do an assignment at the lowest cost or at the highest quality are increasingly not available nor interested in the obligations that come with regular full-time employment. To tap those workers may require detaching the assignment from the employment relationship.
- **Flexibility:** Regular full-time employment can be rigid in ways that may severely limit the options for workers and their clients. Detaching the assignment from the employment relationship can unearth more options. For example, the contests that platforms such as Tongal and Topcoder run usually exist outside the employment relationship. As we saw, workers at Tongal and Topcoder submit their work, the best submissions get chosen to go further, and the bulk of the rewards go to the few chosen submissions. While contests can certainly be a part of employment relationships, the uncertainty about which workers will advance through the contests would often strain an employment relationship, by making rewards much more uncertain for workers who expected more consistent and predictable paychecks.
- **Shifting risk:** Attaching work to employment places greater responsibility for the workers' welfare with the employer. A world of increasing uncertainty makes it more difficult for the employer to predict the future well enough to take on such responsibility. Witness the virtual demise of defined-benefit pensions, in favor of defined contributions plans that largely rest with the individual employee. It may be best for both worker and the client to detach the assignment from employment, and shift both the risk and the responsibility to the worker themselves (a free agent) or to another employer (in the cases of alliances and outsourcing, or other intermediaries).

Unlocking the Code: Applying the Three Dimensions of the Assignment

We can understand these three dimensions of work best by looking at examples and seeing how organizations have turned up the dials on deconstruct, disperse, and detach to achieve their mission.

The Case of Agents at JetBlue Airways: Low Deconstruction, High Dispersion, and Moderate Detachment

JetBlue is famous for having success in an industry where the vast majority of players struggle. One of their innovations is in how their phone agents work. These agents carry out the "assignment" of taking customer calls and providing advice and assistance. Typically, airlines frame the decision as a choice between hiring regular full-time employees for an in-house call center versus using an outsourced call center, possibly employing lower-cost workers located outside the United States. The in-house model constructs the assignment as a traditional job, collects the workers at a call center with fixed hours, and attaches the work to a regular full-time employment role. Similarly the outsourced call-center option constructs a traditional job, collects workers at a call center, and uses an employment relationship—but in this case the employment is between the agent and outsourcer, not the agent and JetBlue.

Instead of either of these options, JetBlue created a hybrid arrangement. They kept the assignment largely intact, with little deconstruction, except a small amount needed to monitor the work remotely. The big change was to dial dispersal way up, by dispersing the assignment to the homes of the workers. They kept the assignment attached to an employment relationship, but they increased the "detach" dial a bit, by making the arrangement part-time. In essence, they created stay-at-home phone agents that were part-time employees. For JetBlue, this allowed them to tap a highly qualified and motivated set of workers that would simply not be available through either regular full-time employment or outsourcing. The ideal agent for JetBlue was a college-educated mother in the midwestern United States working part time. Such workers had excellent English, an American demeanor that was familiar to most JetBlue customers, were savvy with remote technology, and had a strong work ethic and predictable if unusual hours (as any mother with children can attest). These workers wanted the benefits of employment but could not accommodate the logistics of working at a central call center at fixed hours.

JetBlue found a better way to get work done by turning the dials just the right way and creating the infrastructure and processes to manage that work.

The Case of Foldit

Foldit (fold.it/portal) is an online video game where players figure out how to fold a virtual protein structures to meet certain objectives and parameters. Foldit was born out of an attempt to deal with a decades-old problem in biochemistry: how to determine the three-dimensional structure of proteins. A protein is just a long sequence of amino acids, and biochemists have long known how to determine that sequence. The problem is that knowing the order of amino acids does not tell you much about how the protein works; what matters is how that long sequence folds up into a three-dimensional structure. Higher scores are earned by "packing the protein" (avoiding empty spaces where water molecules can penetrate), "hiding the hydrophobics" (surround water-sensitive parts with protective layers), and "clearing the clashes" (avoid placing parts too close together because two atoms can't occupy the same space). A solution is scored based on how well it "minimizes biophysical potential energy," and by an expert review. New puzzles come out every week and players strive to get the best score.[9]

Determining how proteins fold is an incredibly difficult mathematical problem, and one way to solve incredibly difficult mathematical problems is to throw as much computing power at them as you can muster. A cheap way of harnessing computer power is distributed computing, where the problem is deconstructed and bits are sent out to individual computers. One of the first wide-scale uses of distributed computing was the SETI@home project, which had people with PCs downloading programs to help search signals received by radio telescopes for signs of extraterrestrial intelligence. Foldit started in much the same way, creating Foldit@home, which allowed thousands of people to share spare computer time on their home PCs to unravel the mystery of protein structures. The protein-folding algorithm was automated; it simply used the collected computing power on people's PCs.

One feature of the Foldit@home program was a screensaver that could be displayed on the PC, showing the computer trying to fold the protein. The humans hosting the program on their PCs were a mix of scientists, graduate students, or just interested amateurs. They started writing in, saying, "The computer is going down a dead end. What it's trying is never going to work." This gave Dr. David Baker, who leads the Foldit project, an idea: Why not let people try their hand at folding the proteins themselves?

Thus was born the video game where people could take a protein and try to fold in up in various ways. The players are motivated by the bragging rights and personal satisfaction in solving a problem that eluded the computer, and has benefit to mankind.

The Foldit program has achieved important scientific results, including ones that may one day lead to a cure for AIDS. An article in *Nature Structural & Molecular Biology* listed Foldit Contenders Group and Foldit Void Crushers Group as two of the authors.[10] In three weeks, the gamers solved a thorny retrovirus enzyme structure problem that had eluded scientists for years. The solution could have significant implications for the treatment of diseases like AIDS.

The universities that benefit from this work dialed deconstruction very high, by taking the job of research scientist, and isolating the particular task of protein folding. They dialed up dispersion very high, by locating the work in a game that could be played from anywhere at any time. They dialed up detachment very high, by relying on volunteers with no employment relationship to the work. The results suggest that this was probably the only way to tap into the relatively few talented protein folders in the world who could solve the problem.

Conclusion

The world is full of shiny objects for leaders to consider as they try to get work done. Someone is running their business from an island in the South Pacific; someone has IT managers in India leading teams of programmers in Mexico; someone is running a contest for free-agent hackers to improve their online security. Such disconnected tales lead leaders to wonder if they should be on the beach getting work done through a talent cloud, or outsourcing to India, or running contests and video games. The three Ds—deconstruction, dispersion, and detachment—provide a decision framework for how the assignment can be reconfigured. They bring some order to the array of options that exist for getting your work done.

The framework shifts the question from, "Should I try that new alternative to regular full-time employment?" to a question of optimization, "What is the best combination of dials for my situation?" Foldit, with the dials all turned way up, is not the future of all work; it's just an option that is optimal for some work. To lead the work, you must learn the dimensions, fit your work into the dimensions, use the dimensions to devise alternatives, and identify the most optimal choices.

Next we turn to the second major dimension of the decision framework: the organization.

Notes

1. Christopher Alexander and H. Neis, *Battle for the Life and Beauty of the Earth: A Struggle between Two World Systems* (New York, NY: Oxford University Press, 2010).
2. Ed Lawler and Chris Worley, *Built to Change: How to Achieve Sustained Organizational Effectiveness* (John Wiley & Sons, 2006).
3. Roger Martin, "Rethinking the Decision Factory," *Harvard Business Review* (October 2013).
4. E. Catmull and A. Wallace, *Creativity, Inc.: Overcoming the Unseen Forces That Stand in the Way of True Inspiration* (New York: Random House, 2014).
5. C. Tkaczyk, "Marissa Mayer Breaks Her Silence on Yahoo's Telecommuting Policy," *Fortune* (April 19, 2013).
6. John Seely Brown and Paul Duguid, *The Social Life of Information* (Harvard Business Press, 2000).
7. R. Bonet, P. Cappelli, and M. Hamori, "Labor Market Intermediaries and the New Paradigm for Human Resources," *The Academy of Management Annals* 7, no. 1 (2013): 341–392.
8. Ibid.
9. The Baker Laboratory news feed, http://www.bakerlab.org/index/ (accessed February 24, 2015).

David Baker, Wikipedia page biography, last updated December 6, 2014, http://en.wikipedia.org/wiki/David_Baker_%28biochemist%29 (accessed February 24, 2015).

10. Firas Khatib, Frank DiMaio, Seth Cooper, Maciej Kazmierczyk, Miroslaw Gilski, Szymon Krzywda, Helena Zabranska, Iva Pichova, James Thompson, Zoran Popović, Mariusz Jaskolski, and David Baker, "Crystal structure of a monomeric retroviral protease solved by protein folding game players," published September 18, 2011, http://www.nature.com/nsmb/journal/v18/n10/full/nsmb.2119.html (accessed March 6, 2015).

8

The New Organization: Permeable, Interlinked, Collaborative, and Flexible

Let's see how our framework and some of the "new age" ideas could play out in a fairly staid and conservative sector. The core of the insurance industry has traditionally been about risk evaluation and mitigation. This remains the case today. At the same time, though, technology is transforming this industry, for example by enhancing their ability to manage risk and capital. In addition, their customers have benefited from greater choice and more transparent pricing. More recently, we have seen social media and big data transform other industries, and insurance cannot be far behind.

These new technologies can offer valuable insights into customer needs, buying behavior, underwriting risks, and pricing strategies. If insurers are slow to react, new, technologically savvy competitors are likely to enter the insurance space.

To capitalize on these new technologies insurance companies are changing the way they operate. Some are embracing cloud-based computing, others are introducing new products such as usage-based insurance, and many are experimenting with social media. Underlying all of these initiatives is the need for a more diverse and technology-savvy workforce. Combine this need with the fact that the insurance industry is characterized by a fairly mature workforce—about 25 percent of U.S. finance and insurance industry workers are 55 or older[1]—and you get an industry that is poised for change in its talent requirements.

Consider the challenge of attracting these technology-proficient employees. According to the Global Talent 2021 study, conducted by Oxford Economics and Towers Watson in 2012, talent shortages in key technical areas in developed countries will increase dramatically over the next 10 years. The issue is further complicated by the fact that insurers will be competing not only with other insurers but also with other industries for the same highly desirable human capital.

If insurers cannot attract sufficient technical talent as employees, what choices do they have? We think that at this point in the book you will be able to guess our answer. The choice is to move beyond employment and borrow the talent from elsewhere, perhaps through talent platforms, perhaps through alliances, perhaps through employee loans. The industry needs a new vision of what an organization is.

Organizational Form

If we step onto an elevator in an office building, it will deliver us to an organization that looks, at first, quite familiar. There will be an office, cubicles, and workers who appear to be regular full-time employees. However look deeper, and you may find that one small cubicle is the entire IT department, with one employee managing work outsourced to India; another cubicle contains not an employee but a consultant on a long-term assignment. The meeting room is packed, but not one person is an employee; they are a mix of alliance partners and free agents in a rare face-to-face gathering. The office looks the same, but it's a different type of organization.

The fundamental change is the move from seeing the organization as being a stable entity behind solid walls, to a much more flexible structure where deep collaboration with outsiders is the norm. The image we used before was going from a permanent brick house to a flexible prefab structure. You might also envision it as a move from a luxury store with heavy mahogany doors that separate those inside from those outside, to an outdoor market where people come and go and the edges of the market are unclear.

It isn't the case that the stable structure is always wrong, and certainly this form has served the insurance industry well for years. However, we need to be able to twist the dials toward flexibility when the need arises, and that need is arising for insurers who require technical talent.

In this chapter, we describe four dimensions that help you understand the patterns emerging in how work is done so that you can better understand what's happening in organizations, and better decide how you will lead the work. The dimensions are permeability, interlinkage, collaboration, and flexibility (PICF).

Here is how we see it in a nutshell. A traditional organization has thick walls and a sharp distinction between insiders and outsiders. As it shifts to a beyond employment model, the walls become more permeable, and people and work cross the walls quite freely. This movement opens up the chance to interlink with other organizations, such as outsourcers or talent platforms; and at this stage it has become natural for the organization to look outward as a way to get work done. Finally, as organizations get adept at working with outsiders, they form true collaborative relationships, sharing ideas, risk, intellectual property, people, and physical assets.

So permeability leads to interlinking which leads to collaboration—and the role of leaders is to understand what's appropriate for their own organization. Another way to think about this is that "permeability" describes the amount of work and workers that flow through the organization boundary, "interlinkage" describes the pattern of connections through which those flows occur, and "collaboration" describes the strength and nature of those connections.

The last dimension, "flexibility," is a bit different. It means whether to allow the boundary to flex to actually encompass those outside. It captures big decisions about mergers, acquisitions, divestures, outsourcing, and insourcing. The more we turn up the dial of flexibility, the more we are willing to change the fundamental structure of the organization.

How Easily to Permeate?

As we said, a look around a typical office won't show you whether work and workers reside inside a relatively sealed organization boundary or flow freely across it. A familiar example is when you discover that someone working in your office is not a coworker at all, but actually a consultant on an extended contract. That's an example of a worker flowing into the organization without an employment relationship. Do some employees stay only a couple of years, to bolster their resume and then move on? That's an example of workers flowing out across the boundary. Do employees leave for a few years, gain valuable experience, and then return? That's an example of workers flowing both outward and then inward through the boundary.

We tend to think of the organization as a place where there's clear inside and outside, and the way to cross it is to become an employee or to terminate employment. In the world beyond employment, work and workers flow through the organization quite freely, and often without an employment relationship.

As a leader, you decide how much of this inflow and outflow fits your mission—how much to allow your organization boundary to be permeable.

Permeability is closely related to the ideas that we discuss in the previous chapter. The better we get at deconstructing assignments, the more we disperse them, and the more they are detached from regular full-time employment, the more permeable the boundary can become, and the more important it becomes for leaders to choose carefully where they fall on the permeability dimension. The same is true for the workers themselves. There is a range of emerging relationships you can have with workers, from regular employees to consultants on secondment to using employees from another firm (perhaps an outsourcer or alliance), and the work they do can flow through your boundary or be contained within it.

For example, a large company valued its HR consultant because he was the only person who had been around long enough to know how and why certain decisions had been made. Many regular full-time employees in HR had come and gone, leaving no one else to match the consultant's long-term connection and institutional knowledge of the company. In this case, the relationship between the work and the worker—the job of continuity in the HR department—had unintentionally been moved outside the firm and into the consulting firm that employed the consultant. Continuity is important, but if we see the organization as permeable, there may be ways to achieve it without relying on employees embedded inside the firm. Leaving such choices to chance, without a framework to guide them, may be risky in the new world of work.

Leading the work means using the flow of talent, work, and workers to sustain and achieve your mission. Making a sharp distinction between how you manage contractors and how you manage employees feels increasingly odd when people and work flow so freely in and out of the company, even if the distinction is important from a legal perspective. Thinking of free agents providing their work from distant locations as "outsiders" seems odd when the regular employees themselves are rarely in the office, and the work of both employees and free agents is intermingled as it flows in and out across the boundary of the organization.

There will be differences in how you treat people who are working for and with you. Some will be in the inner circle and some, like the MTurkers, will be completely anonymous. Some will merit investment to cement a long-term relationship; others will do a microtask and disappear. The point is that increasingly the work they do flows across the boundary called your "organization," that is demarcated by a regular full-time employment relationship. Your key people and your closest advisors need not be employees "inside" the boundary. You may shield trade secrets from employees who are inside yet share them with a trusted contractor who is outside. You may work hard to retain the work of uniquely skilled free agents yet accept the fact that less-uniquely skilled employees may leave. Leading the work means focusing more on how the work and workers flow through the boundary than on whether or not it is done by regular full-time employees sitting inside that (increasingly) imaginary boundary.

How much should you allow work and workers to permeate your organizational boundary? Dialing this dimension to zero means that no work will be done unless it can be done by regular full-time employees residing inside the boundary. Dialing permeability a bit higher might involve encouraging some employees to become onsite independent contractors, or offsite free agents working through a talent platform, or to form a microbusiness to which you outsource the work. That's letting the work and workers flow out. Conversely, you could offer a talented free agent the opportunity to become a regular full-time employee, so they build more enduring ties with your organization. That's what happens with the most talented coders on Topcoder; they are frequently offered regular full-time employment with companies like Google, Twitter, and Amazon.

In Chapter 4 we related the story of the owner of a small company who hired what turned out to be a very talented software coder. The owner wanted to keep this talented employee but could not compete with Topcoder's variety of projects, high pay, and visibility for talented coders. If you think of work as happening only inside the employment boundary, the inevitable result is that the programmer will leave forcing the small company to hire someone else. The owner was more creative. He encouraged his young programmer to work for Topcoder on the side. The employee was so pleased with this arrangement that he actually turned down a lucrative offer to work for a high-tech firm, to stay with his current employer. Seeing the organization boundary as permeable means that the owner could allow work to flow through the boundary, even when it flowed outward to the Topcoder platform, as long as the coder's work for the small company was still useful. Dial up permeability a bit, and nonobvious solutions emerge for keeping top programming talent happy and close at hand.

The idea is to dial permeability up and down optimally. An organization boundary, with "insiders" that are regular full-time employees and "outsiders" that are not, matters less now; and leading the work means being more savvy about how freely work flows through the boundary.

The solution for the insurance industry's talent shortage will be to embrace a greater flow of technical expertise outside the organization. It will not be able to hire all the technical workers it needs as employees; so its optimal solution may be to get better at finding outsiders to do the work.

How Strongly to Interlink?

The organization can be unlinked to the outside, getting work done by focusing on internal relationships and processes, or it can be strongly interlinked to the outside, with lasting connections to workers and providers beyond the boundary. When interlinkage is dialed down, worker interactions are with other employees, and the issues involve coordination among employees within their unit and with other groups of employees in other units. In this kind of unlinked organization, the outside world sometimes seems like a distant rumor. Everything that matters is happening inside the walls.

When interlinkage is dialed up, workers may go for long periods with little contact with other employees and spend their days working with workers that are employed by the company's allies, competitors, media partners, technology vendors, and consultants. In the highly interlinked organization, the work relationships more often exist outside the boundary defined by employment.

Interlinkage is often complementary to permeability, but it goes farther. A permeable organization allows work and workers to flow more freely across the boundary. An interlinked organization also has work and workers flowing across its boundary, but now it forges actual connections with one or more individuals, platforms, or other employers to make those flows easier, more systematic, and more predictable. It's one thing to send your work out to a freelance designer that you find through a job board. That's permeability. It's another to repeatedly connect with a talent platform like Tongal, to have an ongoing source of such free agents. That's interlinking.

Leading the work through an interlinked organization includes lasting connections with alliance partners, outsourcers, and free agents. Organization design principles like reporting structures, decision rights, information sharing, trust, and collaboration must now be applied as much to the interlinked ecosystem of workers, work, and external entities as they are to more traditional organization units such as employees and divisions.

Consider what the map of interlinkages might look like for your own work and workers. Where does the work come from, where does it go to? With whom do you spend time communicating, employees or "outsiders"? There is an entire social science discipline devoted to mapping such connections, called "social network analysis." What it often reveals is that work gets done through social connections that span traditional boundaries and often involves workers that are not formally designated as gatekeepers or liaisons. Imagine what a social network analysis of your organization would look like if it fully measured all those interlinkages that cross the organizational boundary; it might give quite a different picture of what your organization "is" than a map that only shows links between regular full-time employees within the walls.

As a leader, when you recognize that you can dial up or down interlinkage to fit your mission and strategy, you begin to think of the organization differently. Rather than a hierarchy made up of boxes with employees in it, the organization is a node in an ecosystem of value creation. The same is true for your individual workers, your team, your department, your division, and so forth. Each is a node that gets work done through links connecting it both inside and outside the organization. Traditionally, leaders distinguish between connections that happen inside the boundary and those outside, with strong emphasis on leading through inside connections. The world beyond employment is a more interlinked world, where leaders must make assertive decisions about when and where to dial up and down the links that span the traditional organizational boundary, and the outside, and manage the linkages between regular full-time employees and outsiders.

How Deeply to Collaborate?

Even when an organization has a good deal of its work flowing through its employment boundary, and through many linkages, collaboration may be dialed up or down. Collaboration is dialed down when the links reflect an insular approach focused on protection and formality. Such connections operate through formal and arms-length relationships often founded in specific contracts and legal agreements. Collaboration is dialed up when the links reflect a more open approach focused on trust, sharing, and informality. Such connections operate through mutual trust, common values, and informal ties.

When collaboration is dialed down, organizations are introspective and more secretive. Employees are discouraged from sharing with competitors, and leaders believe their ideas and processes are valuable intellectual property that must be shielded from the outside. It's a world of "us" surrounded by the world of "them," with connections made only when they can be well defined and codified. When collaboration is dialed up organizations reach out frequently to connect their work and workers with others. Their leaders emphasize sharing ideas rather than hiding them.

This spirit of greater collaboration with the outside world shows up in how organizations think about innovation. An article by Boudreau and Ziskin noted the evolution from an emphasis on intellectual property to what they call "agile cocreativity."[2] It has its roots in traditions such as Total Quality Management where all workers are asked to suggest improvements. It has evolved to a more boundaryless idea where any product or service offering is seen as a prototype, the object of gathering criticisms and improvement ideas from users and others, supported by a system to prioritize and implement the changes. Traditionally, innovation is seen as occurring within the organization, in designated roles such as product developer or designer. These roles guide innovation through specific, sequential process "gates," leading to results that can be identified and protected through patents or other intellectual property rights. This idea is giving way to a reality of agile cocreativity, the concept that creativity can come from anyone and anywhere, and that traditional organization boxes or job roles are no longer the sole repository of creativity.

Creativity is becoming less of an ownership-based endeavor and more of a community-based one. This means that creativity and innovation occur both inside and outside of the organization. Creativity may arise from many different roles and levels, and it happens in nonsequential and often unpredictable processes. In the agile cocreativity model, innovation produces transient results that are more like experiments than finished products to be claimed and owned. Wikipedia is one prominent example. In such a collaborative world, getting work done depends less on a concept of "us" and "them" and more about understanding and defining how collaborative the organization should be.

The idea of dialing collaboration up and down applies to individual workers as well. We build relationships at work, and when those people leave, or we leave, the relationships remain. Yes, the person may be working for a competitor, but they're still our friend and perhaps even our future collaborator. Many coworkers will be free agents, leading to sharing significant amounts of information and goodwill with people outside the firm. Alliances may deliver a large share of our revenue, and when someone is filling half your rice bowl, it's hard not to view them as family. Not only are "they" feeling more like "us," but we as employees are not feeling so much like "us" anymore. Is there really a special bond between employer and employee when the employee is working remotely, most of their linkages are outside the firm, and they plan to stay in this gig for only a few years? As CEO of Me, people have their set of loyalties to individuals and organizations, and their current employer may or may not be included in that group.

We normally frame the loss of the feeling of "us" as a loss of loyalty, however, in the world beyond employment, the flip side is that, with the loss of "us," we move toward being open to and collaborative with the outside world. It's a different attitude that may increase the risk of leaking competitively valuable intelligence, but offers greater access to the intelligence and capabilities of the outside world.

Collaboration fits well with human motivation. People often are more engaged by affiliation with ideals than by commitment to a specific company. This has been observed for a long time among scientists and engineers in places like Silicon Valley. For example, an engineer may see herself as building the "Internet of things" or "the world of augmented reality"—that broad ideal matters more to her than what company she happens to be working for this month. The same definition of loyalty and engagement applies in television and movie production, where teams of collaborators move from project to project, employed by different companies, but engaged and loyal to their team, not the institution that employs them. When you combine the employees' desire to contribute to something bigger than themselves, and to have a hand in inventing and reinventing their environment, the potential to harness the collective creativity of those within and outside the organization becomes clear.

The insurance industry's best bet may be to drop their inward focus and turn up the dial on collaboration and begin working with cool organizations that are able to attract the technical talent insurers need.

How Extensively to Flex?

Leading the work clearly means making decisions about the extent to which the organization boundary will be permeable, interlinked, and collaborative. Sometimes, however, the decision is not so much how extensively work and workers should move across the boundary, but how much actually to move the boundary itself. This is flexibility. The idea is that even when you get work done with regular full-time employees, you may choose to extend your boundary to include formerly outside entities, and contract the boundary to send formerly inside employees outside it. Flexible organizations stretch and contract as needed by acquiring and divesting other organizations, outsourcing or insourcing processes, and engaging or disengaging in alliances. A flexible organization reshapes itself to fit the most profitable niches in an evolving ecosystem.

Flexibility often applies not to individual workers, but to larger units like departments or processes—the big building blocks of organizational structure. We can move work around the world within our organization, or move big blocks of work right outside of the organization. We can use the

Lego metaphor: an organization as a set of interlocking blocks that can be reconfigured as needed. The IT function may sit inside the firm now, but a flexible firm sees no fundamental reason why it might not be detached from the structure and moved outside—which is exactly what Bharti did with its own IT function, unplugging that department and shifting it over to IBM as part of their alliance. John Boudreau and Peter Ramstad in their book *Beyond HR* (2007) described how Boeing organized the work of building aircraft out of composite materials by forming a web of interlinked collaborations among a global supplier network, dialing up interlinkage and collaboration. Boeing eventually acquired some of those outside suppliers, which is a good example of dialing up flexibility. The supplier employees became Boeing employees, essentially surrounding the supplier company with the Boeing boundary. This is increasingly common as organizations stretch to acquire small startups (sometimes to get the talent inside), and then shed much of what they acquired, keeping only what makes sense for the long term.

Scott Sherman, formerly the executive vice president of human resources of Allergan and now at Ingram Micro, said that pharmaceutical firms (and others) increasingly flex their boundary to actually acquire early-stage companies that have developed promising therapies to an appropriate level of risk and return. The employees of the early-stage company become company employees. However, the employees and leaders of an early-stage startup are well suited to the high-return and high-risk environment of startups. Companies cannot offer all the elements of that work. So, it's not unusual for the leaders and employees of the startup to leave after the transfer of the ideas is complete, to found a new startup that develops new therapies. Allergan's boundary stretches to encompass the startup leaders and employees and then contracts to allow them to depart.

Are Private Equity Firms Playing the Game of Flexibility?

Private equity organizations acquire companies, to enhance their value. In the process, private equity firms reshape their own organization by stretching the old boundary out to encompass the new firm. Once the captured company is inside the private equity firm, the old boundary becomes completely permeable, and talent can flow across to set up effective systems. For example, for the private equity firm Blackstone Capital, the HR leader of the acquired company is absorbed into the broader community of HR leaders working for Blackstone companies. It's also not uncommon for some private equity firms to isolate parts of the acquired company to sell or divest.

The process works in reverse when Blackstone prepares to sell a unit. A new boundary is set up, links with the rest of Blackstone weakened, and then that unit goes off on its own.

There are few areas that are not potential targets for flexibility. Some might say that "core functions" must remain inside the firm. Yet design firms routinely move their design work outside to talent platforms. If you name a core function that must always stay inside the walls, someone will come along with an example that proves you wrong. Choosing what sits inside and what sits outside, and what is partially in and out, is one of the biggest strategic issues an organization faces.

Reshaping the organization is never easy, but in the world beyond employment it is increasingly possible. Indeed, writers on organizational agility like USC professors Edward Lawler and Chris Worley would argue that constant reshaping or being "built to change" may be the key to sustainable performance.[3] When it comes to leading the work in a world beyond employment, this means that a leader's task is to optimize choices about when to stretch your organization boundary to pull in other organizations, or contract the boundary by spinning them off. It all depends on the optimal way to get the work done. This focus on the work helps to clarify the dimensions that should drive such decisions.

Making Decisions about the Organization: Permeate, Interlink, Collaborate, and Flex

How do we view outsourcing? We see it as dialing up permeability and interlinkage. When a clean chunk of work can be moved outside the boundary then outsourcing may make sense.

How do we view alliances such as the one where Siemens engaged employees at Disney to market its hearing aid? This dialed up permeability a bit, in that the project was not a full function and didn't involve moving vast amounts of work across the boundary. Interlinkage was also dialed up a bit, involving a link to only one organization, not an entire ecosystem. The key here was to dial up collaboration to a very high level. Siemens and Disney could not rigidly or comprehensively define the legal relationship to get the work done. They had to rely on their history of trust and sharing, for something as creative as marketing a child's hearing aid.

So, a typical question in leading the work is, "What capabilities do we need and how can we best get them? Do we build, buy, outsource, or ally?" Yet, there is a complementary question, "How can we generate the greatest value from our own capabilities? Who needs these capabilities and how can we structure things to get the most value from that need?" Consider IBM. If you look at the IBM mainframe days of the 1960s and 1970s versus the IBM of today, much of the value is created in the cloud, and through an ecosystem of entities. IBM's professional services group looks a lot like a consulting firm, where their internal work routinely flows through their boundary to be accomplished with deep collaboration and on the sites of their customers. IBM flexed its boundary quite dramatically when it divested to Lenovo its assets devoted to the PC, including the employees, who became Lenovo employees. IBM's innovation process reflects a web of many interlinkages between corporations, universities, and even a global community of freelance or volunteer puzzle solvers. IBM is constantly asking, "Where do we generate the most value?" and where they don't bring something special to value creation (such as building PCs) they move it outside the boundary.

PICF Pictured

For convenience let's introduce the acronym PICF to stand for the permeable, interlinked, collaborative, and flexible organization. Figure 8.1 captures all these elements. With all the dimensions set to zero (the images on the top), the organization is a fixed structure with all the parts welded into place, and all the work and workers residing inside. On the bottom, permeability is dialed up, as shown by the organization boundary as a dotted line,

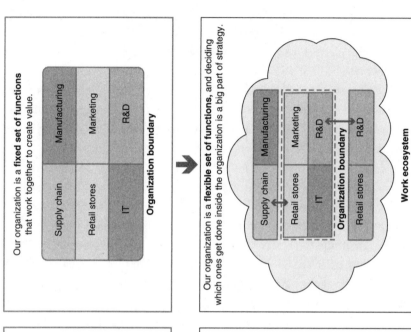

Our organization is a place containing employees doing work.

Task Task Task Task Task Task Task Task

Organization boundary

Our organization organizes work and talent.

Task Task Task Task Task Task Task

Organization boundary

Work ecosystem

Our organization is a fixed set of functions that work together to create value.

Supply chain	Manufacturing
Retail stores	Marketing
IT	R&D

Organization boundary

Our organization is a flexible set of functions, and deciding which ones get done inside the organization is a big part of strategy.

Supply chain	Manufacturing
Retail stores	Marketing
IT	R&D

Organization boundary

	R&D
Retail stores	

Work ecosystem

Figure 8.1 PICF in Pictures

with individual workers (depicted as faces) and tasks (depicted as boxes) moving work across it. Interconnectedness is dialed up as shown in the arrows that connect outside functions with those inside. The outside functions might be done by outsourcers, contractors, and so forth. When collaboration is dialed up, think of it as handshakes connecting boxes, rather than simply arrows. Finally, flexibility is turned up, as whole departments may slip outside the organization or slip inside. Or, even if parts stay within the organization, they're freed from the traditional bounds of hierarchy.

Another way to see the organization when you dial up "permeable" and "interlinked" is to zoom in on the organization chart of one department. The diagram below (Figure 8.2) shows a portion of the organization chart under a hypothetical vice president of marketing. Only two of the boxes— Joe and Mary—represent employees. At least half the work is done by people outside of the firm, a free-agent assistant to handle administrative tasks, a consultant to handle social marketing strategy (who might be a free agent or an employee of a consulting firm), and a PR agency, which has had a big chunk of work outsourced to them. In this case, the VP of marketing is well aware that more than half of his work is being carried on outside the organization. The organization chart includes both internal and external work with equal emphasis.

When it comes to leading the work, if you draw the organization chart to include only the employees (Joe and Mary), you miss the full picture. What would your set of direct reports look like if you included all external relationships?

Figure 8.2   Organization Chart Including External Relationships

Finally, consider what the value chain might look like in a highly inter-linked and collaborative firm (Figure 8.3). A firm can pick the parts of the value chain where it wants to operate (in our diagram this includes Brand/Mission, R&D, Product Marketing, and Customer Support), and have the other steps in the value chain handled by outsourcers, allies, or talent platforms. The opportunity to focus exclusively on what your firm is really good at is sitting there waiting to be grasped.

To lead the work, not just the employees, requires envisioning the organization as a set of options beyond simply containing regular full-time employees to do the work. Fortunately, the familiar tools that you already use, such as organization charts and value chains, can help you describe and communicate this new vision—you just need to extend these dia-grams beyond the walls of the company. Instead of trying to figure this out armed only with examples such as Wikipedia, IBM, or Allergan, the PICF framework allows you to use these tools to map the evolution from an organization with all the dimensions dialed down, to an organization that can dial them up selectively, to crack the code of achieving your mission.

Let's return to the insurance industry story we started this chapter with. Can the industry meet their talent challenges by embracing the Lead the Work framework? For example, could the evolving work of the actuary be deconstructed and performed on talent platforms? Could the organization

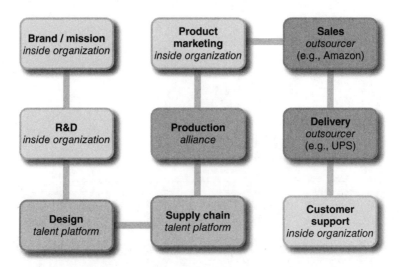

Figure 8.3   An Interlinked and Collaborative Value Chain

outsource its marketing activities to a world-class digital marketing company? Could the insurer leverage its core capabilities to "trade" for technology talent? Even prestigious high-tech firms are suffering from a shortage of skills, albeit of a different kind. While they may have the best software engineers, they don't have the best risk managers. The best risk management talent is at insurance companies. This disparity in skills and needs presents an interesting arbitrage opportunity, perhaps insurance companies can share their risk experts in exchange for high tech's software experts.

One possibility in a PICF world is a staffing model that pools the talent needs of several noncompeting companies. A corollary would be a collaborative production model in which companies pool resources based on their competitive advantages to collectively produce greater value than they might have been able to separately. For example an insurer, a global retail bank, and a high-tech company could collaborate and pool their staff's expertise. In such a collaborative model, the insurer could look to the high-tech company for the talent to harness social media and big data. The high-tech company, for its part, gets risk management expertise to protect itself from change and uncertainty. Likewise, the insurer could look to the global retail bank for help with customer-relationship management and marketing. In return, the insurer could share its risk optimization skills with the bank. The high-tech company, interested in creating a global presence, could draw on the customer-relationship skills of the bank, which could, in turn, use some help in building its digital platforms. In each case, these symbiotic partners are looking to one another for access to the kind of talent and expertise they could never attract on their own. By using this collaborative model, these noncompeting companies can attract the talent they need to fuel growth and innovation without building infrastructure and taking on cost and risk.

How PICF Makes Leading the Work Easier

Turning up the PICF dials of the Organization may seem complicated. Isn't it much easier just to define the organization as a relatively fixed container with regular full-time employees in it? Actually, when you try to lead the work by assuming that all the PICF dials are turned down, it can be much harder. The potential solution to many familiar problems becomes clearer when you can envision turning the PICF dials up.

When permeability is zero, you must get work done with people you hire as regular full-time employees, even if your needs change. Dial permeability up a bit and you can envision letting some work flow across the boundary as needed so that you can reserve employment for the work that does endure.

Assume zero interlinkage and collaboration, and planning your future work needs is beset with rigidity. Imagine if you must prepare a plan for how many delivery drivers to hire over the next couple of years. Even if you could predict delivery demand, some periods are much busier than others, and staffing up to meet average demand would leave you overstaffed half the time and understaffed the other half. Dial up interlinkage and collaboration, and you can tap other organizations that can provide talent on demand. Leading the work by forging good linkages and collaborative agreements with those other organizations is how you mitigate the risk of volatility.

Assume zero flexibility, and the work must include things that you are not very good at. If you're going to distribute, manufacture, brand and service your product, you need to do all of that within your boundary. Dial flexibility up a bit, and your boundary can flex. You can carve out entire departments or processes and give them to someone who excels at them. Dial flexibility down, and you must take on challenges and big risks single-handedly. Dial flexibility up a bit, and you can extend your boundary to acquire small companies after they have taken the early-stage risks and developed their products and services to a less risky stage; and then you can contract the boundary to free the entrepreneurs up to start new firms.

Notes

1. W. Jean Kwon, "Human Capital Risk and Talent Management Issues in the Insurance Market," *Geneva Association Newsletter* (January 2014).
2. Ian Ziskin and John Boudreau, "The Future of HR and Effective Organizations," *Organizational Dynamics* 40, no. 4 (October–December 2011): 255–266.
3. Ed Lawler and Chris Worley, *Built to Change: How to Achieve Sustained Organizational Effectiveness* (San Francisco, CA: Jossey-Bass, 2006).

9

The Reward:
Short-Term,
Individualized,
and Imaginative

Leading the work means thinking differently about the rewards that you provide your workers. A world beyond traditional employment offers leaders the opportunity to actually redesign rewards to give workers more of what they want, and cost you less. At the extreme, more work is being done by attracting volunteers. Recall the example of Foldit, where volunteers used the web-based application to help solve protein-folding problems. They did it gladly, for the reputation of being the winner, and for a good cause. Your organization won't likely get all of its work done by volunteer gamers, but, with the right framework, you can better optimize your work rewards. In Chapter 4 we showed how a small Midwest company retained a top programmer who had Bay Area job offers, by encouraging him to play and work part-time on Topcoder. Is your reward system savvy enough to create that kind of offer? If not, how will you retain top talent?

Leaders must get involved and not assume that if work is not done by regular full-time employees, then they can leave the reward question to the procurement department negotiating the price. Even MTurk clients, dealing with anonymous Turkers, must make sure that they offer attractive rewards. Sites like Turkopticion now call out bad clients. Earn a poor reputation, and you may find it hard to attract enough Turkers to do your work the next time.

You need a way to navigate work rewards that are unbound from the traditions associated with regular full-time employment.

Consider what it takes to attract one talented marketing professional. Mark Harrison is CEO of AH Global, a small but powerful marketing company serving clients like Greenpeace and Mitsubishi. His story starts in Zanzibar where he founded the company while finishing up a two-year international development stint in Tanzania. He had no intention of renting an office and hiring employees there, he did what felt obvious: his office was his laptop, and when he needed workers he tapped free agents wherever they happened to be in the world. In any case, he did not want to stay in Zanzibar, he wanted to live in both Berlin and Mauritius (Berlin in the winter isn't quite so great). This became Harrison's life for five years: he spent half his time in Berlin and half in Mauritius. He built up a network of excellent free agents spread across the globe doing work they loved. It was one heck of a life. And that good thing gave way to another good thing: a California girl won his heart and wooed him back to the United States. Harrison now runs his company from Silicon Valley.

Harrison reinvented his own reward package. He wanted freedom, mobility, and a chance to work on what he likes. It is hard to imagine how any traditional corporation could woo him away from that, no matter how rich their package of stock options.

Harrison not only crafted a rewards package for his own life, he believes he must lead the work by crafting equally imaginative and individualized rewards for his free agents, a diverse group spread across four continents. He says, "I pay people in the currency they value." One worker may want fun projects, another stability, another respect and responsibility, and another to be paid a lot of money for their unique skills and proven performance reputation. Harrison sets up the work to achieve that. These are not just one-off arrangements. Harrison works with some people repeatedly and others on single projects. The rewards are individualized, imaginative and often short term, related to the specific project.

Harrison's company succeeds in part because he deconstructs and disperses the work, but that works best if he also rethinks rewards to attract and motivate the best from his army of workers, none of whom are employees.

Navigating Rewards beyond Employment

The Lead the Work framework can help you understand what's going on in these examples and how to use it to rethink how you reward your workers. The framework describes three vital questions:

1. **How small a time frame to shorten?** Are the rewards built on the idea that the relationship will endure for a long time, or are they built to reflect a relationship that is short term and changeable?
2. **How specifically to individualize?** Are the rewards meant to fit into a single system that is applied to all workers, or can they provide different arrangements for different groups or even for specific individuals?
3. **How creatively to imagine?** Do the reward elements include only traditional things like pay, benefits, work conditions, health, and security, or do they encompass nontraditional elements such as prestige, purpose, reputation, and fun?

With regular full-time employment, the dials on these dimensions are turned to the left. Rewards are long term, part of a single system for all, and traditional. This makes sense when workers and their employer are willing to assume they will be together long enough to reap the long-run benefits (such as a pension fund or vested stock options), if the relationship is similar across jobs and workers, and if workers don't require nontraditional elements.

However, with more alternatives to regular full-time employment, combined with workers that are increasingly accustomed to customization and constant improvement in products, services, and lifestyle, there are more opportunities, if you're willing to dial the dimensions to the right. Leaders like Harrison have built entire successful businesses in part because they moved the dials to the right. Leading the work requires that you consider whether you can improve your work reward equation in ways that give workers more of what they really want, and often in a way that costs you less.

How Short the Time Frame?

In a world beyond employment you see lots of examples of rewards that are extremely short term. MTurk rewards its taskers as soon as they finish tagging a set of pictures. Tongal and Topcoder reward their freelance designers and coders as soon as the client approves the result or chooses a winner from the contest. It's easy to fixate on the timing of the rewards—how fast they are delivered as the work is done—but that's only part of the answer. The more important and fundamental question is whether you design rewards that assume or require a long-term relationship or a short-term one. Traditional reward systems for regular full-time employees are often constructed based on the implicit assumption that workers will stay. Rewards such as stock options that only vest if you stay five years, pension-fund matches that only build up if you stay a long time, and career paths that materialize with long tenure are just a few examples. As we have seen, it's not that long-term work relationships will completely go away, but it is increasingly difficult for either workers or clients to count on a long-term relationship. The world changes too fast and too unpredictably. Thus, even traditional companies have mostly shifted from an employment deal that assumes long-term employment for good performance, to something more like a commitment to do their best to help workers remain qualified as things change, with the understanding that if things change too much, anyone is expendable. Many companies long ago started shifting from defined benefit pension plans that reward a lifetime of service with a guaranteed income after retirement, to defined contribution plans where the company contributes some fixed amount while the worker is employed, and the accumulated nest egg is portable to other companies.

By necessity, the reward structure of free agents reflects the reality of a short-term relationship and the need to allocate rewards immediately. For free agents impermanence is a fact of life: they go from gig to gig. Each gig is a separate relationship, not expected to last beyond that one project. The reward deal must reflect the reality of that short-term relationship, and it can change with each project. Even a free agent organization can twist the dials to get to the right time frame. Tongal wanted to extend their relationship with their talent community beyond a single project, so it introduced the Seasons bonus rewarding a longer-term relationship. That was a smart move that shows the value in understanding the reward relationship you need, and being creative in finding a way to deliver it.

Many writers lament the loss of "good jobs" that lasted a lifetime and provided high levels of income security. Yet framing this as a loss misses the point. Instead, we can think of the time frame of rewards as something that leaders optimize based on their situation. With the right strategic situation, a company might differentiate themselves because they are willing to offer relative security of employment (see the case of SAS later in this chapter). Even Tongal, a platform that gathers 70,000 free agents, builds in some security for their talent community by working hard to bring in enough "winnable" work so that a good performer can feel confident they can earn a decent amount of work year after year. The rewards of money and reputation are given as soon as a project is complete, but even Tongal has reward elements that may last a long time.

One reason for building long-term rewards is that a worker is motivated to look beyond the immediate project to consider longer-term implications and connections. Many believe that long-term incentives like stock options, deferred bonuses, and so forth foster a sense of ownership and an appreciation for the long run. Long-term incentives don't need to disappear just because job security has. In the entertainment industry, free agents like television actors and songwriters can get royalties that extend far beyond the initial engagement. There's no reason one couldn't construct rewards for free agents that pay out past the end of the assignment based on whatever measures of success matter to the company.

Can you create a long-term approach to rewards when work reflects specific projects that must be paid on delivery and may change over time? One way is to see your relationship with the worker as renewable. If an organization has received good work from a free agent, they will want to continue to work with them. Once you find a good worker and the worker finds they want to work for you, it is efficient to return to that worker for future projects. It's easy to think that this requires that the worker be employed, to guarantee that they are available when those future projects arise. However, you can also accomplish this by being the "project of choice," not the "employer of choice." Many free agents work repeatedly for the same client for just this reason. Just because the worker and the client don't get married, it doesn't mean they can't go steady.

Impermanence creates challenges that in the past have been confined to workers like rock stars: you are only as good as your last record. Many writers have noted that all workers, whether they be free agents or employees, must increasingly take responsibility for their own capability and their own brand. Being CEO of Me means continually staying on your game and being prepared for turbulence. When the work-worker relationship is more short term, income will be variable and uncertain, and that becomes a fact of life to be managed. Those who fail to manage it—like the rock stars that squander wealth in the good times—will suffer for it. Risk expert Nicholas Taleb recommends the barbell risk strategy. With this strategy, you get some of your income from low-risk, low-reward ventures and some from high-risk, high-reward ventures. The idea: build a kind of safety net, freeing yourself to take on some risky ventures.

How small should you shorten the time frame of rewards? As we've seen, the answer depends on your situation and objectives. The important thing is to recognize that you have choices. You can dial up and dial down the time frame to optimize the work. It's not simply a matter of choosing between rewards that require a long-term relationship and those that assume immediate and short-term relationships. It's not simply a matter of recognizing that an increasingly volatile and unpredictable world makes it hard to fashion rewards when you can't predict the future. In an age when organizations are generally making the rewards less permanent, organizations may carve out unique market niches by offering selected elements of permanence in their rewards. Thus, your challenge may be to recognize not only how to craft rewards that don't rely on the assumption of permanence, but where you can offer elements of permanence that make sense for you, and make you unique in a work environment increasingly crafted to be nonpermanent.

When to Shorten the Time Frame of Rewards

- The work is fully encompassed in a short-term deliverable that doesn't depend on long-term connections or integration.
- The work is highly changeable and may not be available in the future.
- The reward elements are things that can be delivered immediately (money, points, reputation credits).
- The worker prefers immediate gratification to delayed gratification.
- Creating a long-term work relationship is highly complex or costly (e.g., due to laws or regulations).

When to Lengthen the Time Frame of Rewards

- The work quality depends significantly on long-term connections or integration.
- The work is relatively stable and likely to be available in the future.

- The worker prefers delayed long-term gratification to immediate gratification.
- Creating a long-term work relationship is reasonably simple (e.g., long-term contractual arrangements are well established and understood).

How Specifically to Individualize?

The foundation of most traditional compensation systems is that the system applies to all the employees. This is reflected in collective bargaining and legislation. Even when not required by legislation, reward systems are often designed to fit the tradition of regular full-time employment. Systems reflect a principle of "pay for the job, not the person." Market surveys are used to estimate what workers in similar jobs are paid elsewhere and then compa-ratios calculate the average pay in a job divided by that market rate. Within the organization, rewards systems focus on aligning rewards across different jobs to achieve both internal and external equity. Of course, even traditional reward systems offer some differentiation. Individual pay varies somewhat within a job, depending on things like tenure and performance. Some jobs (such as sales) have a greater amount of pay based on incentives than regular salary. High-potential employees may receive different development opportunities than others. Yet, even these variations are subject to the overarching reward system, designed to apply to all the employees. Even when variations exist, the idea is that they exist within a system that applies similarly to all workers.

A vital role of HR systems is to preserve fairness in rewards, and that often translates into ensuring that every individual is included in the same rewards system, that everyone is treated similarly within that system, and that any differences in rewards between individuals are carefully assessed to prevent bias, and to ensure that they can be explained. This makes sense in a world of regular full-time employment, because it is expected that workers will remain for a long time, that they will interact and compare their rewards with each other, and that they must know that in the long run they will reap the rewards that others receive when they eventually take those jobs or perform at those levels.

These are laudable goals, yet all leaders have experienced situations where the system creates a tendency simply to reward all workers similarly, perhaps to avoid any appearance of bias or simply to avoid difficult discussions with workers about why some workers get something different from others. A good example is the well-documented tendency for managers to give performance ratings and incentives that are clustered at the middle, making only small distinctions for performance, skills, or individual needs and desires.

Contrast this with the world of free agents. It is much more individualized. Free agents and their clients craft reward elements that are best suited to the individual workers. In addition, because the relationship is not expected to last a long time, and because the worker and the client know that it is an individual arrangement, there is much less expectation that the system used to define the rewards for one free agent must be consistent with the system used to define rewards for another. With free agents there is much less pressure to have a "set in stone," "same for all" system. It becomes easier to tune the reward for the specific individual, project, or task. It becomes easier to experiment, because how you reward free agents this week does not need to extend to next week.

Leading the work means understanding these distinctions, but it means more. It is not as simple as using individualized rewards for free agents and collectively consistent rewards for regular full-time employees. In a world beyond employment, employees look more like free agents, and they will be more open toward (and perhaps more demanding of) individualized treatment. In Chapter 1, we mentioned the case of a brand strategy VP who has been allowed to remain president of his own consulting firm. That company broke the mold a bit, making an exception in this case, as a way to retain valued talent. You won't be able to turn the dial up on individualized rewards for employees as far as you can for free agents, but you can certainly turn the dial up from zero.

Individualizing rewards integrates with other dimensions of the Lead the Work framework. When you deconstruct work it is feasible to pay each part appropriately. For example, the job of managing a website might be deconstructed into design (high value and therefore high reward), content management (medium value and therefore medium reward), and routine maintenance (low value and therefore low reward). In an organization where all those tasks are lumped into the job of "website manager" then the reward will be less finely tuned.

Individualized rewards are often a reflection of a change in negotiating power that comes with deconstruction, dispersal, and impermanence.

We have seen that when the work can be deconstructed into tangible deliverables, performance differences across individuals become much more visible to everyone, workers and clients alike. Freelance platforms like Topcoder, Tongal, and Upwork work hard to measure and track performance levels, and to celebrate the best. That means that the best performers know who they are, and their value is public. In a world of individualized rewards, savvy high performers will negotiate rewards that reflect their true value. Indeed, the leaders of talent platforms tell us that one reason the best performers are attracted to freelance work is that their rewards are specifically not limited by organizational reward systems. Many traditional reward systems certainly reward high performers more. Yet, on a talent platform, the performance and rewards of top performers can be many times that of average performers. It is a rare organization whose pay system would accommodate paying high performers five or ten times as much as others doing the same job.

An advantage of individualizing rewards is that you pay no more than necessary for a given parcel of work. Yet, managing differentiated rewards across a wide variety of tasks can increase the administrative and mathematical complexity of the reward package far beyond traditional systems that set rewards based on a finite set of defined jobs. It becomes even more complex if you also allow rewards to vary with the individual qualifications and desires of each worker. This complexity may lead organizations to turn the dial on individualization down, even for free agents, and even for tasks that have been deconstructed. This is a challenge for HR leaders and the HR profession, to optimize the individualization, and not reject important opportunities simply because the current systems cannot deal with the complexity.

How to Optimize Individualizing Rewards: Watch the Curves

How should organizations "solve" for the right amount of individualization in the amount, differentiation, and cost of rewards? When should you dial up individualization, and when should you dial it down? Thinking of three curves can be helpful:

1. The curve that shows how different work performance levels relate to organizational value, called "return on improved performance" (ROIP)
2. The curve that shows the number of workers at each different performance level, called the "performance distribution"

3. The curve that shows how different work performance levels relate to the cost of the rewards needed to motivate that performance, called the "cost of improved performance"

The interplay of these three curves helps you decide how to optimize the cost and return to individualization. Figure 9.1 shows three examples.

In Figure 9.1, the top graph shows that every increase in the value of performance provides a similar positive benefit for the organization. The middle graph shows the distribution of performance as a bell curve.

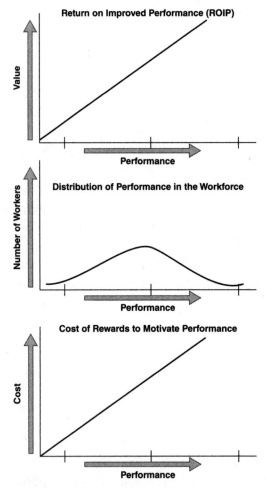

Figure 9.1   Traditional Individualization Is Optimum

The bottom graph shows that the cost to motivate higher performance is also a straight line, such as when performance incentives are paid based on sales levels. In this situation, the objective is to make the middle group better, and because the ROIP and cost curves are linear, it's probably possible to set up one system that applies to everyone. If a worker performs better, they get a linear increase in their reward, and that relationship is the same for everyone. A piece-rate pay system in a production line would fit this model. These assumptions are often implicit in most reward systems, even though they are only one of many possible situations. Assuming that this is the situation across all jobs, projects, and work can lead to missed opportunities.

Figure 9.2 shows a very different situation, where individualizing rewards for top performers is actually not optimal.

In Figure 9.2, we have changed the ROIP curve at the top. Now, increasing performance from very low to where it reaches a certain standard has a high payoff, but once that standard is achieved there is little value in going beyond it. Examples include filing tax forms, piloting commercial aircraft, or basic cleaning. The key is to avoid low performance and mistakes, but not to strive for excellence beyond the standard. As in Figure 9.1, the cost of the rewards in Figure 9.2 is shown as a straight line in the bottom graph. High performers still demand more. However, in this case, there is very little advantage to differentiating rewards for high performers. Dialing up differentiation in this case is far less valuable, particularly among workers who are already at standard.

Finally, the third set of curves shown in Figure 9.3 shows a situation where individualization and differentiation should be dialed up to a very high level. It is typical of many situations where regular full-time employment simply cannot accommodate the needs of the work.

In Figure 9.3, the top graph shows an ROIP curve where the value of high performance is far greater than that of moderate or low performance. This situation occurs in work that is very creative or where the right answer to a problem is extremely valuable, while moderately creative or partially correct answers are not. For example, in creating an Internet advertisement, the vast majority of ideas are not very effective, but if you can find the idea that goes viral or becomes a catch phrase, the value is exponentially higher than for average ideas. The middle graph in Figure 9.3 is different from Figures 9.1 and 9.2, and shows a distribution of workers that is very different

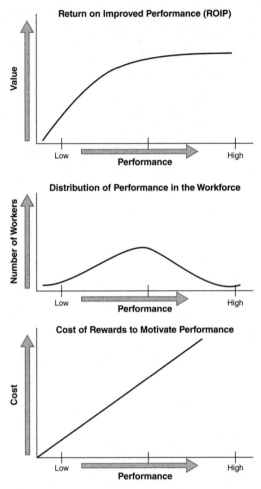

Figure 9.2   Individualizing for Top Performers Is Not Optimal

from a "normal curve." There are a large number of workers who would
be low performers, and a few who are extremely high performers, which
might be typical of situations where those who can create a winning idea
or solve a thorny riddle are rare. Finally, the bottom graph shows that the
cost of motivating low or moderate performance is relatively low, but
the cost of motivating high performance is much higher, such as when the
elite designers or Internet videomakers know how valuable and rare they are.

In this situation, extreme individualization makes sense, with high
performers receiving more rewards and a reward package that is highly

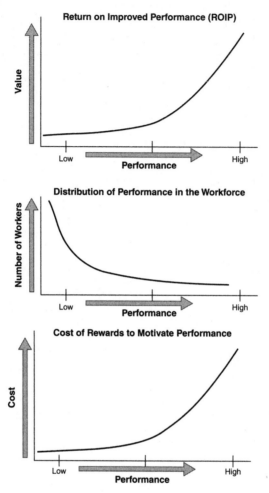

Figure 9.3   Value of Higher Performance Is Much More Than the Value of Moderate Performance

tailored to their individual desires. It's worth it because the value of that rare performance is huge, and because those who can deliver it are so rare.

You don't have to be able to measure and draw the curves precisely for them to help you lead the work by optimizing how much you individualize. Many organizations find it helpful simply to categorize their work according to whether ROIP and the cost of improved performance are highly sloped or flat, and whether the distribution of performance is a bell curve or something different. The point is that whether work is done by employees, free

agents, alliance partners, outsourcers, or by other means, fitting individualization of the reward to the work can reveal important opportunities for you.
This challenges leaders to get involved in optimizing individualization, and
the HR profession to prepare systems and capabilities to advise and support
those leaders.

How Creatively to Imagine the Reward?

Being imaginative about rewards is one of the great opportunities for organizations to offer employees more while spending less. A world beyond
employment makes imaginative rewards more apparent and more appropriate. It was freelance platforms and crowdsourcers that most visibly demonstrated that lots of folks would work for the sheer enjoyment of the game or
the reputation for being the smartest puzzle-solver. It is easier to be imaginative when rewards are more individualized. It is easier to experiment
when reward elements are not expected to endure. Yet, even with regular
full-time employment you can dial up the imaginative scale, to consider
rewards beyond those that are most traditional. In his book *The Purpose
Economy*, Aaron Hurst struck a nerve, suggesting that the "currency" of
the economy may well be individuals' desires for meaning in their work.[1]
Certainly companies with products that save lives or improve health have
long understood the power of such nontraditional rewards.

Here's a list of rewards ranging from those that are traditional to emerging rewards that are more imaginative:

- **Money:** There is no question that the money will remain important,
  including how it is delivered and for what purpose. While "show me the
  money" is unlikely to be irrelevant, limiting your leadership to thinking
  about how to allocate money will miss many options.
- **Reputation:** People want to be the known as the best in their field,
  the winner of the contest with their name in lights. Reputation serves
  a function in improving a person's ability to acquire work in the future,
  but it is also an end in itself. In traditional systems, special titles such as
  "Research Fellow" are used to recognize top inventors or scientists.
- **Glamour:** Some roles are inherently glamorous, whether it's being a
  rock star or working with movie stars, or being part of a project sending space probes to the stars. The job of professional cheerleader carries lots of glamour, even though it involves long hours and low pay.

Being a professional cheerleader may also pay off in launching higher-paying careers in modeling or acting. Yet, even without those potential rewards, professional sports teams would still easily attract people to fill cheerleading positions thanks to the glamour inherent in the role.

- **Meaning:** Meaning or significance has been recognized as a fundamental motivator among workers for more than 75 years. People can find meaning in work as varied as saving the environment to helping others to being excellent in one's own craft.
- **Learning:** The opportunity to learn is a powerful reward, partly because it increases future earning opportunities, but also as an end in itself. There is an intrinsic pleasure in mastering something that was at first difficult. Indeed, evidence suggests that workers are willing to trade off money for learning opportunities. This is particularly true when the learning can clearly drive career advancement and even mobility to future work. In Towers Watson's Global Workforce Study, which looks at what drives employee engagement, attraction, and retention, among other things, career advancement has been among the top three drivers of why employees join a company since 2008.[2]
- **Community:** People strive to belong, and being part of an "in group" is a powerful motivator in both work and life. When work is seen as a sign of being a member of a community that one desires to be a part of, that can be a powerful motivator. Indeed, people typically perceive the group they see as their "in group" as being smarter, more attractive, and more honest.
- **Discretion and control:** When they can, workers naturally gravitate to the work they enjoy. Having a choice can be reward in itself. No one likes to feel trapped in doing one sort of work. You can see this vividly in the free agent world, where actors strive to win awards so that they have choices among projects with excellent directors, great fellow actors, and a cool script. Even when the work is less glamourous, choice matters. One of the earliest findings from research about work motivation was that variety and autonomy were key elements. Some retirees work as Walmart store associates, or they do tasks on MTurk, not just for the money but because they find the work entertaining and interesting. They are motivated and content in part because it was their choice.
- **Flexibility in time and place:** Where you work and when you work has a big impact on the quality of your life. What had traditionally been known as work-life balance is rapidly becoming work-life integration, because both work and life are accessible 24/7 through technology and social connections. This blending of work and life places an increasing value on the flexibility to manage the balance as you desire.

While these rewards are not all new or different, the list matters because the new world of work offers you much greater opportunity to combine and innovate with these rewards than in regular full-time employment. Freelance talent platforms let computer coders, designers, and videomakers do their work in any location; they can accommodate someone's desire to work a few hours a day when it suits them, and to work on the projects that they find most interesting. Traditional employment arrangements might possibly accommodate such an imaginative approach, but they are not built for it. The traditional employment system can tap only the work projects of one organization; it can afford only to build a platform that extends to its most vital locations, and it must not appear to be giving special favors to any one person.

Reputation Systems

An important element in many talent platforms is a reputation system that reports the ratings that clients give to free agents after they complete a project. Talent platforms like Upwork have these built in, and they are an important part of their service to companies. Reputation systems provide a clear signal about the quality of the free agent. LinkedIn has made a serious attempt to build its own reputation system in which a person's skills are attested to by people in their network. Reputation systems for free agents parallel the reputation systems for consumer products that one finds on Amazon and other e-shopping platforms. In both the consumer product and free-agent domain, reputation systems are imperfect, and of course some people attempt to game them, yet they are very important to those using them. In particular, they serve to warn buyers of bad products and warn companies about less than stellar free agents.

Reputation systems are also part of the reward structure. Do good work and you will see your reputation score go up. It is a good motivator and workers who have earned a good reputation on one platform will want to stay with that platform.

The world beyond employment boasts an impressive capability to free the imagination. Yet, will something be lost? Are any rewards uniquely available or better delivered through traditional employment? The typical candidates include

- Income security
- Career progression
- Pensions
- Health and other benefits
- Community and belonging

Today, these rewards are arguably less available outside traditional employment, but that may be changing. People working outside traditional employment increasingly have options to create the same sort of income security and "career progression" that any company has. If they run a good business, they may feel pretty secure and see the business progress the way they like, whether toward higher income or more interesting work. As for pensions and health benefits, individuals will have to find alternatives, either through governments, cooperative organizations (such as the Freelancers Union in the United States), or private enterprise.

One might argue that community and belonging are the exclusive province of traditional employment. In 1955, the novelist Sloan Wilson lamented the fate of the "man in the gray flannel suit" who had sacrificed his identity to the corporation.[3] However, for many people, being an employee of a large corporation is a positive thing. People take pride in being Googlers and IBMers. Individuals often identify with their employer, and organizations go to great lengths to create compelling and desirable company and employment brands. Working for Medtronic means being a part of the company that extends the lives of heart patients and banishes the symptoms of epilepsy. Working for Unilever means being a part of the company that promotes a healthy body image among women worldwide.

The key is to understand that this need not be limited to employment. Every year, an elite group of the free agents who work with Tongal gather to show off their videos, films, and commercials at an award ceremony called the Tongie awards. Just like the Academy Awards, the winners thank their crew, families, and so forth. Unlike the Academy Awards, almost every winner thanks the employees and leaders of Tongal. It is not unusual for a Tongie winner to say, "Thank you for creating a way for me to fund my career" or, "Thank you for creating a way for a small video maker in Kuala Lumpur to pitch an idea to Budweiser." When Topcoders attend a Topcoder Open they surely wear their Topcoder identity proudly. Foldit volunteers can create a team, and enjoy the camaraderie of tackling a tough problem together. The Bill & Melinda Gates Foundation routinely offers contests to devise things like toilets that can work without water or electricity, things that are sorely needed to improve and save lives in emerging countries.[4] The contest winners are seldom employees of the foundation but perhaps share as much pride in their affiliation with it as its regular employees.

The Value of the New Rewards for Leaders, Clients, and Workers

Making rewards more individualized, impermanent, and imaginative can bring significant value:

1. **Getting talent at lower costs**: Imaginative rewards are often nonmonetary, meaning you can attract better talent for the same pay (or the same quality of talent for lesser pay). In addition to saving on pay through imaginative use of rewards, if the work is being done by a free agent offsite then there are also savings in real estate and likely in administrative overhead.
2. **Paying only for results**: Part of the core value proposition of many talent platforms is that you pay only for results. For example, with MTurk when you pay to have a microtask completed, you do not need to worry about how productive an individual worker is since you only pay for results. Free agents often work the same way and will set a fixed price for a given product or service.
3. **Paying only when you have work**: One of the main burdens of rewards that are relatively permanent is that you end up paying the worker whether or not there is valuable work to be done. As one turns up impermanence, one naturally ends up paying workers only when there is important work to be done. For situations where workload is volatile, impermanence makes sense.
4. **Paying as much as performance is worth, but only what it's worth:** When reward systems are not individualized, companies normally end up paying low performers too much and high performers too little. This approach both wastes money and puts the company at risk of losing the best talent. Individualized rewards can be more closely matched to performance; it would be odd to pay one of your employed programmers 10 times as much as the one sitting beside them, however

it can be quite natural to pay one free-agent programmer 10 times as much as another. Traditional pay structures assume a long-term employment relationship that calibrates rewards to the average of a relevant labor market, and restricts those rewards to a set range for everyone. Yes, better performers can be paid more, but because the system must endure long employment periods, it typically cannot allow wide differences in rewards among jobs or among individuals in a particular job. In fact, recent Towers Watson research[5] suggests that pay differentiation has decreased over the past four years, suggesting that organizations are struggling to differentiate between high and low performers in a low inflationary environment.

5. **Tapping better talent**: Finally, the new rewards may offer ways to attract a quality of talent that may otherwise be unavailable. When you give yourself flexibility in the design of rewards, then even the greatest stars can be seduced. When Chilean film director Alejandro Jodorowsky wanted Orson Welles to act in a film, the iconic Welles showed no interest.[6] Jodorowsky, knowing Welles's love of food, offered to bring Welles's favorite Parisian chef to the set to cook him lunch. That was an offer Welles couldn't refuse. Your organization may not need the likes of Orson Welles and Parisian chefs, but Jodorowsky's instinct for finding something uniquely valued by star talent was admirable. You also don't have to choose the best and highest-paid performer for every task. If the work requires only moderate capability, platforms like MTurk, Upwork, and Topcoder allow you to adjust your pay level to the qualifications you need and the available supply of talent for that particular task. Again, in a world beyond employment, there is less requirement to justify rewarding high performance less where performance is less pivotal, while others receive higher rewards when they perform very well on more pivotal tasks. In concept, employment systems can also do this, but designing a system equipped to routinely calibrate and explain these differences is difficult, as evidenced by the many organizations who struggle to identify the roles that are pivotal to their business and to differentiate rewards accordingly. In the world beyond employment, just as in casting a movie, the relationship is renewed with each project, offering differentiation opportunities few traditional systems can match.

Individuals will need to learn to navigate this new world and negotiate their way to rewards that suit them. The traditional employment reward is not open to a lot of negotiation; individuals choose an overall package—usually focusing on salary—and live with it for an extended period of time. In a free-agent relationship, however, there's more opportunity to craft an optimal mix of rewards. You can't always get what you want, but the freedom to try is enormous.

One of the common boasts of successful free agents is that they only work with clients they like. If that element of rewards—only working with people you like—is important to you, then it can be pursued in the free agent world much more vigorously than it can within an employment relationship. A free agent who wants 10 weeks holiday a year will have to make trade-offs to get that, but that reward element is on the table if it's what they want to pursue.

In the traditional employment relationship, a worker often had to accept "that's just the way it is," and maintaining a certain passivity toward the rewards was essential. That passivity will get in the way of making the best of the opportunities that exist in free agent world.

Optimizing the Reward Dials to Lead the Work: Netflix, Foldit, and SAS

We end this chapter by looking at how three organizations—Neflix, Foldit, and SAS—have turned up their reward dials to match their strategy.

Netflix

Netflix operates in a turbulent space and so has thoughtfully shortened the time frame of its rewards, even as it gets work done through regular full-time employees. Netflix makes it clear that employees are, at least in spirit, on one-year renewable contracts. Company leaders put it this way: "Adequate performance gets a generous severance package."[7] The philosophy isn't meant to be harsh, but with the company moving at a breakneck speed Netflix executives believe that everyone must row hard enough to pull their weight, with no passengers in the boat. The company has honed their employee separation approach to be as humane as possible. They do not drag out the separation with a long, involved process to try to make a case that a worker's performance has slipped. They simply say thank you very much, offer a nice package that the employee won't want to refuse, and everyone moves on. There is no shame in being let go, and it may not even be about performance, it may simply be that Netflix's needs changed.

Netflix has a similar reward system for all of its employees, so it is more collective than individualized. The employment rewards Netflix offers are attractive pay and benefits, and also a more imaginative one, because Netflix is becoming "cool" and glamorous as it extends its business model to make award-winning films and television. Netflix shortens the implied duration of the relationship by making security simply not part of the rewards.

Foldit

We met Foldit in Chapter 1. It's the game whose object is to solve tricky problems in structural folding, including that of proteins. One of the truly surprising outcomes of this game is that the peer-reviewed journal *Nature Structural & Molecular Biology* listed two Foldit teams (the Contenders and the Void Crushers) as authors on a paper addressing a problem that has implications for the treatment of AIDS.[8] Some game! Foldit rewards workers by packaging the work as an interesting puzzle that advances science and may lead to curing disease. It is work they can do at home, whenever it suits them, and they can work alone or in teams. There is no pay and no benefits, yet it is an attractive-enough proposition to attract and retain talented workers. Foldit has turned the dial way up on imaginativeness and that has really paid off for them. Interestingly, while permanence is not baked into the reward scheme, most of the volunteers are long-term "workers" (game players) for Foldit.

SAS

SAS, the leader in business analytics software and services, has what many would think of as the traditional reward plan of a big established corporation. It offers good pay and comprehensive benefits that meet the needs of a diverse population and strives to retain employees as long as possible. It's a deal that works for the company, producing an estimated million-dollar benefit for the company by reducing turnover.[9] As a conscious part of the competitive strategy, SAS has turned the dial on permanence just about as high as it can go for a company in the United States, and it works for them.

This is a good example of why you need a framework to lead the work. It is easy to become fixated on companies and talent platforms that have embraced impermanence, individualization, and imagination in reward. However, SAS conveys the real lesson for leaders: you need to tune the rewards for your own competitive situation.

Notes

1. Aaron Hurst, *The Purpose Economy: How Your Desire for Impact, Personal Growth and Community Is Changing the World* (Boise, Idaho: Elevate, a Russell Media company, 2014).
2. http://www.towerswatson.com/en/Insights/IC-Types/Survey-Research-Results/2014/08/the-2014-global-workforce-study.
3. Sloan Wilson, *The Man in the Grey Flannel Suit* (London: Reprint Society, 1957).
4. Bill & Melinda Gates Foundation press release, published August 14, 2012, www.gatesfoundation.org/media-center/press-releases/2012/08/bill-gates-names-winners-of-the-reinvent-the-toilet-challenge (accessed April 3, 2015).
5. Towers Watson's 2014 Global Talent Management and Rewards Survey.
6. *Jodorowsky's Dune*, film, directed by Frank Pavich (2013).
7. Presentation by Netflix CEO Reed Hastings, posted August 1, 2009, www.slideshare.net/reed2001/culture-1798664 (accessed February 10, 2015).
8. Firas Khatib, Frank DiMaio, Seth Cooper, Maciej Kazmierczyk, Miroslaw Gilski, Szymon Krzywda, Helena Zabranska, Iva Pichova, James Thompson, Zoran Popović, Mariusz Jaskolski, and David Baker, "Crystal structure of a monomeric retroviral protease solved by protein folding game players," published September 18, 2011, www.nature.com/nsmb/journal/v18/n10/full/nsmb.2119.html (accessed March 6, 2015).
9. Wayne F. Cascio and John W. Boudreau, *Investing in People: Financial Impact of Human Resource Initiatives* (Upper Saddle River, NJ: FT Press, 2008).

PART THREE

Implications

10

Future HR Practices in Leading the Work

Achieving an organization's mission by getting work done through others is the job of leaders. All leaders should consider how their role will change when they lead the work, not just the employees. Yet, in most organizations, there is a person, team, or entire function devoted to "human resources," or HR. HR professionals are leaders in their own right, so much of this book applies to them. The disruptions we describe here have and will affect how HR does its work, such as using contract trainers, tapping outside consultants for specialized expertise, and running contests to create employee recruiting campaigns.

However, beyond how HR processes are accomplished, the discipline of HR has a special place in leading the work. Many leaders will look to HR for guidance in navigating a world beyond employment. This may be framed as a legal or transactional role: "HR should decide if we should use employees, free agents, or alliance partners." "HR is responsible for making sure we don't run afoul of the law when we use contractors, and that we avoid crossing the line that requires us to make them employees."

Yet, to see these decisions as legal or cost-based transactions misses the point. It is the discipline of HR as a decision science that is key to navigating a world beyond employment. Boudreau and Ramstad defined a decision science as something that improves pivotal decisions and is grounded in a scientific approach to logic and data.[1] It includes logical frameworks, decision support systems, mental models, data and analytics, and a focus on optimization.

As a start on developing that decision science, this chapter describes implications of this new world for the programs and practices of HR. Such programs and practices are, today, the most familiar manifestations of the HR profession, so they offer a useful starting point for contemplating the step-change that will be needed for HR to reach its full potential.

However, this chapter is not exclusively for HR leaders. Rather, it is a call to action for leaders inside and outside of HR. For leaders outside of HR, the chapter will offer ideas describing what leaders should expect from HR in the future. For leaders inside HR, the chapter offers a glimpse of the role they can and should play in this emerging world. Leading the work in a world beyond employment is one of the trends that will most profoundly challenge our notions of what HR means. It offers immense opportunities, but also immense challenges to leaders inside and outside of HR.

The discipline of HR is where expertise should exist about vital issues such as values, engagement, rewards, work design, and the employment "deal." The discipline of HR should house the "decision science" devoted to optimizing the connection between work, workers, talent, organization, and strategic success. Thus, leading the work in a world beyond employment should usher in a brave new era for the discipline and profession of HR. Sadly, as Boudreau pointed out in an article in *Organizational Dynamics* in 2014, evidence suggests that the profession of HR is not advancing rapidly enough to capitalize on this opportunity.[2]

Here, we suggest how HR can accelerate its evolution to meet the challenge.

HR Beyond Employment: Work Engineering

HR is steeped in a language of employment. HR systems focus on how people move into, through, and out of the organization, primarily as employees. HR maps that movement with a set of jobs that are stable collections of tasks. HR leaders define their work in terms like *"employment" brand,* "*employee*" *engagement,* "*employee*" *turnover,* and the "*employment*" *deal.* HR creates reward systems that are designed to apply to a collective set of employees, and work best when those employees stay for the long term. When HR considers the labor market, it is through comparisons between the organization's jobs and employees, with the jobs and employees of others. Training and capability development are couched in terms of what can be delivered inside the organization and in terms of gaining experience by moving through a series of jobs. Employment relations is framed as the relationship with a union that represents employees, or employees gathered into collective bodies like works councils or even affinity groups.

Can HR apply to the world beyond employment that we have described? It's a world where the concept of a job is irrelevant or inadequate for describing how work can be deconstructed and dispersed. It's a world where a reward system based on traditional elements carefully constructed and monitored for equity and motivation of the people inside the organization boundary is inadequate. That reward system doesn't reflect a world where rewards are often nonmonetary and where the most relevant workforce exists outside the organization boundary on a talent platform. It's a world where work and workers are expected to move seamlessly back and forth over the organization boundary, or never even join the organization, making concepts like "employee turnover" and "employee careers" too confining to capture the reality of the options available to workers and those receiving the work.

To be sure, we see today's HR systems incorporating ideas from a world beyond employment. Today's HR systems can count work that will be done by contractors or freelancers in the currency of full-time-equivalent (FTE) employees. The costs of such workers can be reflected in HR budgets. It may also be that for some organizations, nonemployment work arrangements will be exceptions, so it is adequate for HR to focus on systems designed to manage regular full-time employees.

Yet, as we have seen, even for organizations that get work done through employees, the drumbeat of change in the work is getting louder. Every day, employees look more like free agents. Every day, some new area of work becomes feasible to do on a platform. Leaders can't escape the evolution of work simply by avoiding nonemployment work arrangements. Even their regular full-time employees are affected. More important, leaders must have systems that help them optimize how they use different work arrangements.

The employment relationship itself is evolving to a beyond employment reality. Organizations and workers face increasing uncertainty and shorter time frames in which they can predict what the work will be and who will do it. Workers demand rewards that are more differentiated and imaginative than can be offered by a typical employment system. Talent platforms can increasingly gather up a far larger and more diverse global population of workers, and allocate work in a more precise way than any one organization could expect to do. Even if a large and sophisticated organization chooses to provide the sort of arrangements that a talent platform can, it will find itself creating an internal talent platform that resembles the one that already exists outside.

As an organization leader, can you really afford to assume that the HR systems you have built to handle "employment" will be sufficient to navigate a world beyond employment? Are you willing to relegate your HR systems to what may be a smaller and smaller set of workers who have traditional employment arrangements? To whom will you turn for expertise and insights to navigate this new world? Today, your procurement or finance function may be the default location for these decisions. Leaders should demand that their HR organization step up to these challenges.

As an HR leader, can you foresee a robust and strategic contribution for you and your colleagues if your focus continues to be on honing systems that presume employment is the way work gets done? Is it not the opportunity and even the obligation of HR professionals to become the experts at navigating this new world beyond employment, or risk that other disciplines with less of the vital expertise will take up the mantle by default? HR professionals and others in the HR discipline have an exciting and momentous opportunity to embrace the challenge of bringing all of their expertise to bear on this new world.

There is much to be learned from the wisdom and knowledge that the HR profession has amassed over decades of research and practical experience. However, that knowledge and those important HR insights and systems are at risk of becoming irrelevant if the rigid assumptions about employment are not questioned and refined to fit the new world.

Our Lead the Work framework is not only a guide for leading the work but a way to navigate the new world of HR as well. For HR leaders, it's both a challenge and an invitation. For leaders outside of HR, it offers a mandate to ask and expect more from your HR leaders and their profession.

As we shall see, the resulting vision of the future of HR is optimistic, has high impact, and is deeply pivotal to organization success. The vision works, whether applied to employees, those outside the employment relationship, or the hybrid workers who will shift between the two roles. Not only does it offer ways to incorporate nonemployment work arrangements into the HR domain, it offers insights about how HR's approach to employment itself can be more creative, optimized, and mutually beneficial to workers and organizations.

In sum, when the focus shifts to leading the work, then even the name Human Resources seems inadequate. A consortium of top HR executives mapping the future of the profession has suggested the new name should be "Work and Workplace Engineering" to reflect the new focus and a new mandate to create an optimally designed ecosystem of workers and workplaces to achieve the organization's mission.

Let's take a tour of this new world, through the lens of the Lead the Work framework, to see the evolving profession that leaders must demand and HR professionals must prepare to deliver. The questions we pose along the way are designed to offer an outline for the vital dialogue that must occur between organization constituents (CEOs, Boards, officers, and investors) and HR leaders (CHROs, professional associations, and thought leaders).

The Talent Lifecycle

The effects of the world beyond employment on the HR discipline and HR functions is complex, so it's helpful to frame it within a familiar metaphor; the "talent lifecycle" (Figure 10.1). Organizations often have their own version, and we encourage leaders to apply the ideas in this chapter using their own depiction of HR, as the principles we discuss generally apply to any variation of this concept.

The talent lifecycle describes HR as a series of employment life stages beginning when a person enters the organization, capturing their experiences as they encounter its rewards and development opportunities, and finally the lifecycle ends when the person separates from the organization.

A typical list of the stages of the talent lifecycle is shown in the outer circle. The cycle starts with planning, through which the current and future supply of workers and demands for work are estimated, while

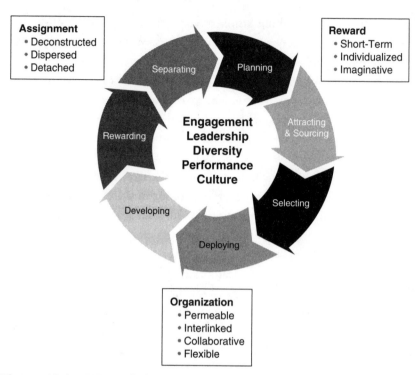

Figure 10.1   HR and the Lead the Work Framework

strategies and tactics are developed to match projected demand to projected supply. Attracting and sourcing identifies the sources from which workers are drawn and the activities to attract workers to engage with the work. Selecting chooses which of the willing workers will be matched with what work. Deploying moves workers among different work experiences, locations, and assignments over time. Developing builds the capacity of workers through experiences, such as training, experiential learning, and challenges. Rewarding conveys an array of benefits to workers through explicit exchange or through implicit experiences via the work itself. Finally, separating ends a relationship between a worker and a particular work assignment or experience.

Traditionally, the lifecycle is expressed in terms of entry, movement within, and movement out of a particular organization, and it's shown in terms of a series of jobs contained within that organization. It's often called the "employment lifecycle," which begins when you join and ends when you leave a particular organization. We have been careful here to avoid referring to a single organization and its jobs. As we shall see, if we use the words "work" and "worker" instead of "organization," "job," or "employee," this familiar model can become a powerful organizing metaphor for a world beyond employment. The idea is that all of these lifecycle stages still occur, but not necessarily within the boundary of a single employer and not necessarily through work experiences organized as jobs.

In the middle of the circle are a set of broad outcomes of the employment lifecycle. Here, we have included engagement, leadership, diversity, performance, and culture. We will take them up in the next chapter.

Surrounding the traditional employee lifecycle in the diagram are the familiar three dimensions of the Lead the Work framework: assignment, reward, and organization. In the sections that follow, we will take each lifecycle element in turn and show how the Lead the Work framework helps leaders fashion a future HR approach that optimizes success in a world beyond employment.

Planning

In a world beyond employment, planning is transformed from employee supply and demand and gap analysis to work and worker engineering and optimization. The unit of analysis becomes the work, not employee head counts or FTEs. The domain becomes the full array of work and workers—not only what is contained within the organization boundary. The scenarios and options that are considered now include not only supply, demand, and deployment but how to dial the dimensions of the assignments, the organization, and the rewards.

When assignments can be dialed up or down on deconstruction, dispersal, and detachment, planning must now ask questions such as, "Could we alleviate a planning constraint or dilemma by breaking up the job into its parts?" and, "What tasks should be kept together and which ones separated?" Sometimes it will simplify planning, because once you deconstruct, disperse, and detach the work of coding to Topcoder or logo design to Upwork, your plan is simply to tap those platforms for a ready inventory of qualified workers on demand. When assignments can be dispersed to workers who are employed by other organizations, then planning systems must extend beyond "counting" work only when it's paid for through an employment agreement. Simply translating outsourced or contracted work into full-time equivalents (FTEs) misses the point. Planning systems must design and consider options that include reaching into other organizations, or considering which individuals would be willing to do the work as free agents. The entire notion of the "supply" of workers changes.

That draws in dialing up and down the organization dimensions. A permeable, interlinked, or collaborative organization boundary means that fundamental planning concepts such as head count, worker availability, movement between jobs, and worker separation must take on very different meanings. The key planning issue may be where to allow the boundary to open and where to keep it closed. When "employment" planning shifts to "work" planning, plans include a connected network of work sources, including platforms, outsourcers, individual freelancers, and contractors. No longer can planning simply define work as "in" the organization when done by employees and "out" when it is not. Contractors, freelancers, and crowdsourced workers don't fit either category. Leading the work means forecasting the number of available freelancers from Topcoder, consultants from Towers Watson, and crowdsourcers available on Tongal, as much as forecasting the number of candidates for jobs.

A collaborative organization means planning must include looking inside competitor or partner organizations for talent. Instead of, "How do we beat them or prevent them from taking our employees?" the question may be, "Where could we form a useful alliance, or trade talent in a way that would advance our mutual goals?" Recall the example of Siemens partnering with Disney marketers to sell the Siemens hearing aid for children. For the Siemens planning system, the question, "How many Siemens marketers are available?" would miss the point. Siemens must include Disney in their talent supply. Indeed, a work planning system must track the available supply of marketers who are employed by others, ready to freelance from a platform, available through consulting firms, and self-employed as contractors for hire. The same thing applies to talent demand. If Siemens partners with Disney to borrow their marketers, then should they consider Disney as a destination for their engineers, perhaps on a project to design Disney roller coasters? Should your planning system include destinations for your workers that are other organizations, platforms, consulting firms, and self-employment? That offers many new options to alleviate worker surpluses beyond layoffs.

That brings us to how rewards could change work planning when the work relationship can be short term (even momentary), individualized, and imaginative. Some things will be simpler. Workers with a contract carrying an expiration date don't require forecasting how long they will stay. When the rewards become more imaginative and individualized, planning only for work done by paid employees will miss the true workforce. Many paid workers will not be counted in the human resource system, but as payments through the procurement system, or contracts with consulting firms or talent platforms. When rewards do not include money at all, how does a planning system "count" talent that is engaged through voluntary crowdsourcing or games? Future planning systems must explicitly incorporate the quantity, quality, and cost of such workers. Indeed, future workforce planning may draw as much on procurement experts as it does on traditional HR experts.

Attracting/Sourcing

Today, attracting, sourcing, and recruiting typically focuses on employment, and companies look for job seekers who want to work for the organization and who fit its requirements. The idea is to attract a pool of individuals for jobs. Leading the work requires a process of seamlessly engaging multiple systems (procurement, contracting, partnering, recruiting) to attract workers for engagements that may not be jobs at all.

When you can dial up the dimensions of the assignment, organization, and reward, you must attract workers for specific tasks, projects, or microtasks, or their combinations. This may simplify things for commoditized work that is not pivotal to the organization's success, such as tagging pictures on MTurk. "Sourcing" is simply putting the job on the MTurk site, far simpler than attracting candidates for full or part-time jobs. Yet, once you let the organization boundary become permeable, and begin to interlink and collaborate, the issue becomes more complex and richer. Do you want the top designers at Tongal or Upwork to work on your projects? What's your "engagement brand" with those employees?

It's unlikely that any company could afford to have a "job" that involved developing advertisements to run on YouTube only during the Super Bowl. However, once you deconstruct that project and disconnect it from the "jobs" of the organization, you can imagine sourcing it with crowdsourcing or freelance platforms, and rewarding it with a huge payoff or fame that could not fit into a traditional recruitment offer. When Colgate or Ford run a contest for an ad to be broadcast on network television, they have the freedom to craft the project and its payoff in ways that might not be possible with employees. A one-off relationship specific to that project allows for appealing to a very specific pool of talent, and with a message and rewards that you might not want to replicate for other employees. The "product brand" of Colgate or Ford may be the key to attracting free agents, not your "employment" brand.

Dial the dimensions to include volunteers, and attracting/sourcing morphs even more. Unilever created a global campaign to encourage improved body image among women and how products such as Dove soap contribute to that image. With missions like these, organizations can tap a vast source of workers who are eager to help, but don't show up as job applicants. This is even true for paid freelancers. If you attend the Tongie awards ceremony, you can see the pride of the freelancers that worked on campaigns funded by the Bill & Melinda Gates Foundation. The Tongalers choose what projects to work on and your "brand" with them may make the difference in whether the best choose yours.

Dial the dimensions to include borrowing and lending employees from other organizations, as we showed with the insurance industry example in Chapter 8, and attracting/sourcing looks even more radically different. In *Beyond HR*, John Boudreau and Pete Ramstad described how supplier relationships became even more pivotal when Boeing decided to construct the 787 out of composite plastics instead of aluminium.[3] The expertise in composites often resided with suppliers, not with Boeing engineers. In essence, when Boeing worked with suppliers, it was borrowing those supplier employees. Boeing's internal magazine featured front-page pictures and stories of supplier employees working side-by-side with Boeing engineers. It was key for Boeing to attract the best of the suppliers' employees to work with them. Think how much more attractive Siemens is for marketers if it can point to opportunities for them to work with Disney marketers on special projects.

Will your future head of recruitment be someone as adept at attracting freelancers, volunteers, and borrowed employees as they are at attracting eager candidates for your regular full-time jobs? Will you need an entirely new sourcing function for workers who are not employees? Will you leave the sourcing of nonemployee workers to procurement? The answer depends on how you dial-up the dimensions of the Lead the Work framework, and getting the answers right may make the difference between attracting the best and the worst workers.

Selecting

Who gets chosen? Today's selection systems largely focus on choosing candidates to become regular full-time employees, often assessing things like cultural fit, to make sure the employees have the potential for a career beyond their first job. When you consider dialing the dimensions of the assignment, the organization, and the reward toward a world beyond employment, the concept of choosing and selecting workers changes. You can choose workers for deconstructed tasks that can be done anywhere and paid instantly. Sometimes, that means leaving the entire selection process to the talent platform. If you interlink with platforms for tasks like coding or logo development, with easily observed results, does that render irrelevant the standard selection qualifications such as education, quality of university, past employment, and test scores? Coders routinely publish examples of their computer code online. Why not just analyse the person's past work? Do you trust Topcoder's evaluation of its talent? Topcoder has gone to great lengths to design contests and even training programs to develop and rate coder capability. MTurk has less sophisticated systems of assessment. Future selection systems will require a way to decide how much vetting is enough when another party is handling it.

If you collaborate with another organization to borrow their employees, will they share what they know about their workers to help you select the right ones to work on your project? Would you share what you know about your employees with them? When rewards become impermanent, individualized, and less monetary, workers may not need to be selected so much for "fit" with an employer, because the reward elements can be fitted to the worker, rather than fitting the worker into the organization. If American Express awards an advertising project to a Tongaler, that person may amass a group of freelance colleagues to do the work. Do they need to "fit" with American Express? Perhaps not, but on the other hand they might create a more appropriate advertisement if they had something in common with the culture and values of American Express.

In a world where you lead the work, what are you really selecting for? It's no longer as easy as saying, "We select for this job," because the work can be deconstructed and reconfigured. What is the common language of work that you can use to communicate with workers that arrive as individual contractors, are provided by a platform, or are borrowed? In *Transformative HR,*[4] we described how IBM's Global Workforce Initiative created a global supply chain of talent, where talent moved freely across global units. That required getting IBM's global leaders to adopt a common language to describe the work, so that one region wasn't defining a job like "project manager" differently from another. IBM ended up requiring all their units to adopt the same common language based on about 100 "roles." IBM then required all of its external talent suppliers to adopt the same language so that IBM could better choose among the external workers and better connect the external supply to IBM's internal supply. Can the language you use to describe the work when you choose your candidates for regular full-time jobs also serve you when you're choosing candidates from talent platforms or borrowing them from other organizations?

If you can turn the reward dial to make individualized deals, then you can do individualized selection. We see this already in industries where reputation and performance are very public, such as entertainment, sports, and investment analysis. A movie studio doesn't just select a really great film director, they select James Cameron. A basketball team doesn't just select a really good player, they select Kobe Bryant. An investment firm doesn't just select a really good technology-sector fund manager, they select the one person who got the highest rating last year. In every case, the deal required to get the talent will likely be highly individualized and often very lucrative for them, compared to others they will work with. Such pinpointed selection will be possible in many more areas of work. Already, you can select the very best computer coder in a certain language on the Topcoder site, as long as you are willing to make him or her a deal commensurate with their reputation. Tongal and Upwork are creating a similar marketplace for top designers.

These examples pose a fundamental question for the role of the selection process in a world where you lead the work, not just the employees: When should your organization's selection systems choose your workers, and when should they be chosen by someone else? Will your head of "employee selection" soon become a head of "worker quality assurance" who is as adept at analyzing the selection methods of platforms, contractors, and partner organizations, as they are at selecting candidates for regular jobs? Increasingly the function that used to be concerned with choosing candidates for jobs must now go beyond just choosing, and seamlessly integrate with how you dial the assignment-organization-rewards dimensions.

Deploying and Developing

Deploying moves workers among different work experiences, locations, and assignments over time. Developing builds the capacity of workers through experiences such as training, experiential learning, and challenges. Development includes other key experiences, such as classroom training and mentoring. Deployment and development are so closely aligned that we treat them together.

When you focus on leading the employees, then deployment and development focus on moving employees laterally and vertically within your organization to fill open positions, give employees jobs they want, and/or develop employees. Leading the work in a world beyond employment means that work and workers move across a network of tasks, microtasks, companies, platforms, and alliances. Development and deployment today focuses on ideas such as promotions, demotions, and transfers. When you lead the work, these ideas give way to concepts like tours of duty, sabbaticals, special projects, and talent trades. Deployment and development systems have always had to balance competing goals such as cost-efficiency, high job performance, and strong employee development. Even today's deployment systems focused only on moving employees are clunky. Often, different units of the organization don't know what sort of talent resides in other units, and moving people from one unit to another is too often the result of fortuitous meetings of managers who happen to each know a good candidate or have an open position. Ignorance of talent needs and availability across organization units can cause leaders to do things like hoard their best talent rather than contributing them to the larger system.

If today's systems struggle even to optimize regular full-time employee deployment and development, they may be dangerously inadequate in the world beyond employment, which will require that they take account of a massively expanded set of options. The limitations will be played out on a much larger stage. Yes, the option to deploy work and workers across a vastly larger ecosystem than just your own organization offers you advantages, but that ecosystem also offers your workers vastly more options to chart their own learning and development paths to best meet their needs. A world beyond employment makes many of those development options available to workers whether their employer provides them or not! So, mastering development and deployment in a world beyond employment is most likely to be a requirement, not a choice. The smart organization of the future will consider embracing them before they are forced upon it.

Systems built on the idea of deployment through jobs and hierarchical levels must give way to be rebuilt on deployment to tasks, microtasks, and projects. The idea of a "career" now may mean not a progression through positions, but accumulation of project and task credits. What does it mean to get "promoted" in such a system? Will workers self-define the value of the work elements and bargain for valuable assignments?

Detaching work from an employment agreement means that the authority to "deploy" talent shifts from an employment contract to a more arms-length relationship with a talent platform, outsourcer, or free agent. Today, this is often handled by service-level agreements focused on specific tasks or projects. However, if the future promises a more fluid and ever-changing configuration, can nonemployee talent be efficiently moved and reassigned by constantly creating new contracts? Does your talent deployment system need to incorporate long-term collaborations that allow for planned projects with a freelance platform or vendor, not only to accomplish the task at hand but to ensure the worker develops to be ready for your next task?

The lines blur between what is meant by worker "selection" and worker "deployment" in the world beyond employment. Deployment can now mean repeatedly crossing the organization boundary, and thus, each return to the organization can be seen as selection, or simply the continuation of career without boundaries. When that happens, the same issues about the language of work come into play. If the arrangement is viewed as outsourcing, then the precision and compatibility of the common language used by the provider of the worker and the user of the worker will become key. Do you trust Topcoder's evaluation of its talent? Would you trust MTurk? As we saw earlier, IBM developed its own common language for work and required its external providers to use it. Can you do that?

For the learning function of organizations, this creates an opportunity and a paradox. Learning functions in today's organizations have adopted an array of virtual and online approaches, well beyond traditional classroom learning. Some have extended their learning mandate to include potential workers at early stages of the talent pipeline, such as providing math and science learning to school children in hopes some will grow up to be candidates for future technical jobs. Yet, the focus of such functions largely remains on preparing individuals for current and future jobs within the organization. In a world beyond employment, workers won't wait for the employer to provide development and education on the new skill, if they can get it more quickly and effectively on a platform like Topcoder. This is a problem if the employer feels they must prevent workers from moonlighting on Topcoder, or that they must match Topcoder's ability to quickly identify and provide training in hot new skills. Yet, if learning organizations can embrace the idea of leading the work, not just the employees, a world beyond employment can alleviate many of the nagging problems plaguing in-house learning organizations for decades. If employers explicitly include and encourage online platforms as an alternative vehicle for employee development, that can free them from trying to compete with the platform and instead embrace it.

Making IBM's "Watson" Even Smarter with Open-Source Learning Contests[5]

In a world beyond employment, the nature of learning and skill development can change fundamentally. When work and workers can flow freely through the boundary, when work can change rapidly, and when workers' motivation to learn will be increasingly driven by its value and cachet to them personally, the old model of building skills among your employees through traditional training looks rather limited. Consider IBM's desire to assure a workforce that is prepared to invent new and valuable uses for what it calls *cognitive computing*. *Cognitive* is best exemplified by IBM's Watson, a combination of algorithms, interfaces, hardware, and software that was capable of playing the television game *Jeopardy* and winning over human opponents. Watson can also interact with physicians researching oncology treatments for cancer, to scan thousands of research studies, and conversationally interact with physicians about the implications and findings. How do you get a cadre of workers—inside and outside of IBM—motivated and qualified to invent new applications for "cognitive"? IBM's answer was to create "IBM Watson Academy," a virtual hub for training on a massive scale, including global challenges and thought-provoking idea exchanges, such as, "What do you think should be the next Grand Challenge in computer science?" The Academy's focus is on cognitive training that is accessible by IBM employees, employees of IBM clients and development partners, and even students in schools and universities around the world. For example, upon its launch, Watson Academy piloted an IBM-made MOOC, adapted from a Columbia University graduate-level course taught by an IBM Watson researcher, and including students and faculty from 19 universities in 10 countries. The Academy has also used contests to get attention and to motivate these workers to train themselves on cognitive computing using tools on the website and then competing to showcase their best solutions. In addition, the Academy has launched an online interface that delivers learning in a broad variety of media, ranging from mastery modeling videos to hands-on guided practice. This creates flexible learning mosaics that appeal to learners and are at the same time easy to maintain and update. The idea is to make IBM's best tools and lessons about "cognitive" available to the entire ecosystem of workers inside and outside of IBM, to rapidly create a qualified workforce ready and willing to develop the next big thing for Watson.

This is not without risks. It's quite possible that the best workers, once they experience life on a talent platform like Topcoder, may be tempted to moonlight permanently, augmenting their income and working on Topcoder as a consistent part of their work life. For a traditional employer, this can feel like a loss of the exclusive relationship with that employee. The employee is now closer to a market that may tempt her away. Yet, such platforms exist whether an employer admits it or not, and such moonlighting is now difficult to prevent. Perhaps the better option is to embrace it. Recall our story about the small company that was lucky enough to find a very talented computer coder locally, but, realizing the coder was unlikely to be satisfied with the small salary that the firm could provide, encouraged him to join Topcoder, while continuing to work with the firm. After he built a reputation on the platform, the coder received offers from Silicon Valley firms, but he turned them down. He liked the open spirit of his boss, and letting him learn, develop, and earn money on Topcoder was pivotal in the coder's decision to stay with the small firm.

The same dilemma and the same solution applies to learning organizations when it comes to alliances formed with other employers that allow talent trading.

Peter Voser, the CEO of Royal Dutch Shell beginning July 2009, retired in May 2013. Voser had more than 25 years of experience at Shell, having joined Shell in 1982. Historically, Shell's top leaders spent their careers at the company. But unlike many Shell leaders, Voser's career at the company was not continuous. He spent two years as the CFO of power and automation company ABB, from 2002 to 2004, before returning to Shell as CFO. In an interview in 2009, when he became the CEO at Shell, Voser said, "I left Shell for a short period to go to work for ABB. The main driver for me was to be CFO of a quoted company. I wanted that experience. I was ready and impatient with myself, and I couldn't see that happening fast enough at Shell. . . . [At ABB] it was about survival, and we restructured the company, while sustaining sharp operational performance. Had we not done that, we would have gone under. I learned that it's better to drive change yourself first than to be forced by external events to do it. So my time at ABB was truly a formative experience."[6]

Taking Development and Mentoring to the Cloud: The Case of Everwise

Mentorship can be a vital part of worker and leader development. Typically mentors and mentees are both employees of the same organization. Employees looking for a mentor might find a friendly manager or leader they know. Perhaps they hit it off with someone from their company at a meeting or social occasion, and the mentor relationship develops from there. Some organizations formalize and systematize the process by allowing employees to request mentors and then tapping fellow employees who have said they were willing to be a mentor. The mentoring pool is defined as regular full-time employees.

The advantages are that the mentors may have deep knowledge about the employing organization, and that the topics discussed by the mentor and the mentee can be kept confidential, within the walls of the organization and governed by the employment agreement. On the other hand, the population of employees can be a very small pool from which to try to make mentorship matches. Many organizations find it very difficult to meet the demand for mentors from among their own leadership. There may be only a few leaders who are skilled and motivated to be mentors. Those leaders may or may not have time to mentor at all, let alone to mentor many protégés that may desire their help. The result can be that many worthwhile opportunities go unmet.

What if you could take mentoring to the cloud? A company called Everwise (geteverwise.com) does just that. Everwise is a platform where those desiring a mentor can be matched with willing mentors, across a wide array of organizations beyond their employer. Everwise has amassed a database of 60,000 relationships, to pair protégés with experienced operating executives from a cross-organization mentor pool. Like other talent platforms, this one takes advantage of the opportunity to learn from the thousands of mentor and mentee relationships occurring in its ecosystem. The platform not only uses multiple factors and algorithms to ensure good mentor-mentee matches but also provides online tools to help make the most of the relationship. The algorithms and tools are constantly updated with knowledge about what works and what doesn't for the mentors and mentees on the platform. Everwise can certainly apply these tools to an organization that wants only to match mentors and mentees from among its employees. However, Ian Gover, the CEO of Everwise, reports that organizations often begin by restricting the pool to their own employees, and then expand it once they realize the significantly greater value they can achieve by expanding the pool beyond their boundary. A permeable boundary, facilitated by a collaboration with Everwise, brings the advantages of cloud-based talent platforms to the employee development activities of HR.

In a world beyond employment, workers will more frequently take "tours of duty" that move them between your organization and others. What should be the reaction to a world where some employers form alliances with Google or a top technical consulting firm that allows them to have their employees tap the training and experiences of those firms as a tour of duty? A traditional organization might see this as competition and try to prevent employees from leaving by offering in-house training, or creating in-house versions of a Google-like environment in the hopes of competing with Google for those workers. However, perhaps the more savvy approach in the future would be to accept that the most effective skill development will occur within the organizations that do it best, such as Google, and rather than try to compete with that, companies should try to incorporate it into their learning strategy instead.

In the Lead the Work framework, such interlinkages can evolve to collaborations. The connections become symbiotic, and the organizations build mutual relationships based on common goals, trust, or economic necessity. Developing your leaders is now a collaborative effort with partners, so your learning agenda must take into account your partners' as well. Moving your people where they are most needed or where they can learn the most is important, but so is accounting for the needs of your partners. Today, learning and development systems focus mostly on what's best for the employer and employees within a relatively closed system. In the future beyond employment, lasting collaborative relationships that span a permeable and interlinked organizational boundary will require asking, "How can we help out a partner or talent provider by giving them some of our talent now so that they're more willing to give us theirs, or provide us a favorable deal on talent in the future?"

Indeed, the potential for collaboration has not been lost on the talent platforms. For a fee, Topcoder will help an employer use Topcoder's expertise in running contests that motivate and evaluate the skills of that organization's own employees relative to each other and the best in the market. Similar collaborative development opportunities occur when an employer hires employees of consulting firms as executives. The consulting firm may heartily encourage this because those executives become great clients for the firm. Time at a consulting firm is a way to have your people experience many more cycles of a skill or project than they ever could within your company. Today's learning and career systems often treat such situations as special cases, but evidence suggests that talent platforms and consulting firms are already creating an infrastructure that will make it easy to incorporate a more permeable, interlinked, and collaborative organizational approach. Chapter 6 described how IBM has developed an internal system to optimize just this sort of talent trading.

Imagine a learning strategy at a financial services firm like American Express that included using Topcoder as the learning platform for new software skills and a tour of duty at Google as the platform for learning the culture and technology of the web. A learning strategy built upon combining the best of what's outside with what's inside requires very different competencies and vision from chief learning officers (CLOs) but is likely to define their role in the future. We see harbingers of this today. At GE's John F. Welch Leadership Center at Crotonville in Ossining, New York, it's not unusual to encounter employees from other organizations that are market partners to GE. Those employees attend classes there to benefit from unique GE learning and experience. That benefits GE's partners as well as providing another way that GE can consolidate its relationships with those partners. This is an analog version of a boundaryless learning philosophy, and it requires that the CLO and learning organization at GE specifically embrace the role of its partners in its learning agenda. It's a small step from that world to one in which CLOs are called upon to embrace and incorporate talent platforms, tours of duty, and talent-trading alliances with competitors or consulting firms as the most effective way to create the learning they need.

Rewarding

Applying Incentive System Principles to Crowdsourced Contests

Contests are a reward mechanism that is commonly used in the Talent-Platform space. For Topcoder, programmers give it their best shot, knowing there can be only one winner. The contest model may seem discomforting ("What? I do the work and then may not get paid?"), but sales departments have long used contests as part of the reward package, and anyone responding to a request for proposal is engaging in a contest. Innovation contests are particularly interesting because they are designed to amplify the quantity of ideas produced, as well as to engage the crowd in evaluating them and combining them into new ideas. However, the rewards and incentives in such contests often actually work at cross-purposes to these objectives, and some fundamental principles from traditional employment incentive systems can make a big difference to their effectiveness.

Professors Arvind Malhotra and Ann Majchrzak, of the University of South Carolina and University of Southern California respectively, reported research showing that innovation challenge contests are most successful when they encourage participants to integrate their knowledge.[7] They noted that such contests must motivate participants to share (post ideas, examples, facts, and trade-offs), highlight the best quality (vote on posts and promote others' comments), and combine ideas (create solutions by putting ideas together from multiple sources and posts). On the one hand, the less successful group received conventional instructions that emphasized posting, tweaking others' ideas, being encouraging and not critical, and voting on whether you liked an idea or not. On the other hand, the more successful group received knowledge integration instructions that emphasized posting ideas designed to stimulate others, comment in ways that modify others' knowledge, integrate with others' knowledge to form complete solutions, and vote based on whether an idea was useful in solving the challenge.

Their findings suggest that when you change the performance definition and give rewards for integration, not just individual ideas, you get a more integrative result. Just as with employees, you get what you ask for and what gains the incentives. In this case the incentives gained were the votes, and the change was to focus the voting on integration and usefulness, not just "liking."

The Lead the Work framework already includes a dimension on the Reward that we have discussed in earlier chapters. Here, let's focus on the concerns directly related to how HR will craft a total rewards approach. How should the perspective of leaders in areas of compensation and benefits change with the advent of a world beyond employment? As with the other elements of HR, this offers a challenge to HR professionals with systems that today focus primarily on employment, but it also offers opportunities to better optimize the contribution of total rewards to the organization's strategy and mission.

At one extreme, rewards might become mostly piecework, because all work will have been broken down into tasks and microtasks, where output is easily observed and rewarded. It's tempting to think that platforms like Topcoder and MTurk are basically just virtualized versions of traditional piecework systems that have been around for hundreds of years. Does that mean simply shifting to a piecework perspective can offer sufficient insights into how to optimize rewards for deconstructed work? Probably not. Even traditional piecework systems implemented by organizations that have a long history of success with them, can fail in new regions or countries. In the book *Redefining Global Strategy,* author Pankaj Ghemawat writes, "[As Lincoln Electric] has expanded abroad, it has done much better in countries that resemble the United States in allowing unrestricted use of piecework.... Where piecework isn't allowed [the company] is thinking hard about mixing and matching policies in a way that strikes the best balance possible between internal consistency and fit with the external environment—rather than naively emphasizing one or the other."[8]

Dispersed work means that even when there are tangible outputs, they are often created in one place and then transported through intermediaries. This creates dilemmas for rewards that require personal contact to deliver. It also creates difficulties if you don't see the work until it is completed, so you can't reward effort, time, and/or motivation.

When you're not the employer, some elements of what you can offer as part of the deal will evaporate, such as employer-based benefits, and perhaps career paths and an affiliation with your organization. Yet, talent platforms, lending employees to iconic partners, and embracing career paths that welcome workers who leave and then return may allow you to entice workers with perks or offers that could not be made if they were employees. This requires new skills. How do you explain to your employed computer coders why their "deal" is different from what they would get if you hired them through Topcoder? How will your reward system allocate highly desirable career opportunities to do a tour of duty with an iconic partner such as Google, Disney, or others?

The fundamental definition of rewards will change more often. New rewards, such as reputation, will enter. Old rewards, such as traditional internal education, will exit. The notion of rewards slotted into an array of "jobs" arranged by hierarchy and market position becomes irrelevant when work is constantly being deconstructed and reconstructed, and when the boundary is constantly changing. For example, if your work system includes getting work done on a talent platform, using consultants, and by allowing trades and tours of duty with other employers, then what is the right "market" for setting pay levels and deciding what array of rewards is competitive? In today's world, these arenas seldom intersect, so perhaps even when an organization uses all of them, it's sufficient to say, "You are an employee, so your deal is different. Those Topcoder folks, the consultants we hire, and the people who work at the organizations where we trade workers are not our employees, so we can't incorporate them into our reward structure." Even today, such a position is rather tenuous, considering that Topcoder pay levels are fully visible, and the emergence of sites like Glassdoor.com, where employees anonymously review their company's management and policies, make it surprisingly easy for your employees to find out what others receive at other organizations. Indeed, Edward Lawler at the Center for Effective Organizations has argued in his pieces on the Huffington Post that the idea of pay secrecy is an outdated concept, and that organizations should just make their pay decisions public to their employees.[9] In the world beyond employment, your organization may actually move workers between their role as employees today, consultants tomorrow, platform-based talent the next day, and talent on sabbatical at another organization on another day. In such a world, it seems reasonable that workers will expect some fidelity in the level and type of rewards offered across these different roles. Yet, most reward systems today operate as if they can be walled off.

Today, organizations apply techniques such as focus groups and zip code analysis to their employees. Soon, they may be applied to scan the vast array of potential workers you might engage. If an organization is your "trading partner" for talent, then their reward array becomes as relevant to your workers as the one in your organization. If you routinely draw on talent platforms, then your employees will justifiably want your reward system to recognize their work alongside the population of freelancers. When you disperse work in time and space, like the JetBlue call-center operators who work from home, regional analysis of different employee needs and labor markets becomes paramount so that you don't risk losing employees by trying too hard to fit every region into the same system, or overpay through ignorance that in some regions nonpay rewards are much more valuable.

The world beyond employment offers the chance to break work down into its smaller components and often to see performance of that work in real-time detail. As we saw in Chapter 9, that means reward systems will need to have a much deeper idea about the return on improved work performance, the costs of motivating that performance, and the distribution of performance among workers. For example, if you don't need the best programmer, then you need to individualize the rewards to attract and motivate one that is "good enough." When mitigating risk is enough, you want to put most of your resources into that, rather than pushing workers to excel beyond the point where risk is minimized. On the other hand, when breakthrough performance creates a large payoff, you want to provide very high incentives for breakthroughs, and perhaps less incentives for average performance. Platforms like Upwork, Tongal, and Topcoder generate vast amounts of data that can allow this kind of reward optimization, across a wide array of reward elements and thousands of free-agent workers. The data are there. Can it be long before such analysis becomes commonplace? It seems inevitable that tomorrow's reward systems will need to seamlessly incorporate the information and insights being generated in the talent platforms and other interlinked sources of work and workers.

When work and workers can move across the boundary, a reward in the future may never happen. It can be seen as a recipe for extreme employment-at-will with little long-run exchange. This is the classic danger being described by those who see the emergence of freelance platforms as little more than worker exploitation schemes. Or, organizations may make permeability a central part of their reward structure by creating rewards that entice and welcome workers to move out and in. Why not an offer of a big cash bonus upon returning to the organization after a worker goes outside to get valuable skills? It ushers in a world of "tours of duty" where rewards need to be portable and visible for things like documented skills and public achievements. Interlinking organizations and collaborative structures take this even further. When explicit connections exist between one organization and others, it makes the cross-organization pattern more predictable, so you can afford to create advanced rewards that actually capitalize on the permeable boundary. That's because if you create strong linkages with external platforms, contractors, or talent vendors that can offer unique rewards, you may be able to amplify your own reward structure through them. If you set up a collaborative relationship with an outsourcer, contractor, freelancer, or platform, you may be able to actually induce them to deliver rewards that are beyond your ability as a single employer, but also do it cooperatively with you.

You need not become an expert at using contests to motivate your workers to get new skills and then track which ones are best at those skills. Tongal or Upwork will run a contest for your employees, giving them internal or external recognition and prizes, perhaps based on your own projects or problems. The symbiosis goes in the other direction when you collaborate with you take on workers from a consulting firm, and that provides rewards to their employees that only you can offer (development or exposure to the latest technology), while having the option to move employees back to them when you don't need them.

In the world beyond employment, the very meaning of an organizational reward changes. The "deal" with your workers becomes boundaryless, more diverse; it can tap imaginative elements that were previously not available, and data that can optimize in ways hardly imagined today. The opportunities and the risks increase and accelerate. HR leaders and their constituents will be wise to begin considering those opportunities and risks now, in time to exploit them and shape them, and before they are surprised when the best talent demands them.

Separating

In the talent lifecycle, the stage of separating is typically seen as the end of the employment relationship. It's traditionally an easily measured event that is indicated by numerous administrative and accounting processes to terminate the employee. Indeed, employee turnover is one of the most widely and well-studied phenomena in organizations, in part because it is so easily measured. To be sure, there is much that the employee-turnover rate does not capture, including whether the departure is functional or harmful for the organization, the costs of the turnover processes, and whether the act of separating one employee to hire another reduces or increases the quality of the group in which the turnover took place.[10] That said, turnover is historically and remains a central concept in human resource systems. Even today, organizations such as Google and Microsoft work hard to predict employee turnover using big data and sophisticated algorithms. It is one of the most frequent applications of big data and predictive analytics.

Is the whole notion of employee "separation" obsolete in a world beyond employment? The end of a project conducted by a contractor or freelancer is hardly a separation when that worker will be available in the future for more work. It is technically employee turnover when a "boomerang" employee departs to embark on a series of career stages in other employers, then returns to the original employer as a more qualified candidate. Seeing this merely as a separation and rehire hardly captures the potential value of such a boundaryless work relationship. An employee who leaves to join a consulting firm or alliance partner and remains closely connected to the work of their original organization, even though they are now employed by someone else, seems hardly equivalent to the traditional concept of employee separation.

Even today, the old model of employees going from "learning to doing to retiring" is certainly passé. Workers are already challenging the traditional notion of full-time employment followed by full-time retirement. The black-and-white boundary of employment followed by retirement is being replaced by phased retirement, where employees transition from full-time employment to part-time employment to semi-retirement to post-retirement employment to job sharing to temporary work. Organizations facing unprecedented uncertainty consider alternatives that involve talent on demand, where workers join at peak periods, then depart, often to work in other organizations, but are on call should future peaks emerge.

A future beyond employment will see organization leaders, planners, and HR professionals fashion the notion of employee separation into new concepts that encompass boundary crossing, outside intermediaries, innovative rewards that include "separating" and "rejoining," and definitions of work beyond the "job." This new approach to the idea of employee separation will make it less the end of a talent lifecycle and more an integral element of an ongoing series of engagements between work and workers.

When you deconstruct the work, the notion of "separation" has less meaning, particularly when it's done through a platform. But the idea of "keeping in touch" may be key. If the best designer on Elance has a falling-out with your organization and won't work with you in the future, does that count as employee turnover? It may be at least as harmful as the separation of a more traditional employee in a less pivotal role.

However, if you can keep a good relationship with them, they are in a way "retained" as part of your available workforce. As long as the worker can be located and is willing to work, he may be counted as not "separated." What might look like "serial turnover" or "job hopping" in the old world is now simply a series of engagements with a worker who is always available, even if he's working part-time for a competitor. The old notion of employee retention is replaced by a new notion of staying in touch for future accessibility.

Rewards that are individualized, short-term, and more imaginative also redefine what it means to join and separate. An individual contract for a screenwriter through an agent, for a consultant through a consulting firm, by its nature is a one-off relationship. Such arrangements naturally incorporate the expectation of separation followed by reengagement. The traditional idea of worker turnover doesn't apply.

In many ways, separation across the traditional organizational boundary starts to look more like "separation" across the boundary of one internal company unit to another. The more you can interlink with external organizations, the more options within this permeable network. The more collaborative you are with the external destinations of those that separate, the more options you have to optimize the separation and return pattern. Malleability creates a similar pattern. When IBM divested its PC division to Lenovo, long-term IBM employees technically separated from the organization, just as in a layoff, termination, or resignation. Yet, because they left as an intact group, the nature of their work, coworkers, and team relationships remained; they just moved outside the original IBM organization.

To illustrate the extremity of the changes, we have portrayed a workforce of people leaving and returning to the same company like so many bees around the hive. This may be well beyond the current experience, and even the future aspirations of most organizations. Perhaps the more fundamental message is that HR systems must rethink separation as a failure. When an organization creates the right ecosystem, the right people will join when it is best for them, and, yes, they will ultimately leave. This won't always be a good thing for the organization. Those workers may not return. That is the nature of the new world beyond employment. Yet, even if you can't count on getting them back, it makes sense to embrace a more boundaryless world. If you are the organization that "gets it," the word will get around, and you will have a natural ecosystem of new talent, even if it's not the specific person that "separated" in the first place.

Leading the Work by "Rewiring" HR

Scott Pitasky, the Vice President of Partner Relations at Starbucks, coined the phrase "rewired" HR to capture the fundamental changes required for HR processes, infrastructure, and systems to meet future demands.[11] We have seen that a world beyond employment is a potent force demanding just such change. Like rewiring the systems of a building to bring it from the era of physical telephone lines to one of fiberoptics and wireless connectivity, the necessary rewiring of HR requires rethinking fundamental assumptions, not just modifying the existing systems and infrastructure.

To meet the future demands of leaders, and to live up to its vast potential contribution will require that HR leaders rethink the very foundations that support today's HR systems. While that observation has been made by many, with regard to developments such as big data and personal technology, there are few frameworks for mapping the specific changes needed and their ultimate purpose. The Lead the Work framework, and the world beyond employment that it embodies, provides one framework for not only envisioning the elements of that rewiring but actually providing the dimensions and principles to help optimize the new designs.

In order to fully appreciate the implications, however, we must complete the picture by examining the outcomes of HR. We take those up in the next chapter.

Notes

1. John W. Boudreau and Peter M. Ramstad, *Beyond HR: The New Science of Human Capital* (Boston, MA: Harvard Business School Publishing, 2007).
2. John Boudreau, "Will HR's grasp match its reach? An estimable profession grown complacent and outpaced," *Organizational Dynamics*, *43*, no. 3 (July–September 2014): 189–197.

3. John W. Boudreau and Peter M. Ramstad, *Beyond HR: The New Science of Human Capital* (Boston, MA: Harvard Business School Publishing, 2007).

4. John W. Boudreau and Ravin Jesuthasan, *Transformative HR* (Hoboken, NJ: John Wiley & Sons, 2011).

5. Personal interview with Obed Louissaint of IBM, March 13, 2015.

6. Peter Gumbel, "Meet Shell's New CEO," *Fortune Global 500*, July 13, 2009, http://archive.fortune.com/2009/07/07/news/international/royal _dutch_shell_peter_voser.fortune/index.htm.

7. Arvind Malhotra and Ann Majchrzak, "Managing Crowds in Innovation Challenges," *California Management Review*, 56, no. 4 (Summer 2014): 103–123.

8. Pankaj Ghemawat, *Redefining Global Strategy* (Boston, MA: Harvard Business School Publishing, 2007).

9. Edward E. Lawler, III, "Why Pay Secrecy Needs to End," *Huffington Post*, January 6, 2015, www.huffingtonpost.com/ed-lawler/why-pay-secrecy-needs-to_b_6425772.html.

10. Wayne F. Cascio and John W. Boudreau, *Investing in People: Financial Impact of Human Resource Initiatives*, 2nd ed. (Upper Saddle River, NJ: Pearson Education, 2011).

11. Personal interview with Scott Pitasky of Starbucks, March 13, 2015.

11

Future HR Outcomes in Leading the Work

Leading the work in a world beyond employment affects the outcomes of HR just as profoundly as it affects HR activities. Recall the talent lifecycle diagram, shown again in Figure 11.1.

In the middle of the circle are a set of broad outcomes of the employment lifecycle. Here, we have included engagement, leadership, diversity, performance, and culture. Engagement refers to employee commitment, loyalty, identity, passion, and satisfaction with their relationship with the organization. Leadership refers to setting a vision and values, inspiring followers, and communicating strategy and mission. Diversity refers to an environment that is inclusive of differences, encourages disparate perspectives, and allows interactions among those with different demographic, lifestyle, professional, and cultural backgrounds. Performance refers to the results produced by individuals and groups, as well as the systems that evaluate, communicate, and track those results. Culture refers to the often-unstated beliefs, norms, values, and customs of the work. Again, these are traditionally framed to focus on a particular organization, with terms such as *employee engagement, job performance, company culture,* or *top [name of the company] leadership.* Again, we have been careful to

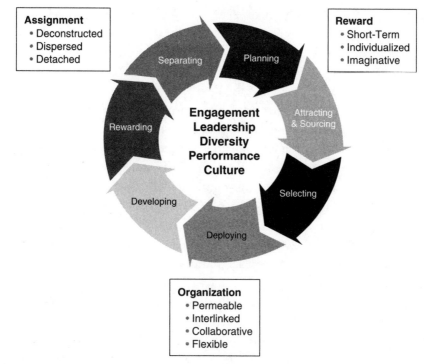

Assignment
- Deconstructed
- Dispersed
- Detached

Reward
- Short-Term
- Individualized
- Imaginative

Separating

Planning

**Engagement
Leadership
Diversity
Performance
Culture**

Attracting & Sourcing

Rewarding

Developing

Selecting

Deploying

Organization
- Permeable
- Interlinked
- Collaborative
- Flexible

Figure 11.1   HR and the Lead the Work Framework

frame these ideas in terms of the work and the worker so that they can become more powerful concepts that can encompass not only traditional employment but a world beyond traditional employment.

Engagement and Culture

We introduced this book by asking whether you should think of Topcoder as a company with 700 or so regular full-time employees, or as a company that delivers 700,000 workers through its platform. Is being rated a "best place to work" by the 700 really a good indicator of Topcoder's success in engaging the workers that really matter? In fact, the leaders of organizations that provide talent platforms like Topcoder, Upwork and Tongal pay close attention to engaging their free-agent workers. If you watch videos of the Topcoder Open, you will see a very engaged group of coders who gather in one place to spend hours watching the best coders in the world solve tough riddles. The attendees literally watch code being written and speculate about who will win. The Tongies are an annual award ceremony, much like the Academy Awards, but featuring the best work by the free agents delivered through the Tongal platform. Awards include the best 140-character idea and the best "wildcard" ideas that were at first rejected by the client, but where the free agent decided to invest their own time in creating a demonstration video, and managed to win the job after all. In the speeches by the winning Tongalers, they frequently thank Tongal for "giving me a way to pursue my career." Many employers would dearly love to have their own regular full-time employees be this engaged!

Does a free-agent platform have a culture? In Rob Salvatore's speech at the Tongie awards in 2015, he reminisced about the early days when the platform had only 200 members and was scrambling around to explain to potential clients like McDonald's, Unilever, and Netflix how the model actually worked. He marveled that today projects that were created through the platform attracted millions of dollars in corporate advertising dollars and were showcased at the Sundance Film Festival. He summarized by declaring, "We used to say that Tongal was going to be the future of how creative work gets done, but today all of you *are* the future!" That message, and the values, norms, and beliefs that it embodies, certainly resonated with Tongal's 48 employees in the room, but it resonated even more powerfully with the thousands of assembled free agents whose lives are being changed by the opportunity that Tongal creates.

Even if you don't lead a talent platform, in a world beyond employment, engagement and culture matter, and it's not only engaging your regular full-time employees. Leading the work means creating engagement with your culture among a workforce that exists well beyond your boundaries. When you use a platform like Tongal, Topcoder, or Upwork? In a world beyond employment, it makes sense to choose a talent platform because its leaders are good at creating engagement among their free-agent workers. Even more directly, you will want to engage workers on the platform with your specific organization, by creating a great reputation among them that your projects are interesting and change the world, and that you are a good partner to work with. How would HR measure that? Can you do an engagement survey of the free agents that work on your projects? It may already be done for you. Freelancers Union has a website that compiles "reviews" of clients and summarizes them into a five-star rating (https://www.freelancersunion.org/client-scorecard/).

Rocio Bonet, Peter Cappelli, and Monica Hamori summarized the research on engagement when it comes to "labor market intermediaries" such as talent platforms, temporary agencies, and so forth.[1] The research suggests that worker attitudes and engagement reflect both the intermediary and the client for the work. Commitment and loyalty toward an employment agency are driven by traditional elements such as career support, communication, quality of facilities, and interpersonal supportiveness, and the average commitment score of workers to their intermediary is "not far below" the averages typically found for traditional regular full-time employee. Interestingly, free-agent workers were also more committed to their client when they felt that their intermediary supported them. They also found that workers who felt their client company treated them fairly showed positive behaviors toward the agency that placed them and vice versa. The bottom line is that how well your talent platform or worker provider engages workers may well affect how engaged those workers are with you.

Are Independent Workers More Engaged and Innovative than Regular Full-Time Employees?[2]

You might expect that independent workers would be less engaged with their work than regular full-time employees, and in particular those regular full-time employees who have been designated as "high-potential" and thus receive more focused attention on their careers and rewards. Is regular full-time employment the way to get innovation, or can independent workers be as innovative? Results from a 2013 survey of over 33,000 employees in 26 countries suggests that engagement and innovation transcend employment. The employees worked at least 30 hours a week, but the independent workers worked for different companies, were often self-employed, and typically were not entitled to the same benefits as regular full-time employees. The report found that independent workers were more engaged with their clients than were regular employees with their employer and that independent workers reported being more satisfied and taking greater pride in their work than not only regular full-time employees but even those regular employees designated as high-potentials. The report found that among the reasons independent workers became independent, those rated highest in importance were "flexible working conditions," "being my own boss," and "interesting, challenging, and fulfilling work." In addition to being more engaged, independent workers may be more innovative. When asked if they take calculated risks in their work, feel free to challenge the status quo, try new things even if they may not work, and feel that promising new ideas will be financially supported, independent workers scored almost as high as high-potentials, and significantly higher than regular full-time employees.

When Disney marketers work with Siemens engineers to market a hearing aid, or when Mitsubishi engineers work with Boeing engineers to craft an innovation in a commercial airliner, culture now spans both organizations. Engagement with the project may be more important than engagement with either organization alone. The mixing of two cultures from two different organizations may be far more pivotal than the culture of either organization. If you measure engagement and culture only among the workers from one organization, you may miss the most important factor in success.

If HR defines engagement only as applying to employees, then the ratings of Freelancers Union, the reputation among free agents on the platform, the attitudes of contract workers, and the passion of employees you borrow from other organizations simply don't factor into decisions. If HR defines engagement in terms of leading the work, those ratings become a vital element of organizational success and leader decisions.

Leadership

Leadership refers to setting a vision and values, inspiring followers, and communicating strategy and mission. When you lose the traditional basis of being "the employer" much of leadership changes. Leading without power, and through intermediaries will become more frequent. Are you the leader that the outsourcers' talent wants to work for? Are an organization's leaders respected enough that free-agent volunteers will go the extra mile? If your HR systems define leadership only as it applies to regular full-time employees, you may miss significant opportunities and challenges that are revealed when you realize that leadership means leading the work.

What does leading the work mean when there are no employees? Recall the story of Mark Harrison, the CEO of AH Global, whose entire workforce consists of free agents he engages remotely. Harrison crafted a leadership approach that kept his workers engaged and aligned. He formulated an approach to rewards that allowed him to "pay people in the currency they value." When the dials of the Lead the Work framework are turned all the way to the right, not only is leadership still vital, but it becomes even more nuanced.

What about leaders in more traditional organizations? Is iconic leadership important to a free-agent community? Consider the power of the names Bill and Melinda Gates or Robert Redford. At the 2015 Tongie awards ceremony for Tongal freelancers, some of the winning projects were completed for the Bill and Melinda Gates Foundation and were featured at the Sundance Film Festival. The Tongal producers that won the award were thrilled to have contributed to the mission and vision of their heroes like Bill and Melinda Gates and Robert Redford. It's certain that the leadership of clients factors into the work and engagement of talented free agents on the Tongal platform. As work shifts toward platforms, collaborations, and alliances, it may be as important for HR to build leaders that are well known and respected outside their organizations, as it is to build leaders that are well respected by the regular full-time employees inside the organization.

This means rethinking leadership in at least three ways:

1. "Leaders" may emerge from any spot in a much larger network than the traditional organization. The best leader of a project or technical team may be an experienced project manager at Tongal, Upwork, or the consulting firm that is working with you.
2. Leaders inside organizations must articulate a vision, create a culture, and generate passion and motivation among a workforce that spans the boundary. Leaders with strong public reputations (perhaps through ratings by those in other organizations that have worked with them) become even more valuable, when they may be the attraction points that get freelancers, consultants, or alliance members to collaborate.
3. Leadership development, as a special case of the talent life cycle, now must encompass sources, development opportunities, destinations, and depart-return possibilities that vastly expand the way you can create

leaders for the future. Leadership now may include creating a culture and vision that easily incorporates contraction and expansion. It means being adept at explaining the nontraditional outcomes that have been outlined above, generally getting organization members to see the logic and fairness of constant stretching and contraction, and the differentiation that must come with it to make it work.

Diversity and Inclusion

Diversity refers to an environment that is inclusive of differences, encourages disparate perspectives, and allows interactions among those with different demographic, lifestyle, professional, and cultural backgrounds. Diversity is typically conceived of as a sort of ratio, with the numerator being the number of different categories represented and the denominator being the total number of employees, such as the percentage of female employees among all employees, or the percentage of different age groups among all the employees on an innovation team. The numerator and denominator of the diversity equation are typically calculated based on traditional employees. In a world beyond employment, the workforce is more likely to include workers that may never interact with the organization's regular employees, or it may involve traditional employees working side-by-side with workers that have no employment relationship.

In either case, the very definition of diversity and its purpose must be reconsidered. Should organizations increase diversity by tapping nonemployment relationships with workers that are different from its regular employees? On the one hand, the emergence of global platforms that allow organizations to engage with workers worldwide might be seen as a boon to diversity and inclusion, because work will routinely be accomplished by workers with varied ethnic and regional backgrounds and who may bring vastly different perspectives to the work. On the other hand, should it "count" as diversity if an organization taps a platform for workers from many different countries or workers of many different ethnic or demographic characteristics? Technically, the work is being done by a very diverse group. Yet, if these different types of workers never interact, is the "workplace" actually more diverse?

It is no longer sufficient to define diversity merely as demographic variety, when the work can encompass global variety with the click of a mouse or a visit to the website of a talent platform. Diversity of interaction may best be accomplished by partnering with an organization whose employees are different from yours. Imagine the diversity of views that arose when Siemens engineers interacted with Disney marketers to create the marketing campaign for Siemens' children's hearing aid. IBM routinely sends teams of its young leaders to work in developing countries, in collaboration with local governments and nongovernmental organizations. It is called IBM's "Corporate Service Corps." Projects can involve helping communities create a system of Internet access, or analyze the spread of deadly diseases. Certainly these teams are often demographically diverse, but the real payoff is the diversity of experiences they receive through encounters with the local population.

For HR leaders and their constituents, a world beyond employment requires going beyond defining diversity demographically, and clarifying the strategic definition and purpose of diversity.

Performance

Leading the work obviously means defining worker performance well beyond the traditional performance ratings of only your regular full-time employees. Earlier sections have illustrated how talent platforms are redefining performance management for their free agents, in a way that allows worker performance to be immediately and publicly available. For HR leaders and their colleagues, that kind of performance assessment makes the traditional yearly performance appraisal interview seem archaic. Can it be long before regular full-time employees expect a performance system that is as transparent? Are you willing to rely on the performance assessments of talent platforms and providers, or should you separately assess the performance of those they provide? When you form alliances or collaborations with partners to borrow and lend workers, are you willing to rely on your partner's performance assessment process when you evaluate the workers you loaned them? Should you be conducting performance assessments for your partner's employees?

While these are complex questions, our earlier sections and chapters have provided examples and guidance about when you dial up and dial down the dimensions of performance assessment and rewards. There will always be a place for traditional performance assessment of regular full-time employees, but the emerging world beyond employment is increasingly unearthing new ways to measure and report performance that HR leaders must account for as they develop performance assessment systems.

So, let us turn to a significant broader social issue: whether the world beyond employment will be one of exploitation and winner-take-all performance or one where the vast majority of workers at the middle performance levels can find good work and equitable rewards. Is the world beyond employment destined to produce a labor force of a few winners that receive a disproportionate share of the spoils, while the great majority of workers are relegated to wishing for a world in which there were "good jobs" that guaranteed good rewards to workers, even if they were not among the elite or best?

A common premise among writers, such as Maynard Webb in *Reboot Work* and Lynda Gratton in *The Shift*, about the world beyond employment is that workers must prepare for a future in which only the fittest will survive and prosper. The idea is that organizations will want the best work possible and now can locate the workers that provide stellar results. Those workers will enjoy high earnings, lots of engagements, and increasing attention from organizations and individuals looking for that sort of work. Some foresee an attractive new world in which workers find or build their strengths, and once they build them they can enjoy a life where they can work only when and where they wish, on projects that are most engaging and for rewards that are tailored to them.[3] The reward for workers accepting the uncertainty that comes with being the CEO of Me is a level of flexibility, freedom, and influence over their work arrangements.

These same writers often note that such a world will no longer allow mediocre workers to hide within traditional employment systems that tolerated or overlooked mediocrity, or that rewarded tenure and loyalty beyond performance and contribution. This has prompted others to suggest that the world beyond employment will see performance and reward systems that commoditize work and workers, resulting in lower costs for those who receive the work, but also lower rewards and exploitive short-term engagements for the workers themselves. This has prompted some to call for laws requiring that nonemployed workers receive similar protections as traditional employees.

There may be a middle ground. In reality, not everyone requires the best performer and not every worker desires to be the best at everything they do. Even in traditional organizations, not every role requires the very best performer. It depends on the relationship between performance and value, which we discussed in Chapter 9 as "return on improved performance" (ROIP). For some roles the ROIP relationship is linear, in that every increment of better performance provides an equal increment of improved value. In such roles, workers that perform better add more value, but in roles where the slope of the line is very low, it may cost more to achieve higher performance than it is worth. In roles where the line is very steeply sloped, it is more likely that going for the best is optimal.

For other roles, the ROIP relationship is highly sloped or "pivotal" as performance goes from low to meeting standards, but then levels off. For example, in most organizations roles such as accounting and legal compliance do not require the very best accountants or attorneys in the labor market, because those organizations do not have accounting or legal outcomes as their product or service. Thus, having accounting and legal systems and outcomes that are at standard is optimal, and it does not pay to try to achieve anything beyond the necessary standard.

For still other roles, the ROIP relationship may be rather flat from low to moderate and then increase exponentially as performance goes from moderate to high. This is often the case in creative endeavors, such as R&D or entertainment, where the costs of mistakes is often not high, but the real payoff comes only with breakthrough performance. In these situations, it is more clearly optimum to engage workers that are truly the best available and at the top of the performance distribution. In such situations, it makes sense to reward such workers aggressively and handsomely.

Of all of these scenarios, only the last one suggests a winner-take-all world in which only the very best workers benefit handsomely and all others are relegated to low rewards and exploitive uncertainty. With many other ROIP relationships, there is ample room for workers that either choose or are not capable of becoming the best performers. In other words, a world beyond employment that more accurately and aggressively tracks performance and capability may have ample room for workers in the middle of the pack. Indeed, the advent of sophisticated platforms that match worker quality with work demands may make the life of the middle-performing worker better. Such systems would routinely and transparently create a match between the return on performance for those receiving the work, and the level of performance of those providing the work, even when that match happens at the middle of the performance distribution. Yes, moderate performers would receive fewer rewards than elite performers, but they might be no less in demand at the right price. For work where "at standard" is good enough, platforms would allow those that want to work at a middle level to find their niche. Indeed, for some types of work there may be more demand for such workers in the middle of the performance distribution than for those at the elite end.

As important as this is to leaders within organizations, it is perhaps an even greater call to action when it comes to the broader talent ecosystem. If the new world of work devolves into winner-take-all at one extreme and commoditization of labor at the other, it cannot be sustained. The HR profession is in a prime position to help shape the debate in a way that is more sustainable, and to help leaders in companies, governments and investor groups better understand both the risks and potential of a world beyond employment.

The New HR Professional: Leader, Architect, Engineer, and Orchestrator of a Boundaryless Global Workplace

Clearly, what we know today as the department of human resources will evolve significantly as the mandate evolves to lead the work in a world that includes employment, but extends well beyond employment. The new name for this profession has not yet emerged, but we believe it will encompass future capabilities resembling those of great leaders, architects, engineers, and orchestrators, who play on the stage of a boundaryless global workforce.

HR leadership will mean extending HR's current mandate by reaching beyond the functional and organizational boundary. It will be necessary for HR leaders to influence social values, legislation, and political debate in new ways. The HR profession can be the repository of evidence-based perspectives on thorny questions about how to maximize the benefits and minimize the costs of the new world beyond employment. Today, the debate is largely focused on jobs and employment. HR can shape a new discussion framed in terms of leading the work.

HR as architect means creating new frameworks to build upon. John Boudreau noted in *Retooling HR* that this new architecture will often take the form of retooled mental models that leaders, workers, investors, legislators, and other constituents use to understand the work and workplace.[4] Today, inadequate mental models about HR are often widely shared (e.g., turnover is always bad and should be reduced, performance follows a normal curve, and all human capital risk should be reduced). Perhaps the most pervasive traditional mental model is that employment is how work gets done. Where might these new mental models for talent and human capital come from? As the previous section described, there is evidence that leading HR organizations may develop such models by retooling HR and talent questions with the models that leaders already understand and trust. As we have seen, a mental model of employee turnover can be retooled to a model of sequential engagement over the course of a career. The mental model of the employment deal can be retooled to a model of differentiated rewards that draw on principles of consumer product optimization and customization.

HR as engineer must become facile with social networks enabled by technology, big data, and analytics. It will mean creating sense from the avalanche of data in boundaryless information systems. It will mean interconnecting data sources as diverse as internal HR information systems; external social platforms like LinkedIn and Facebook; organization systems such as operations, marketing and finance; and decades of scientific research that is retrieved in milliseconds. It will mean harnessing technologies as diverse as virtual meeting spaces, personal access points, artificial intelligence, and games.

Ian Ziskin, a former chief HR officer, suggests that future HR leaders will be more like orchestra conductors.[5] The conductor need not be proficient on every instrument but must locate and assemble single-instrument virtuosos into an ensemble. This is how to accelerate HR leadership in a world that requires rapid adaptation through multiple disciplines. The future HR leader will often not be the expert but will be adept at locating and assembling the capability to address complex and fast-changing strategic human capital issues. HR leaders and the HR profession must become comfortable with a permeable professional boundary—a professional boundary that welcomes expertise from other disciplines. Traditional HR disciplines such as industrial and organizational psychology and labor economics are valuable, but HR organizations must reach out beyond these traditional areas. Google employs analysts in its People Analytics organization with disciplinary backgrounds including operations, politics, and marketing. Human capital planning and strategy is increasingly supported by those with deep training in competitive strategy and scenario planning, whether they exist within the HR function or in a separate strategy group.

At its heart, HR will remain a profession with a soul.[6] Issues such as sustainable employment and balancing personalization and consistency are deeply humanistic. They require the art of HR, to be sure. Yet, they will not be accomplished by an HR profession that functions like a mysterious wizard, who can work magic with talent that no one else can understand. Future HR leaders must codify and share their frameworks so that those outside the profession can usefully engage. The future needs the HR profession (whatever it will be called), so HR professionals and their constituents must create a necessary step-change to meet the challenges. If progress remains slow and complacent, HR's reach may soon so exceed its grasp that it can't catch up. If HR progress accelerates through rigor, humanism, and collaboration, the HR profession will rightfully maintain and extend its stature into a world beyond employment.

Notes

1. Rocio Bonet, Peter Cappelli, and Monica Hamori, "Labor Market Intermediaries and the New Paradigm for Human Resources." *Academy of Management Annals,* 7, no. 1 (2013): 341–392.
2. Rena Rasch, *Your Best Workers May Not Be Your Employees* (Somers, NY: IBM Corporation, 2014). https://www14.software.ibm.com/webapp/iwm/web/signup.do?source=swg-US_Lotus_WebMerch&S_PKG=ov28393.
3. Maynard Webb, *Rebooting Work* (San Francisco, CA: Jossey-Bass, 2013).
4. John W. Boudreau, *Retooling HR: Using Proven Business Tools to Make Better Decisions about Talent* (Boston, Mass.: Harvard Business Press, 2010).
5. Ian Ziskin, "HR as Orchestra Conductor," chapter to appear in the HRCI eBook, *The Future of HR.*
6. Boudreau, "Will HR's Grasp Match Its Reach?"

12

Governance and Stakeholders

The advent of these myriad choices for getting work done raises some confounding questions for companies. How do our existing governance protocols apply and, perhaps more fundamentally, who is responsible for work? HR has traditionally focused on employees, while business leaders look at joint ventures and alliances, and procurement might focus on vendors and contractors. If we believe that winning organizations will seamlessly traverse these options as opportunities arise and market conditions change, then the decision rules we have previously touched on need a governance framework; one that ensures coherence and consistency, and reflects the shifting realities facing each stakeholder and their role.

Let's define six key governance principles organizations will need to consider in a world beyond employment:

1. Ownership and protection of intellectual property
2. Knowledge management and capability development/preservation
3. Work quality control
4. Risk management, including liability and indemnification
5. Time horizon
6. Logistics and control systems—talent movement, payment, taxes, and so forth

Current and Likely Future States for Governance Principles

Governance Principle	Typical Current State	Likely Future State
Ownership and protection of intellectual property	Confidentiality agreements, contracts, patents, restrictive covenants in employment agreements	Shared ownership of intellectual property (IP), open-sourced development as more companies begin to recognize that the competitive advantage is increasingly in the ability to execute versus being in the IP itself. Continued use of contracts to govern the rights of various parties.
Knowledge management and capability development/ preservation	Training of employees, closed-loop knowledge management systems to preserve capability within the organization	Crowd sourced innovation, shared/cloud-based knowledge management systems to encourage others to use and contribute to the overall knowledge pool (e.g., Wikipedia). Enhanced knowledge management and collaboration tools to manage work and the flow of information from free agents, contractors, outsourcers, and so forth.
Work quality control	Mix of input- and output-based performance management and professional excellence standards for employees with compensation tied to proficiency; service-level agreements (SLA) and contracts that specify a mix of inputs and outputs for all others, with remuneration tied to SLA/contract fulfillment	Typically output based. As work moves more freely across various delivery solutions, organizations will increasingly focus on creating a common standard for assessing quality with the cost (compensation, fees, etc.) associated with delivery increasingly tied directly to output.

Governance Principle	Typical Current State	Likely Future State
Risk management, including liability and indemnification (e.g., what happens if a free agent causes property damage while executing a project for the company? Does the company bear any of the liability?)	Codes of conduct, errors and omission (E&O) insurance policies for employees, standardized contracts with limits of liability for all others	Expanded use of insurance products to govern the risk associated with potential liabilities in multiple types of relationships (i.e., ensuring the organization has no increased exposure whether the liability was incurred by an employee or a free agent)
Time horizon	A mix based on the specific nature of the relationship (long-term for employees versus short-term for contractors versus rolling, renewable agreements for outsourcers)	A mix based on the nature of work (e.g., long-term relationships with free agents for strategic projects versus short-term relationships with employees for execution of core capabilities)
Logistics and control systems—talent movement, payment, taxes, and so forth	Highly structured control systems to ensure consistent, efficient execution for employees; all other entities left to their own devices and have separate, less-evolved systems with fragmented governance	More integrated control systems to bring the same level of oversight to multiple types of relationships (e.g., vendor management systems). For example, Upwork offers corporations a freelance management system (FMS) with tools/modules and reporting functionalities that provide a great deal of visibility, analytics, and insight into an organization's scope and spend.

As can be seen from the "current and future state" box, these governance principles have always been considerations in how we manage employees and their work, but the number of variables and the permutations grow significantly when you contemplate a world beyond employment. Let's examine them and some potential scenarios.

What about protecting our IP? Companies go to great lengths to protect what they believe to be their proprietary knowledge and capabilities. How do we stop people from stealing our talent? What does that even mean? Could a competitor just follow our use of talent platforms like Topcoder and get the same people to replicate what they did for us, but cheaper and better since it is the second time around? What information do we have to keep hidden from nonemployees? Does it even make sense to think of it that way? How do we stop information we shared from being stolen? For example, if one of our free agents in Egypt working on a brochure design comes to understand some secrets of our business model, how do we stop her from setting up the same business? If we invest in innovation and most of the knowledge sits in free agents' heads, we may have spent a fortune getting them to solve our problem, but now that they have, how do we prevent them from selling their knowledge to competitors? The answers may well come from how open-sourced technology is developed and managed where the focus is on shared ownership versus individual rights.

Scenario: You find that the free agent you hired to build your sophisticated website is reusing the code for other clients of his.

Preventative action: As part of due diligence, identify any areas of sensitivity around IP (exploitation of yours versus use of someone else's) and have a discussion with the free agent on those issues. Don't rely only on a standard nondisclosure agreement; you need to be able to give the free agent concrete examples of what they must and must not do.

What about knowledge management? When all your work is done within the bounds of the organization by employees, the biggest challenge is formalizing knowledge management and transfer. This becomes immensely more challenging in a world beyond employment

Scenario: Over the years more and more of the engineering work on your company's specialized marine pumps have been done by free agents. With the retirement of two internal engineers, it becomes clear that their specialized knowledge was essential to organizing and directing the work of the free agents. Almost all of the work had been done outside the walls of the organization, but what was done inside was crucial. Not only is it proving impossible to hire people with deep intelligence about marine pumps; you don't even know who the free agents who worked on your pump design were. They were all hired via a talent platform that has since gone bankrupt. Critical knowledge about your line of marine pumps has been irretrievably lost.

Preventative action: Knowledge management must be a disciplined process since one can no longer count on the natural diffusion of knowledge from senior engineers to juniors that occurs when long-term employees are housed in the same office and work together. Furthermore, knowledge management must treat free agents the same way it treats employees, some of them are the holders of business critical knowledge, the knowledge management function needs to know which workers have critical knowledge and take the necessary steps to document, catalog, and appropriately disseminate it.

Now let's take a look at work quality control. Organizations typically focus on measuring and rewarding both inputs (like values, behavior, culture, etc.) and outputs (financial outcomes, operational performance, etc.). While it may be easy to specify the exact output you expect from a developer on Topcoder, it becomes quite challenging to ensure consistency of management decision making.

Scenario: A freak flood wipes out your alliance's production facilities in a remote part of China. Since there was no history of floods in the area, the factory was not insured against this calamity. The head of the alliance, who incidentally is an employee of the partner company, immediately borrows $50 million from a Chinese government development agency to get the factory back online. Your company, which is facing hard times, had been planning on phasing out of the alliance and now faces half of a bill it can't afford.

Preventative action: Attempting to set down every contingency in a contract can strangle an alliance, especially in a fast-moving industry. How do you ensure consistent output/behavior from a distance? Furthermore, assume in the case above that your company is a family firm that has a strong tradition of giving a great deal of decision authority to managers in overseas locations. That tradition worked when managers were long-term employees with strong internal networks that ensured they would make the same decisions the owners would have made in their place (i.e., the output was ensured because of the consistency of the input). The tradition fails when the manager is the "disconnected" leader of an alliance. The company needs to hire an experienced alliance manager who can ensure appropriate governance; communication and decision rights are established when the alliance is formed—alliance management is not a job for amateurs.

Let's examine risk. As noted, we have strong protocols for managing the risk associated with getting work done by employees. But what happens when more of the work is being done by free agents and the distinction between employees is fuzzy in the eyes of consumers and regulators? Where might we fall afoul of employment law? To what extent are we subject to the employment laws of other countries when work is dispersed there? What if we don't even know who is doing the work? What happens if a free agent incurs a liability that they are not able to absorb? Does the company now become liable? Let's examine how a company should respond to this very real—and highly plausible—situation.

Scenario: You hire a free-agent filmmaker via a talent platform for a corporate video on safe driving, and one of the free-agent actors working for the filmmaker accidentally runs over four people during the filming. The injured people try to sue the filmmaker, but he is only 18 years old, so that lawsuit is going nowhere. The lawyers turn on you, and social media plays this up as a corporation exploiting a teenager.

Preventive action: Don't plan to hide behind some legality that the kid is responsible, and the corporation is not. Don't assume the free agent (or the talent platform you used to find him) have sufficient or appropriate insurance. As part of due diligence in working with the platform, make sure all their free agents have sufficient insurance in place, or ensure that your insurance covers both your employees and your free agents.

What about time horizon? The traditional mind-set that work was done by employees and all employees are here for a long time allowed unions to flourish and grow to protect the interests of employees. With the time horizon increasingly being driven by the nature of work rather than the employment relationship, how might this affect traditional employee-based constructs like unions?

Scenario: You are head of a lathe operators union, and you are seeing membership collapse as robotic lathes, which can be controlled remotely, replace the older technology, which required at least one operator per lathe on site. More than half the work done by employees has been shifted to free agents—many of whom used to be members of your union. You hear through the grapevine that these free agents are being treated badly, being denied future work if they take time off sick and of course there is no maternity leave or provision for a pension. Your union is dying and the free agent lathe operators are suffering from a loss of bargaining power.

Preventative action: Think about organizing the free agents differently, inventing new forms of union membership that are not predicated on tenure or employment. Look for lessons from groups like the Screenwriter's Guild. Invent new services, such as a pension fund, that is not predicated on it being provided by an employer.

What about logistics and control systems? For employees, the company typically handles all the direct and ancillary logistics of the deal (taxes, movement of talent to where the work is, or vice versa). Other providers, however, are strictly on their own. Contractors pay their own taxes, procure health care and pension benefits on their own, and must manage the cost of getting to the work. In the future state, the contrasts between the management of such logistics will likely not be quite as stark. Consider the previously referenced Freelance Management Systems (see Chapter 4). As Staffing Industry Analysts frames it, "Unlike online staffing platforms, which facilitate direct one-to-one or 'one-off' engagements between an individual buyer and an individual worker, FMS facilitates an enterprise-wide engagement and deployment model. This arrangement still allows for direct engagements between companies and workers, but the key difference is that the rules and processes of the FMS platform will be uniformly enforced across an organization. In other words, with online staffing platforms, each engagement is a one-off experience; with an FMS, although the engagement is still 'direct,' it is managed under the enterprise's rules and system of control."[1]

Scenario: A class-action suit in a South American country rules that any free agent who has received at least one payment from your firm for five consecutive years is an employee with the right to certain benefits. Some of your managers (you are not even sure which ones) had used a talent platform to get perhaps tens of thousands of microtasks (you don't have any clear idea on the number) done by workers in that country. While you don't have any idea how many of these microtasking free agents might be deemed employees, you know the total cost could be stomach churning.

Preventative action: All payments to workers, whether to employees, free agents or free agents via a talent platform, should be managed on a single system, handled by a single department (HR, procurement, or finance) in the company. The company needs to treat its relationships with free agents with the same discipline it treats its relationships with employees. In cases where there are legal uncertainties the company may wish to seek out insurance.

The sidebar "Governance in Action: Making Collaboration Work" illustrates these principles in action.

Governance in Action: Making Collaboration Work

If you believe our arguments about the permeable, interlinked, and collaborative organization then complex, intermediated arrangements between organization and worker will become more common and perhaps even the norm. What are the considerations required to govern relationships where collaboration leads to sharing or loaning employees? Let's illustrate how a general set of decision rules might help bring appropriate governance to this situation.

- **Ownership and protection of IP:** A key pain point is the risk of loss of confidentiality. This can be mitigated as follows:
  - Signing nondisclosure agreements (as is currently done with independent contractors).
  - Sharing employees should only be possible between different sectors and not between direct competitors.
- **Knowledge management and capability development/ preservation** $\left(\frac{1}{2}\right)$**:** To mitigate the potential poaching of employees by participating companies
  - Employees should sign a contract stipulating that after the agreed time frame, the employee stays with the supplying organization for a certain amount of time.
  - When companies hire an exchanged employee during the exchange period or shortly thereafter, a predetermined transfer fee (e.g., two times the annual salary) should be paid to the current employer depending on the level of the employee. This would protect the interests of a company contributing talent to such an exchange and recognize its investment in the acquisition and development of that employee.
- **Knowledge management and capability development/ preservation** $\left(\frac{2}{2}\right)$**:** For knowledge-transfer assurance, knowledge sharing is tied to the length of the exchange. The longer the exchange, the more impact the exchange can have.
  - Introducing job shadowing, with the exchanged employee functioning as a mentor to other in-house employees. This would help ensure that the skills and experiences of the exchanged employee can be transferred to the employees of the "borrowing company." Involve the exchanged employee in recruitment efforts, so she can help assess the talent being acquired and ensure that the right skills are being brought in.
  - Involve the exchanged employee in learning and development decisions, thus helping to ensure that in-house employees have a learning curriculum and training opportunities that are relevant to cultivating the skills of the exchanged employee.
  - Create a transition phase in which the exchanged employee reviews and supervises while in-house resources do the

actual execution. This provides in-house employees with the opportunity to "practice" in a safe environment.

- **Work quality:** Given the nature of these relationships, quality is typically assessed based on achievement of predefined objectives. For example, a short-term project may involve the development of a specific capability for the receiving company (e.g., a project related to developing an app). For a longer-term exchange, the work may relate to the building of a specific capability for the receiving company (e.g., creation of a risk-management function). In all cases, the quality is more easily defined (and judged) by the outcome.

- **Risk management:** The talent broker who helps manage the movement of talent between collaborative companies needs to ensure a clear match between the organizational culture of the companies, the participating organizations, and the employees being exchanged.

- **Time horizon:** Exchanges typically last between six months and three years. The amount of time is correlated with the impact of the transfer on the organization and employee (Figure 12.1).

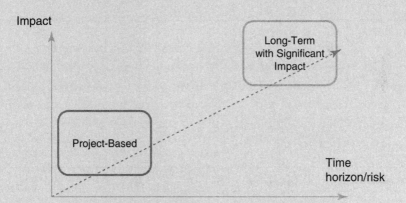

Figure 12.1 Longer Exchanges Have Greater Impact

- Six months would be project-based assignments with the potential impact being fairly limited beyond exposing an employee to a new business model, culture, and so forth, and for the organization to inject some fresh thinking into its operating practices.

- Longer-term exchanges will have a more strategic impact on both the organization and the individual. For example, development of specific skills in leaders, acquisition of new, pivotal skills for an organization, and so forth.

- As with all exchanges, the longer the term, the greater and more diverse the risks.
- **Logistical challenges:** These include issues related to cross-border transfers, taxes, payroll, and so forth.
  - Employees stay employed by their current organization, keeping an identical pay package. The organization to which the employee is exchanged should pay a predetermined fee to the supplying organization.
  - There is an actual transfer from one organization to the other with a clear stipulation that the assignment ends after a predetermined time. The remuneration and support of the individual will therefore be the responsibility of the organization that receives the talent for the determined time frame.
  - The broker functions as an intermediary and is responsible for the talent that is put in the talent pool and exchanged. The talent pool is constantly refreshed, and companies can withdraw talent when needed and when not loaned out to other organizations.

As can be seen, the governance considerations become increasingly complex as we look at a future for work that lies beyond employment. Governance involves stakeholders; and, as we see in the car-sharing industry, it can get quite messy, but the role of each can be assessed and defined (see sidebar). How will the role of each stakeholder evolve? Will they all continue to be relevant?

Stakeholder	Typical Current Role	Likely Future Role
Owner/ shareholders	Provide financial capital, and value the return on such capital based on the traditional model of the firm (i.e., a self-contained entity with the vast majority of revenues, costs, liabilities, and capital captured on traditional financial statements)	Provide multiple forms of capital (financial, social, intellectual, etc.) while measuring the return through alternative measures (e.g., the strength of the leadership team's social networks, the flexibility of the organization to utilize multiple platforms for getting work done, etc.)

Stakeholder	Typical Current Role	Likely Future Role
Leaders/ Managers	Define the work, ensure sufficient supply/skills of employees to do the work, manage alliances and partners, ensure engagement of employees and execution of work at the desired cost to produce the targeted revenue at an acceptable level of risk	Continuously (re)define the work and build the capability to assess the very essence of the operating model and seamlessly deploy work where it can be most optimally performed at a particular point in time
HR	Hire, develop, engage, reward, and retain employees	Will HR evolve its remit to manage how work gets done versus enabling the management of employees?
Procurement	Manage contractors and vendors	Will procurement extend its current tools and framework to encompass the management of employees?
Workers	Perform the defined work in exchange for current and future rewards, including the skills needed to be relevant as an employee	Multiple forms of relationships with companies over the course of a career, with increased accountability and ownership for "future-oriented" reward elements (e.g., pension, retiree medical benefits, skill acquisition)
Unions	Protect the interests of workers through bargained work rules and rewards that are provided by the company	Leverage scale to provide services (e.g., advocacy, bulk buying of benefits, etc.) to providers (employee, free agents, etc.) of a particular craft (see the future of unions sidebar)
Customers	Purchase bundled services with limited opportunities to disaggregate them	Access to an infinite number of options for any particular service (see the car-sharing sidebar)
Governments	Focus on provision of benefits and protecting the interests of employees	Provision of safety nets for all citizens regardless of work relationship

(continued)

Stakeholder	Typical Current Role	Likely Future Role
Brokers/Talent Platforms	Focus on organizing free agents to provide services to companies	Integral partners to enable corporations to continually access the resources to get work done: free agents, third parties, employees at noncompetitive companies (e.g., collaborative production), current and future employees

You might well wonder how we could be so apparently definitive about the possible future states for so many stakeholders, yet rather less so about the two that we know so well: human resources and procurement. The reason is the potential interdependency between the two in a future beyond employment. We see clear roles, and some early signs of adaptation, by owners, leaders, workers, unions, customers, and governments to the future state. Yet, with some exceptions, we do not see much change on the part of HR and procurement. Given their deep legacies in helping organizations ensure compliance and mitigate risk in specific domains, how will HR and procurement change? As companies build the capability to seamlessly traverse these various options for getting work done, who will be responsible for analyzing, understanding, and managing the movement of work from one platform to another? HR? Procurement? Or some other function?

A Perspective on the Future of Unions

The role of unions in society is a deeply political issue, and we are going to sidestep the power politics and hopefully the emotions that surround them. We like to think of unions as key stakeholder organizations that provide a set of services to workers. With unions, the noun "organization" clearly follows from the verb "organize." Unions organize otherwise disconnected workers. Thus, a union might be called a guild or an association.

Probably the single most important service of the U.S. Freelancers Union is to provide health insurance. This is a service that otherwise unorganized freelancers need. However, it is some distance from the traditional role of unions in negotiating pay, work rules, and work conditions.

Management's biggest complaint about unions has long been their view of what a job is. To a union, a job is a sharply defined construct that is to be done by a specified person and no one else. One manager told us the story of a machinist whose lathe stopped because the electrical connection, sitting in the floor beneath the machine, had come loose. He stooped down to correct it, only to be swiftly stopped by a union colleague. "Hey, that's electrical work," he said. "You can't do that." Once an electrician had been found, the issue arose as to whether he was allowed to disassemble the appropriate part of the wooden floor, as that was carpentry work. The whole area came to a halt as everyone stopped to see how management and the union steward would resolve this fascinating problem. The story sounds apocryphal, but it's a real one; and no doubt some readers experienced with unions are thinking, "I can top that story!"

What happens to unions as our sense of what a job is dissolves under the potent solvent that is the Internet? They need to focus not on jobs within a tightly defined skill set, but on the needs of the workers within a more broadly defined craft, and in the future the workers most in need of this support will be free agents. Free agents will need help knowing what to charge, to avoid being exploited by bad talent platforms or bad employers, to manage their finances, retirement, and wellness, and insure against risks. Unions won't be the only organizations attempting to address this need. Profit-making businesses will sell their services to free agents.

Will unions be able to negotiate higher wages in a world of deconstruction and dispersion? It will be harder, but already groups like the Writers Union attempt to do so by setting out guidelines on what to charge. Interestingly, the unit of measurement they use gets right down to the microtask level: they suggest charging by the word. These are guidelines, not rules, and encouraged, not enforced. That does not mean they are not helpful. But this discussion about the challenges facing private sector unions pales in comparison to the broader issues facing society when you consider the implications for public sector unions. Consider these statistics from the Bureau of Labor Statistics on the percentage of workers belonging to unions:[2]

- in the United States 11.1 percent
- in the private sector 6.6 percent
- in the public sector 35.7 percent
- in local government 41.9 percent

One doesn't have to look beyond the average daily newspaper in the United States to realize that cities like Chicago and states like Illinois are on the cusp of bankruptcy in part due to the unfunded liabilities associated with pension and health care obligations for unionized public sector employees. So as private sector companies evolve toward flexible work arrangements, unions can expect the decline in their membership to further accelerate unless they fundamentally alter their basic philosophies. The 6X contrast between union representation of public sector employees versus private sector workers will become increasingly visible to voters as the disparity in the "cost of work" increases between these two sectors. How should unions respond as the 84 million millenials in the United States who are now eligible to vote start to question the rationale for the public sector "deal"?

Free agents need protection from precariousness. Unions often lean toward forcing everyone back to the old world where people have full-time permanent jobs working for a single employer established in a single country. As long as they take that tact they are fighting the tides of change.

Some Closing Thoughts on Governance and Stakeholders

Current talent governance frameworks such as legislation, regulation, and professional excellence standards will likely need to change to encompass the tide of new work relationships. Most employment legislation and regulation relies heavily on the assumption of employment as the main engagement method and the primary means of delivering value in the economy (compensation, health care, retirement, etc.), and even goes to great lengths to rigidly categorize such things as full-time employment, contracting, temporary-labor suppliers, and so forth. Increasingly, regulations that rely on the notion of an identifiable organizational boundary and employment transactions may need to morph to include protections and regulations for those who are not employed by any single organization, or even those who contribute ideas without getting paid. It is obvious to the casual observer that the vast majority of labor protections are afforded to the employed, with less consideration for alternative ways of contributing to the overall economy.

For the United States, the introduction of the Affordable Care Act of 2010 represents one of the more significant steps forward as it relates to the decoupling of rewards from employment. By enabling talent who are not employees to access the health-care benefits traditionally associated with employment, a significant barrier to the growth of alternative platforms has been eliminated. It's worth asking the question of what rewards should be governed and legislated versus left to the market. Categorizing these rewards into direct versus indirect rewards may be useful in this regard. Direct rewards associated with work would include salaries, bonuses, long-term incentives, recognition, reputation, and development opportunities. Indirect rewards include health care, retirement, and other family benefits. Should regulation cover both categories of rewards? Are there minimum protections that should be afforded to any one category (e.g., minimum wage)? How will such protections recognize the trade-offs that individuals might be willing to make across the various categories (e.g., trading of short-term compensation for reputation scores on a talent platform that might ultimately result in higher compensation in the future)? Since the dawn of the first industrial age, unions have played an important role in protecting the interests of labor, but do they have a future in the information age?

When it comes to ensuring the quality of work, most organization's professional excellence standards presume that the work of the organization will be done by either an employee or contractor. There is little discussion of how the work of other entities will be assessed, managed and governed, as these are typically managed through service-level agreements and contracts. What white space and inconsistencies might exist between these different governance frameworks? Are there opportunities to structure these as part of a single continuum of standards that govern the risks, capabilities, and costs associated with every different type of relationship? When the "how" matters, not just the "what," then that makes the relationship with a contractor more difficult to manage. Yet, many an employer will tell you that she sometimes feels she has more control over a contractor than an employee. A quick scan of any "professional excellence" manual will reveal an intense focus on how work is done, and say very little about the output of work. Often this is left to the performance management process (for employees and contractors), or service-level agreements for all other third parties. Interestingly, many organizations struggle with the philosophy of paying for individual output instead of time, as evidenced by recent research from Towers Watson that indicates a weakening linkage between pay and individual performance.

A final consideration related to governance involves the investment markets (i.e., the enablement of ownership). Given the significant percentage of a company's market value that is accounted for by intangibles, and the value of its human/knowledge capital, there will likely need to be a radical rethink of how we evaluate and measure "employment"-related relationships, and the cost of work. The current categorization of costs does not allow for consistent analysis and visibility into the total cost of work. The P&L structure provides inconsistent detail of the cost of employment (pay, benefits, etc.) and virtually no detail on the other categories of work (usage of talent platforms, offshorers, etc.). As the diversity of means with which work gets done increases, financial analysts will have progressively less insight into the true cost of work.

What about the forward-looking valuation of the company? If future leadership is as likely to come from outside the organization as inside, and depends more upon the web of social connections outside the organization than the formal hierarchy or candidate slates within, then should the value of organizations depend in part on the social presence of organization leadership and key influencers? How will investors and boards assess "key man risk" (i.e., the risk that a significant percentage of an organization's success is due to the contributions of one individual? Think Steve Jobs and Apple in the early days)? Does the number of Twitter followers for the CEO or leadership team matter more than the number of employees, or the slate of in-company successors? As exchanges have removed the friction associated with the movement and utilization of financial capital, so too can they reduce the friction associated with the movement of human capital. Talent exchanges can allow different entities to collaborate in pursuit of mutually beneficial outcomes. Just as financial exchanges require a "market maker," so too do the human capital exchanges. Consider the example of collaborative production, as presented in Chapter 8. For talent to move seamlessly from one entity to another with minimal disruption to work and the shortest possible time to productivity requires an intermediary who can source the right talent, slot them into the right job at the right career level, ensure that pay and benefits are appropriate, and handle all the external requirements of work permits, taxes, and the like. In such networked architectures, the role of "brokers" to reduce the friction associated with such interorganizational movement will be critical to governance. Will analysts have insight into such relationships, and, perhaps even more challenging, how will such complexities be factored into company valuations?

Car Sharing

What are we to make of this proliferation of ways to get around? The techno–utopians speak of these developments in breathless terms of freedom and efficiency. Pessimists point to problems with safety and workers being thrown into the Internet of serfdom. Both have a point. Car sharing in all its forms offers great efficiencies. However, the lack of regulatory control is a concern. Uber drivers have staged protests against the company, and some governments have temporarily halted the service as they figure out the obligations of the company to its various stakeholders (drivers, customers, competition, etc.). Outside this debate, managers tend to shake their heads in wonder at all the things "they" are inventing, then go back to business as usual.

For managers, the important thing is to recognize that this confusing array of new services fits into a relatively tidy framework, a framework that will ultimately help in their own decision making. The stakeholder arrangements are particularly interesting. For car sharing, the two main factors are how the work gets done and who owns the asset.

Let's try to understand asset ownership by mapping the options. The shaded rows are "old world," the unshaded ones "new world."

	Who Owns the Car	Who Does the Work of Organizing	Who Drives	Who Is Driven
Taxis	Corporation	Employees (corporation?)	Employee/ Contractor	Consumer
Rental	Corporation	Employees (corporation?)	Consumer	Consumer
Private ownership	Consumer	Consumer	Consumer	Consumer
Uber X	Free agent	App	Free agent	Consumer
Zipcars	Corporation	App	Consumer	Consumer
Getaround	Free agent	App	Consumer	Consumer
Self-driving cars	Corporation	App	Technology	Consumer

In the old world, private ownership is the special case where the consumer does it all, with the inefficiency being that 90 percent of the time, the asset (the car) sits unused. In the old world, cases of taxis and rental corporations and their employees sit at the center of the action, with the inefficiency being the unavoidable overhead of a corporation and labor costs.

What makes the new world possible is apps that do much of the organizing, allowing free agents or corporations to leverage their assets with fewer employees.

Looking at the 3D framework, the work is usually deconstructed in the same way: there is the overall organization of the service, and there is the driving. How it is distributed (is the driving part done by an employee, free agent, or consumer?) is a major strategic decision. How it is detached is a battle between corporations using employees and apps, and it looks likely the apps will win.

Now, to step back to our mea culpa that we've oversimplified. Of course, Uber is a corporation and has some employees, and, yes, taxi drivers are often not exactly employees, but their relationship with the corporation is close enough to employment for our purposes. So while there is simplification, it does not undermine the value of the framework.

The first takeaway for managers is that the world of car sharing is not some magic place where anything goes. There are a few dimensions, in particular where the work is done and who owns the asset, and strategy is largely about finding the right place on those dimensions.

The second takeaway is that these principles are general enough to apply to almost any business. Very often, if it is possible to deconstruct work and disperse it to free agents and consumers, then that's the most efficient way to get it done. That's why we were drawn to and toyed with the title "End of Employment" for this book—because so often, getting rid of a good deal of employment is the best strategic option. With assets, as well in the case of automobiles, where there is a huge base of woefully underutilized assets already out there, not owning the asset seems to make sense. That doesn't mean Zipcar and its ilk won't succeed in the long run. Perhaps as the alternatives to car ownership expand, the number of owners willing to participate in Uber and Getaround may fall to the point that it undermines that strategic choice around asset ownership.

The third take-away for managers, and for governments, is that governance of the whole ecosystem matters and is hard to do. In a column on TaskRabbit, Josh Bersin of Bersin by Deloitte revels in the fact that not only did TaskRabbit allow him to cheaply and easily get a free agent to do a hunk of work, that free agent was "vetted by TaskRabbit." Yeah, well, maybe. It's unlikely that anyone from TaskRabbit met this person, or even spoke to them on the phone. They may have some papers saying this person is not a criminal or lives at a certain address, but the vetting is only as good as that piece of paper. And just as people may need some protection from dishonest TaskRabbits, so too the TaskRabbits will need protection from exploitation by the whole system.

Consider the recent challenges being faced by Uber in a number of countries. Uber is increasingly under scrutiny for potentially violating rules about contractors and employees. Might other organizations employing free agents face similar challenges? Yes, it is quite likely. Uber is also under scrutiny for its obligation to protect its customers against the risk of driver misdeeds. Are you liable for the behavior and/or negligence of your free agents or intermediaries? Yes, your stakeholders (customer, governments, etc.) may well hold you liable. These problems are by no means unsolvable; but it will take time and effort from companies, the government, and civil society to sort it out.

Notes

1. Tony Gregoire, "The rise of freelancer management systems," Staffing Industry Analysts, published November 15, 2014, http://www.staffing industry.com/Research-Publications/Publications/IT-Staffing-Report/Nov. -6-2014/The-rise-of-freelancer-management-systems (accessed April 8, 2015).
2. U.S. Department of Labor, Bureau of Labor Statistics press release, posted January 23, 2015, http://www.bls.gov/news.release/union2.nr0.htm (accessed April 20, 2015).

13

Nations, Citizens, and Children

In this book, we have tied together a number of innovations in the world of work to show that they fit together as part of a more systemic and broader trend. This trend already has significant traction; we're describing the world as it currently is through a new lens, not imagining some future world. However, we also feel that this trend toward 3D (deconstructed, dispersed, and detached) work, PICF (permeable, interlinked, collaborative, and flexible) organizations, and new rewards (shortened, individualized, and imaginative) can go much further. Recent business history is full of examples of concepts that started as interesting innovations—moving some manufacturing to China, selling a few books online, streaming some songs to a PC—and then went on to overturn entire industries. Employment is still the norm in most economies, but that may not be the case in the future.

One cannot talk about the world beyond employment without people wondering what it will mean for them, their children, and the nation. We won't pretend to be experts in predicting the future; however, we couldn't end this book without touching on the debate about how these forces will affect society.

The overarching questions about the world beyond employment are

- Will it exploit workers or empower them?
- Is it really good for organizations, or is that an illusion?
- Is it economically efficient so that, overall, it creates wealth?
- Is it good for some countries but bad for others?

From there we need to ask what individuals and governments should do:

- How should we as individuals respond to a world beyond employment?
- How can our children prepare for a world beyond employment?
- What should governments do to best serve their citizens?

The Bright Side of a World Beyond Employment

If you talk to a typical engineer in Silicon Valley, he will tell you how the innovations around a world beyond employment could lead to a host of positive outcomes for all stakeholders. If we put on our optimist's hat, we can envision a scenario where individuals, organizations, economists, and nations are all happy about the changes discussed in this book.

Why Workers Will Be Happy

Individual workers can see lots of upside in this new world. Workers may find that to a far greater extent than in the past they will get to work on what they want, when they want, and where they want. This freedom could lead to a far higher quality of life. Some workers who were shut out of the employment market because they live in the wrong country or are unable to leave the home for long periods may find the world beyond employment to be a lifesaver. And rewards could be far more aligned to the unique needs of individual workers versus the homogenous, often inflexible, rewards typically received by employees.

Why Organizations Will Be Happy

For organizations, the beyond employment world looks delicious. The organization gets to access all the talent they need at the right price and only for the period of time they need. Organizations should be able to focus on what they truly do best and move the rest outside the organizational boundary.

Why Economists Will Be Happy

For economists, the beyond employment world looks efficient. While they will have some areas of concern, such as the amount of labor poured into a particular competition and the potential knock-on consequences for the rest of the economy, they will likely see the new world as a place where talent and work are matched far more efficiently than in the past.

Why Nations Will Be Happy

If workers, organizations, and economists are happy, then nations should be happy too. It is true that developing countries have more to gain from dispersed work than wealthy countries, but it is hard to argue that helping close the income gap between the old world and the developing one is really a bad thing.

In this scenario, the world beyond employment is the best thing ever.

The Dark Side of a World Beyond Employment

If you talk to a single parent with a mortgage in Madrid, she is unlikely to be thrilled by the news that employment may be dissolving. If we put on our pessimist's hat, we fear the world beyond employment will harm many people and benefit just a few.

Why Workers Will Be Concerned

The average MTurk task pays less than $2 per hour, which adds up to less than $4,000 per year for full-time work.[1] If that's the future of employment, then workers have a right to be worried. There is widespread concern that moving work outside employment is simply a means for escaping laws on minimum wage, liability, safety, and security.

The issue of income security is one that bedevils even successful free agents. A free agent never knows from month to month how much they will make or when the work will appear. There is a continual fear that one day the work will, without warning, dry up. Employees can lose their jobs too, but it doesn't happen quite as often and at least they get severance.

The concerns of low-skill workers will be somewhat different from high-skill workers, and the concerns of on-premises workers will be somewhat different from virtual workers. However, we can still list three broad categories of threats that worry all free agents to some extent:

1. **Dramatic drops in hourly wage.** There is no minimum wage for free agents, and in particular if people face competition from workers in poor nations they may find their hourly wage is much lower than it was in the past.
2. **Insufficient volume of work.** For many free agents, the hourly rate is less of a concern than the inability to get enough work. This can be especially true if you need to compete for work via contests that you only occasionally win. For on-premises part-time workers, the commute time may dramatically cut into the time available to do paid work.
3. **Income insecurity.** Even if a free agent is doing well, there's the constant fear that next week could be a bad one. Free agents may be hesitant to plan for time with family or holidays because they feel a need to always be on call for potential clients. Some landlords in the UK won't rent to people on zero-hour contracts because they see them as high risk.[2]

Why Organizations Will Be Concerned

Organizations may find the turbulence of the world beyond employment undermining their ability to operate. Some may go too fast or too far, and inadvertently cut some of the essential rigging that holds the organization together. Others won't move fast enough and get caught with unsustainable overheads. Perhaps everyone will spend a fortune trying to adapt to change and build more agile and nimble organizations instead of serving their customers and improving their products.

Furthermore, social concerns are business concerns, too. If people cannot earn a decent living in free agent world, then that will be bad for business as their ability to spend money on goods and services will be diminished.

Why Economists Will Be Concerned

Thoughtful economists can imagine all kinds of situations where the changing approach to work leads to inefficient outcomes. If free agents spend most of their time competing for work, and only a little time actually doing the work, that's not an efficient use of talent for the economy. If 11 designers create 60 webpage designs and only one gets paid $600 (a real example), is that not at least 90 percent waste?

There is also the risk that a world beyond employment will amplify the winner-takes-all economy where there are a few winners and many losers, and that will lead to an even more unequal distribution of wealth. In his popular book *Capital in the Twenty-First Century*, French economist Thomas Piketty argues that unequal distribution of wealth causes social and economic instability.[3]

Why Nations Will Be Concerned

In the book *Rebooting Work*, Maynard Webb writes about the virtue of being the CEO of our own destiny, and how he worked his way up from a job as a security guard to be the CEO of the cloud-based contact center LiveOps.[4] It's a great story, but should it interest a government policy maker? A policy maker knows that a small percentage of people will always succeed regardless of the obstacles they face. However, governments need to address the risk that a significant percentage of the population will not have the capability to thrive in a free agent world.

Furthermore, there is the risk that dispersing work will move a lot of it to low-cost markets. According to PayScale.com, the median salary for a civil engineer in Indonesia in 2015 was around $5,000. If that becomes the going rate then developed countries will have to deal with a lot of unemployed engineers.

Nations have leaned heavily on labor legislation to create a good life for their citizens. That legislation is now being outflanked as work is being sent to the people, instead of people coming to the work. Nations are right to be concerned about how disruptive the beyond employment world may be, leaving governments to pick up the pieces. In the words of Gary Swart, former CEO of oDesk, "There are very few laws about bringing work to the worker as opposed to the worker to the work."

When I Grow Up, I Want to Be a Rabbit

Parents have long dreaded hearing their kids say they want to grow up to be a rock star. Now they can also start worrying if their kids say they hope to be a TaskRabbit.

TaskRabbit is a talent platform designed to find people to do short-term, low-skill, in-person tasks like cleaning a room, helping someone move a couch, or delivering a sandwich. The pitch to workers sounds appealing at first: make some easy money doing the tasks you choose, when you choose.[5] In practice, since one is always competing with other TaskRabbits for tasks, it can be hard to secure work, particularly work you like that pays reasonably well, fits your schedule, and is convenient to get to. Furthermore, TaskRabbit can change the rules at any time (they made some significant changes to how workers found tasks in 2015), and that could derail a successful Rabbit's career.

TaskRabbit illustrates the challenges in dispersing some kinds of work. The TaskRabbit work is generally low skilled, onsite, and F2C (free agent to consumer). That kind of work just doesn't have any economic levers working in its favor. Some TaskRabbits will do well, and some will be happy to pick up a few dollars on the side; however, the type of work (low-skilled and in-person) is not well suited to generating a good living, especially since you don't get paid for searching for tasks or commuting to the job.

TaskRabbit is a good illustration of how the glowing marketing pitch of a talent platform may hide a less pleasant reality. If your teenager wants to be a TaskRabbit, you might do well to steer him or her back toward being a rock star.

The Wild Card of Automation

We can't talk about the scenarios of free agents replacing employees without addressing the issue of automation replacing employees. Automation has been replacing workers ever since the industrial revolution; however, the topic has gained renewed attention due to advances in the cool area of robotics, the everyday area of self-checkout, and the surprising world of smart computers. In particular, smart computers are able to do tasks, such as reading medical images, that we thought would always be the domain of humans.

Why Now?

Automation may be on the verge of rapid acceleration now because of the evolution of a number of complementary technologies. Robots have better sensors (and senses), especially vision and touch; physical objects have smart tags that allow them to communicate with robots and each other; machine learning is enabling computers to recognize complex patterns and predict human behavior; Wi-Fi makes it easy to communicate without wires; GPS lets everything know where everything else is; the Internet connects everything and computers, thanks to better hardware and software, are much smarter.

What all that means is that many tasks that machines found hard or impossible to do are becoming relatively easy. In fact, it's hard to identify jobs that couldn't potentially be done in large part by a machine in 10 or 20 years. One job routinely identified as challenging even for an advanced robot with artificial intelligence is that of a housemaid. Perhaps dusting shelves will be the only job left for humans.

But machines don't need to do everything to have a huge impact on workers. If self-serve checkouts can handle three out of four customers, they eliminate 75 percent of cashiers, one of the most common jobs in the United States. If robots can handle half the tasks in a surgery, then a lot of surgeons are going to be serving fries (or perhaps dusting shelves).

Does It Matter?

The initial reaction to the possibility of tens of millions of jobs being lost to automation is fear and wonder. It's amazing to imagine a world where cars are driverless and artificial intelligence replaces lawyers—but the idea that we would lose our own job is sobering.

Will the free market somehow create new jobs for all? There is some evidence for this. The invention of agriculture eliminated most hunter-gatherer jobs, but created many new jobs. Similarly, the industrial revolution eliminated most farming jobs, but they, too, were replaced by new occupations. But two successes in a row is not proof that the same thing will happen a third time.

Even if the long-term prognosis is good, in the short-run, this kind of massive economic change can cause huge disruption. One potential problem is a demand drought. If a tsunami of automation eliminates too many jobs too quickly, it could lead to a lingering depression as workers with irrelevant skills struggle to retool themselves and become economically relevant. In that scenario, robots will staff the stores, but there will be no one who can afford to go shopping.

What It Means for Leaders and Individuals

Consider a company like Amazon: it has various options for distributing its products. It can hire employees, outsource, or use free agents. It can also use robots and drones. Automation is one of the very important options that is now getting stirred into the mix.

More so than the other options, automation involves many unknowns. Any new technology is unproven, with its full implications hard to predict. If you invest in a fully automated factory, what happens when the next generation of technology makes it obsolete? It's like investing in the coolest smartphone only to find that it's become out-of-date a year later.

How to manage in a world of rampant advances in automation? That's the subject of another book. However, it's clear that it will require careful assessment of the risks—both of leaping in and of not doing so.

> For individuals, the biggest lesson is not to invest heavily in a narrow career. Someone with fairly general skills like a manager, analyst, technologist, or laborer has a decent chance of moving laterally in the face of economic change. No one place is safe, so agility becomes the key currency.

Who Is Right, the Optimists or the Pessimists?

The optimists have a strong case. Innovation always brings some discomfort, but individuals, organizations, and economies are adaptable. Where the beyond employment model makes sense, organizations will turn up the dials and reap the benefits. Where the beyond employment model is not effective, we can expect more traditional arrangements to remain.

The pessimists also have a strong case. Profit-seeking organizations, by their nature, are always striving to get more from workers while paying them less. In some cases, detaching work from employment is appealing to organizations not because it enhances effectiveness or competitive advantage, but simply because it allows them to escape labor laws, and that comes at the expense of the worker.

Where the pessimists have the strongest case is that even if one were to prove that on the whole a shift away from employment is a force for good, there may still be too many losers. That there are already a large number of people who certainly appear to be in worse shape than they would be were they in full-time employment only strengthens their case:

- In the UK, about 1.4 million workers are on zero-hour contracts (part-timers without any guaranteed minimum number of hours per week), according to figures from the Office for National Statistics.[6]
- Also in the UK, workers without a set number of working hours earn on average £188/week (around $285) compared with £479 ($725) for permanent workers.[7]
- The Canadian newspaper *The Globe and Mail* reported in 2013 that "Barely half of people working in the Greater Toronto and Hamilton areas have permanent, full-time jobs that provide benefits and stability. Everyone else is working in situations that are part-time, vulnerable, or insecure in some way."[8]

What Should We Do?

The real issue is not so much whether we should be optimistic or pessimistic but what we are going to do. Clearly the beyond employment world creates opportunities and costs. How should we seize the opportunities and mitigate the costs?

What Nations Can Do

There is an entrenched school of thought that the free agent world is all about employers exploiting workers and that it should be stopped. It's seen primarily as a way for employers to skip out on their obligations to employees. Those who believe this view call for governments to crack down on these new practices and draw everyone back into the familiar world of employment.

This is far too simple a way to frame or respond to the issue. Yes, sometimes free agent world leads to exploitation, but often it can serve the free agent well, and often it's a more effective way to get work done. Furthermore the vision of a world where everyone is employed in secure, well-paid, full-time jobs is a myth even in rich countries with strong labor laws. Countries like France do a good job of protecting employees; however, this protection has created a two-tier world with some people in secure work and others in precarious work or unemployed. Besides, readers of the Dilbert comic will know that the traditional office is hardly a paradise of human happiness.

We might think back to the industrial revolution, where the invention of the factory led to dangerous and unpleasant conditions for workers. Governments could have tried to ban factories and draw workers back to the familiar world of farms and crafts. But the actual outcome was better than that. Governments came to recognize the harms that arose from industrial work and addressed them, creating extensive legislation and institutions to deal with the following issues:

- Unsafe working conditions
- Unfair wages
- Unduly long work hours

- Unfair time-off policies
- Arbitrary dismissal
- Discrimination

Rather than try to suppress free-agent work and rely on existing law and institutions, nations need to update those laws and institutions so that they address the problems arising out of this new world of work.

Here is some specific advice:

- **Get good data**. Is MTurk underpaying workers, or does it provide a niche for hobby work for people who are otherwise idle? Is the precariousness of the competition system on Tongal and Topcoder hurting workers or are the vast majority doing okay? What actually are the biggest problems facing workers today? Without good data, we can't make good policy decisions, so the first step for governments and civil society is to improve the ability to gather and analyze data on the new world of work. With good data, we can identify just what harms need to be addressed. Interestingly, many of the problems addressed by existing labor laws may be less important in free agent world. Certainly, issues like unduly long work hours, unfair time-off policies, and arbitrary dismissal seem moot for free agents who make the decisions about what work to do and when to work. Unsafe working conditions and discrimination are less likely to be problems when so much work is virtual and often done at the free agent's location of choice. Maybe TaskRabbits do need to unionize and we may need to make that easier to do, but we won't know without good data.
- **Be bold, be inventive**. Our existing laws and institutions arose because of a willingness to be bold and inventive. Perhaps we need a guaranteed minimum income (e.g., a living wage); perhaps the state should act as an employer of last resort; perhaps we need to reform taxation; maybe we need to promote cooperatives over corporations—let's test some new initiatives to see how they work. No major government initiative is without downsides; however, government initiatives have led to excellent train networks in Europe, moon landings by the United States, and efficient health care in France. So let's not discount the ability of nations to find means for adapting to a world where employment is not the norm.

We should also remember that there is more to a nation than government. The U.S. Freelancers Union helps address many problems freelancers face, and Turkopticon helps warn Turkers about exploitive companies.

We should look to civil society to identify and address problems that arise in the new world of work.

One of the main limitations of government action is that it tends to operate at a national level. If workers win protections in one nation, what is to prevent companies from simply moving work to some other country? Countries that have tried to rein in risk-taking behavior in the financial services industry know how hard it is to act individually. Sweden introduced a tax on equities trading in 1984, and by 1990 more than half of all Swedish trading had been moved to London. In 1991, Sweden abandoned the tax.

While global collective action is not easy, there are many global institutions that address global problems. Global health institutions eliminated smallpox, and global collaboration among banks makes it possible for you to withdraw cash from your account even when you are standing at an ATM in Borneo.

There is much skepticism regarding the ability of global institutions to be effective and to address the interests of the average citizen as opposed to special interests. This skepticism is well founded. However, if we choose to live in a global economy, then there's no avoiding the need for global institutions and global collective action. It's not so much a question of acting or not acting globally, it's a question of how do we get better at dealing with issues that extend beyond the boundaries of the nation state.

Germany Faces Up to the Digital Challenge

Many political leaders understand that the digital revolution is affecting how companies produce goods and how consumers buy them, but far fewer seem to have faced up to how the digital revolution is affecting the labor market. Germany may represent an exception. Andrea Nahles, German Federal Minister for Labor and Social Affairs, has said, "the labor market will also undergo radical change, . . . we want to be pioneers and mold tomorrow's world of work." In other words rather than condemn or exult in the digital revolution's impact on labor, Germany intends to manage it.

To spark a productive national debate on the issue, Nahles presented a 90-page green paper at the "Work 4.0" conference in Berlin in April 2015. The paper raises issues such as whether the Federal

Employment Agency should be proactive in training people so they stay employed, rather than reactively trying to deal with unemployment. Another big issue is the need for a clear legal framework to deal with flexible work. Then there is the question of how to fund pensions for online free agents (often called "clickworkers" in Germany). All in all it is a matter of coming to a new social agreement so that citizens, organizations, labor and government collaborate in adapting laws and institutions so that they suit the new world.

It is an encouraging example of forward thinking from a country that has a good track record of developing a highly capable workforce.

What Organizations Can Do

Organizations should recognize that they have a duty to their workers whether those workers are employees or not. In fact, legal scholar Lynn Stout has shown that even profit-making corporations need not put shareholder interests ahead of the well-being of workers.[9] Organizations need to break down the mental walls that treat employees as "talent" and free agents as "widgets." All workers are people, and organizations should be concerned with the well-being of all their workers.

What We Can Do on Our Own

Probably the most important thing an individual can do is avoid clinging to the idea that success is about getting a traditional job. That option may still exist in the future, however, it may be that the best or only work available is for free agents. Simply seeing the world in this way should motivate you to start developing the skills and knowledge necessary to succeed as a free agent. This means adopting a mind-set of continuous learning and skills acquisition to ensure your continued relevance.

Financially, the life of a free agent can be fraught with uncertainty. There simply is no guarantee of making money week to week or month to month. Risk expert Nicholas Nassim Taleb argues that this model is not so bad, that it is actually "antifragile."[10] It may feel insecure to be constantly searching for work, but Taleb argues that this helps us continually adapt to a turbulent world. A free agent may go through a dry spell, but she is unlikely to lose all her revenue streams and is in a good position to adapt and find new work. In contrast, an employee who loses his job loses all his income and may find himself with outdated skills and no ability to find new work.

A free agent has to embrace income volatility as a fact of life, and in the absence of a secure stream of income, will be wise to avoid debt even if it means delaying gratification. Some old notions about the merit of saving money and being frugal seem all the more relevant for a free agent's life. Lots of people do live good lives as free agents, and lots more may need to learn from their example.

What Your Kids Can Do

"Kid, let me show you the ropes." That's a phrase you won't hear much in a world beyond employment. One of the most valuable purposes of traditional employment in traditional organizations is that it can take a young person with no particular skills and turn them into a skilled, productive individual. They might even cost more than they are worth for the first year or so, but that's okay, because they're the young plants you nurture. What is the equivalent in the free agent world? Kids need to seek out coaches and mentors to help them develop the skills to thrive in a free agent world. In today's world it is easier than ever to connect to people with the expertise you need so there is no excuse for not reaching out. There are even talent platforms to help you access the right mentors.

Free agents have to be skilled at technology, sales, marketing, and self-development. Kids need to accept this as a reality and recognize that mastering some specific discipline (whether that be English or Engineering) is only one part of what they will need to thrive. If schools do not help kids get the free-agent skills they need, then they need to get that education elsewhere. There are endless sources of help online; and kids need to understand they need to go out and find them.

The next generation will have to ponder if it is better to pay to get an undergraduate degree or spend those four years learning how to navigate the talent platforms. A kid out of high school can't expect to earn much on a talent platform when starting out. But after four years, she will probably have gotten quite skilled at acquiring work and won't be sitting on a pile of student debt. Imagine groups of young people connected via Internet chat, playing the talent platform world much like they play team-based video games like Call of Duty. In the world of work, they will "level up" as they develop new skills, a stronger portfolio, and a better brand.

Another great opportunity for the next generation is to use the myriad of talent platforms to explore the enormous variety of work in the world. Children say they want to be a teacher or a pirate, not because these are the best jobs, but because those are the only jobs they know. A young man in Texas would never have known how lucrative playing with Legos could be had he not discovered the world of Lego-based commercials through Tongal. Young people have the most to gain, and the least to lose, from embracing free agent world.

The main thing for kids to recognize is that they may never get, nor need, a regular job. Sure, many will end up employed, but everyone should embrace being CEO of Me; whatever that means to them. Let's stop grooming kids for a world that won't exist.

Conclusion

We believe the days of employment being the only important means for getting work done are passing. This will lead to a host of dislocations for us as individuals and citizens. It's natural and appropriate to worry about how this will affect our children. If we just let economic evolution take its course, there will be some good and some bad, but no guarantee of anything close to an optimal outcome. If we're smart individually and collectively, we can ensure that the good outweighs the bad. Being proactive in managing the change is undoubtedly better than trying to hang on to the past.

Notes

1. G. Paolacci, J. Chandler, and P. G. Ipeirotis, "Running Experiments on Amazon Mechanical Turk," *Judgment and Decision Making 5*, no. 5 (2010): 411–419.
2. H. Osborne and S. Butler, "Zero-Hours Contract Workers Turned Away by Some of UK's Biggest Landlords," *The Guardian*, October 31,

2014, www.theguardian.com/uk-news/2014/oct/31/zero-hours-contract-workers-turned-away-britains-biggest-landlords.

3. Thomas Piketty and Arthur Goldhammer, *Capital in the Twenty-First Century* (Cambridge, MA: Belknap Press of Harvard University Press, 2014).

4. Maynard Webb and Adler Carlye, *Rebooting Work: Transform How You Work in the Age of Entrepreneurship* (San Francisco, CA: Jossey-Bass, 2013).

5. TaskRabbit website homepage, https://www.taskrabbit.com/ (accessed March 25, 2015).

6. P. Inman and A. Monaghan, "Number of Zero-hour Contracts Reaches 1.4m," *The Guardian*, May 1, 2013, www.theguardian.com/uk-news/2014/may/01/huge-increase-workers-zero-hours-contracts.

7. Lianna Brinded, "Zero-Hour Contract Workers Earn £300 Less per Week Than Permanent Staff," *International Business Times*, December 15, 2014, www.ibtimes.co.uk/zero-hour-contract-workers-earn-300-less-weekly-permanent-staff-1479496.

8. Susan McIsaac and Charlotte Yates, "Half of Toronto-Area Workers Have Fallen into 'Precarious Employment': Study," *The Globe and Mail*, February 24, 2013, www.theglobeandmail.com/globe-debate/columnists/half-of-toronto-area-workers-have-fallen-into-precarious-employment-study/article9003680/.

9. Lynn Stout, *The Shareholder Value Myth: How Putting Shareholders First Harms Investors, Corporations, and the Public* (San Francisco, CA: Berrett-Koehler, 2012).

10. Nicholas Nassim Taleb, *Antifragile: Things That Gain from Disorder* (New York: Random House, 2012).

About the Authors

John W. Boudreau, Ph.D., professor and research director at the University of Southern California's Marshall School of Business and Center for Effective Organizations, is recognized for breakthrough research on how decisions about human capital, talent, and human resources affect sustainable competitive advantage. He has more than 100 publications, including over 10 books as well as articles and chapters published in scholarly journals like *Journal of Applied Psychology, Personnel Psychology, Organizational Dynamics and Human Relations*, and features in *Harvard Business Review, The Wall Street Journal, Fortune, Fast Company*, and *Business Week*. His books include *Beyond HR*, with Pete Ramstad, (Harvard Business Publishing, 2007), *Investing in People*, with Wayne Cascio, (Pearson, 2008), *Achieving Strategic Excellence in Human Resource Management*, with Edward Lawler (Stanford University Press, 2009; 2012; 2015), *Retooling HR* (Harvard Business Publishing, July, 2010), *Transformative HR* (Wiley Publishing, 2011). He holds a BBA from New Mexico State University, and a masters in management and Ph.D. in industrial relations from Purdue University's Krannert School of Management. http://ceo.usc.edu/research_scientist/boudreau.html

Ravin Jesuthasan, CFA, is the global practice leader of Towers Watson's Talent Management Practice. He is a managing director of the firm and is based in the Chicago office. Ravin has published numerous articles and led several global research efforts on the topics of measurement and analytics, human capital management, rewards, labor cost optimization, and talent management. As a recognized global thought leader, he has been a featured speaker on these subjects at conferences in North America, Europe, Asia Pacific, and Latin America. He has also been featured and quoted extensively by leading business media, including *CNN*, *The Wall Street Journal*, *Business Week*, *CNBC*, *Fortune*, *FT*, *Human Capital* (China), *Les Echoes* (France), *Valor Economico* (Brazil), *Business Times* (Malaysia), *Globe and Mail* (Canada), *South China Morning Post*, *Dubai One TV*, and *The Australian* among others. He has been recognized as one of the top 25 most influential consultants in the world by *Consulting Magazine*. He is also the co-author of the recently released book, *Transformative HR*. His recent article in the *HR People and Strategy Journal* entitled "Performance Management as a Business Discipline" received the 2014 Walker Award for making the most original and valuable contribution to the HR profession. Prior to joining Towers Watson 21 years ago, Ravin was a consultant with the strategy practice of a major management consulting firm.

David Creelman is CEO of Creelman Research. He helps organizations identify, make sense of, and address important new issues in human capital. His work with Andrew Lambert on one such issue (board oversight of human capital) won the Walker Award. Another important topic is leadership transitions in knowledge-based firms—Creelman works closely with Dr. Wanda Wallace on this subject. Finally, one of the most important new issues in HR is analytics and evidence-based management; Creelman leads a community of practice of Fortune 500 companies on those topics with Carnegie-Mellon's Denise Rousseau as the academic lead.

David has spoken about reporting on human capital at the World Bank headquarters in Paris, worked with the Etisalat Academy in Dubai, and helped leaders from Japan's Recruit Co. tour the U.S. HR tech industry. He is a long-term member of the Workforce Institute's advisory board in Boston and regularly does research for the Tokyo-based Works Institute.

Prior to his current role David helped launch HR.com as chief of content and research; earlier still he worked as a management consultant for the Hay Group in Toronto and Kuala Lumpur and taught an HR course at the University of Malaya.

He began his career with corporate jobs in the resources and finance industries in Canada and the UK. He has a BS in chemistry and biochemistry and an MBA. He now lives in Toronto, Canada, with his wife and daughter.

Index

Page references followed by *fig* indicate an illustrated figure.